01283

McFarland, John W., ed.
   Lives from Plutarch, The modern American
edition of twelve lives edited and
abridged, with an introduction by John W.
McFarland, Pleasant & Audrey Graves.
Random, c1966.
   284p.

   1. Plutarch, A.D. 46?-ADc 120.
2. Greece--Biography. 3. Rome--Biography.
4. Greek literature. 5. Roman literature.

Lives from Plutarch

Lives
from Plutarch

The Modern American Edition of Twelve Lives

Edited and Abridged, with an Introduction by

JOHN W. McFARLAND

PLEASANT & AUDREY GRAVES

Random House   New York

C 1966

A Note on This Edition

We have worked from the Dryden translation and the
Clough revision, and have consulted a number of others.
At the end of Plutarch's life of Cato and at the beginning
and end of the life of Julius Caesar, we have included
brief comments, set in small type, that are original for this
edition. At the end of the life of Pericles, a portion of
Pericles' famous oration at the funeral of Athenians is
included. We are indebted to Edmund G. Berry for many
references in our introduction drawn from his powerful,
scholarly EMERSON'S PLUTARCH, published by Harvard University Press in 1961, which contains the only substantial
modern treatment of Plutarch in English.

Contents

Introduction

We write nearly two thousand years after the time of Plutarch. Plutarch was born in Greece about 45 A.D.—a few years after the death of Jesus and several centuries after the political power of ancient Greece had collapsed. Greece had become a province of Rome. Nevertheless Greek thought, absorbed and projected by Roman genius for organization, dominated the Mediterranean world; it followed the Roman legions as they spread over Europe and established the foundations of our western world.

While Plutarch lived to old age under several Roman emperors—Nero, Domitian, Nerva and Trajan, perhaps even Hadrian—the blend of Graeco-Roman civilization was producing the last great pagan era. By that time most of the men of action, the thinkers and writers of the ancient world had done their great deeds, thought their great thoughts and written their great works which have so profoundly influenced the development of the West. Plutarch considered that he had inherited them all, both Greek and Roman. It is through him that our present civilization knows many of them best.

For fifteen hundred years this most renowned of all biographers apparently escaped the focus of other biographers. From the Renaissance to our time, scholars have attempted to detail his life, alternately adding and subtracting inferences and deductions based primarily upon incidental references scattered through his own works. Much is conjecture; much is disputed.

It is known that Plutarch came from a respected Theban family long established in the small city of Chaeronea on the plains of Boeotia—a place historic in his day as the site of the Macedonian victory over allied Thebes and Athens, a victory which weakened the independence of the Greek city-states. His interest in history was stimulated by the reminiscences of his great-grandfather, who had been forced with other Greek citizens of Chaeronea to carry on their backs, like beasts of burden, huge sacks of Boeotian corn commandeered for the support of Antony's army; the Greeks had happily dropped their burdens when Antony's officers fled the port upon news of his defeat at Actium.

As a young man Plutarch studied philosophy in Athens, where he recorded that one of his fellow students was a descendant of Themistocles. Plutarch traveled in Greece, Italy and Egypt, collecting manuscripts and noting the thoughts of scholars he met and the traditions of wise men. He studied the records and public documents preserved in Sparta, Thebes and other cities to learn about their government, their leaders, their soldiers, their women, their ceremonies, their memorable deeds, and their way of life in both peace and war.

Plutarch was a welcome visitor, lecturer and diplomatic representative in Rome, which his contemporary Juvenal indignantly called "that Greek city." There Plutarch was recognized and respected as a teacher; there he established friendships with eminent men, and he is even said to have been granted honorary consular rank. Most of his life, however, he spent in provincial Chaeronea, where he married and became the father of five children—a happy, responsible domestic figure. In Chaeronea he held many municipal offices even into

INTRODUCTION

his old age; there he studied and wrote, preferring, as he said, to live in his own little town "lest it should become less by even one."

Plutarch was a Hellenist—a lover of all things Greek. He was a pagan; he was initiated into the Mysteries of Dionysus, and served as a priest of Apollo at Delphi. Although he deplored atheism, he scorned superstition. He was rather a polytheist who saw the lesser gods as aspects of the one God of all men and of the whole universe, pure and absolute, the source of the idea of good, and of reason and fate. In his work Plutarch stressed immortality and sensed universality in various religions.

As a philosopher Plutarch was eclectic and occasionally inconsistent—the product of wide reading and various influences. He was identified with the Neo-Pythagoreans, yet he was more a Platonist subscribing to the Platonic concept of the duality of the material world with a world of pure ideas, and of an evil world soul in opposition to good. He went beyond Plato in his admiration of reason and in his insistence that vice is ignorance, virtue is knowledge and can be taught.

To reconcile his Hellenistic polytheism and Platonic dualism, and to bridge the gap between man and God, Plutarch anticipated some of the ideas of the later Neoplatonists. Between man and God he saw the "spirits" or "daemons,"—part man and part God—controlled by fate, able by their divine nature to reveal divine purpose to man through prophecies, oracles, omens and dreams; the daemons could help the man, who, by the use of his reason, accepted their divine revelation.

But Plutarch's ethics reflected Aristotle. He rejected the Epicurean doctrine that the attainment of pleasure is the aim of man and he also opposed the Stoic doctrine that pleasure has no bearing upon human happiness. Plutarch considered human desires and emotions as divine gifts; he insisted that man has free will which, properly directed by reason, can free man's desires and emotions from the influence of evil. He argued that only in this way may man make great and necessary contributions to the good life. Although Plutarch criticized the Stoics, he resembled the later Roman Stoics in his keen and dominant interest in the practical ethics of everyday life and in his admiration for self-reliance and calm endurance.

Politics, the practice of statesmanship, was for Plutarch the noblest human occupation. He believed man's greatest happiness comes from participation in social and political activities to the best of his ability. He respected most the man with authority who worked unselfishly for the good of the community. He stressed the great responsibilities of such men. He had a concept of natural law and championed representative government, studying and comparing various forms of democracy and representative political institutions in ancient civilizations.

Plutarch was a prolific writer who treated an enormous variety of subjects, all in relatively brief form. His *Moralia*, a collection of essays, and his *Symposiacs*, or *Table-Talk*, a series of less formal dialogues, include discourses on ethics, politics, natural science, education, philosophy and religion. The diverse but related strains which thread his essays come into sharper focus in his later and most popular work, the *Parallel Lives*. It was for the instruction of others that Plutarch wrote the first group of his biographies. He continued with a second group, he said, for his own sake "by the study of history . . . to accustom my memory to receive and retain images of the characters of the best and most worthwhile men. . . . The virtues of these great men serve me as a sort of looking-glass in which I may see how to adjust and enrich my own life." He chose to write not of philosophers or artists,

INTRODUCTION

but rather of virtuous men of action. In remarks introducing
the life of Pericles, Plutarch explained: "Man's intellect has
the power of choice, and can turn itself to whatever it pleases.
It ought, therefore, to employ itself in the best pursuits, not
merely for the sake of contemplating what is good, but that it
may be itself strengthened. The mere statement of great actions of good men inspires both admiration for the things done
and the earnest desire to imitate them . . . Moral good draws
man powerfully to itself and forms in him a dominating purpose."

Plutarch wrote a third group of biographies to emphasize
virtue through negative examples of vice and weakness, and a
fourth to extend his survey of famous men back into legendary
prehistory. He is believed to have written as many as sixty-five
Lives, of which only fifty survive. He arranged them in pairs,
one Greek and one Roman, generally followed by a comparison—perhaps as some have thought, to prove to each nation the merit of the other, but more likely as a device to draw
the reader beyond the exploits of his subjects to the author's
real but more abstract interest in their ethical qualities.

Plutarch was not a great stylist, yet he made substantial contributions to letters, and to biography in particular. He brought
new talent to the conventional form of biography which already existed, avoiding the traditional rhetoric of the Greek
and the tiresome eulogy of the Roman. He was absorbed with
word usage and wrote that he "did not so much gain the
knowledge of things by words, as words by the knowledge
. . . of things." A particular element of his style was his effective use of terse epigrammatic expressions and pithy sayings
which he had collected; these gave power and vigor to his
prose. He was casual and intimate, a skilful story-teller, a
master in the art of digression.

Because he was determined to create vivid portraits, Plutarch worked from a wide variety of source materials although he recognized them as of unequal authority. Plutarch outlined for the first time a technique sometimes used by biographers; he contended that when a story is celebrated, and more important still, when it is so much in keeping with the character of the subject, it should not be rejected merely because it might be in conflict with the so-called rule of chronology. He had great sensitivity for selecting anecdotes and incidents which seemed unimportant in themselves, but which clearly revealed the character of his subjects. He had unusual power to portray men's motives and thoughts; he illuminated his subjects with the warmth of his own personality, the breadth of his own humanity, and his understanding of human nature.

The Renaissance scholar Theodorus Gaza said that if it were possible to preserve the works of only one author, he would choose Plutarch. The French King Henry IV wrote that his mother gave him Plutarch so that he might not be an "intellectual dunce." The King said: "It has been like my conscience, and has whispered in my ear many good suggestions and maxims for my conduct and the government of my affairs." Montaigne, perhaps more than any other major figure, assimilated Plutarch; he admired him as "a philosopher who teaches us virtue," and wrote that Plutarch, "of all the authors . . . has best mixed art with nature, and judgment with knowledge." Racine developed techniques from Plutarch. Rousseau, writing of his own youth, said significantly that Plutarch "became my favorite author . . . cured me a little of my taste for romance . . . and formed in me the free and republican spirit." Madame Roland remarked that "The *Lives* are the pasturage of great souls."

In Italy Gioberti compared Plutarch with Dante. Plutarch was a favorite with the Italian revolutionaries. In Germany, the dramas of Schiller reflect Plutarchan themes and make

INTRODUCTION

reference to his work. Plutarch was a substantial influence upon Goethe, who read his *Lives* frequently and found Plutarch "a wise, learned man of Chaeronea, presenting the greatest of heroes . . ."

In early sixteenth-century England, Erasmus spread knowledge of Plutarch and presented to King Henry VIII a translation of Plutarch's essay "How to Know a Flatterer from a Friend." Queen Elizabeth I as a young woman proudly translated from Plutarch to display her accomplishments. Sir Thomas North, her subject, completed in 1575 the first translation of the *Lives* into English, from the French translation by Amyot. Plutarch's *Lives* influenced plot structure for Shakespeare and provided him with outlines of such characters as Coriolanus and Antony. Among those who respected Plutarch was John Donne, who called him "the oracle of moral men"; the Neostoics used Plutarch's anecdotes and epigrams as a Bible. Bacon quoted Plutarch; many of Bacon's anecdotes and apothegms derive from Plutarch, either directly or through Montaigne or others. Even the preachers of seventeenth-century England freely used the ethical wisdom of the pagan Plutarch to enrich Christian doctrine with philosophy.

When Dryden wrote a *Life of Plutarch* in 1683 as an introduction to a new translation by members of a group of Oxford scholars, he described Plutarch as sociable, a lover of conversation, candid, humane, humble, happy to praise virtue, eager to teach others but always ready to learn. His arguments, Dryden said, "drawn from reason, work themselves into your understanding and make a deep and lasting impression in your mind." Thinking in terms of Plutarch, Dryden saw history as a "perspective-glass . . . which helps us to judge of what will happen . . . For mankind being the same in all ages, agitated by the same passions and moved to action by the same interests, nothing can come to pass but some precedent of the like nature has already been produced . . ." Again thinking in terms of Plutarch, Dryden argued that of all history, biography gives perhaps the greatest pleasure and instruction because examples of virtue gain vitality when compressed into the life story of one man; ". . . you are led into the private lodgings of the hero; you see him in his undress, and are made familiar with his most private actions and conversations . . . The pageantry of life is taken away; you see the poor reasonable animal, as naked as ever nature made him; are made acquainted with his passions and follies, and find the demigod a man."

The eighteenth century viewed history as moral; history was biography, and Plutarch's *Lives* was the popular textbook of classicism, of history, philosophy and ethics. The influence of Plutarch as historian and moral biographer was dominant in England, not only in court circles but for the ordinary man, who had learned that ordinary humans can be heroic in the ancient pattern—the pattern of the *Lives*. The new philanthropy or humanism of the Age of Reason responded to the humanity of Plutarch. His human heroes were current popular symbols in thought, literature and politics, not only for those who read the works of Alexander Pope, but for the larger audiences of orators and pamphleteers. *The British Plutarch* was enormously popular; the word "Plutarch" came to be the common name for any collection of biographies. In 1770 a new translation of the *Lives* by William Langhorne appeared. Wordsworth knew Plutarch well; so did every scholar, statesman and schoolboy.

The Puritans had brought Plutarch to America in the seventeenth century. Cotton Mather had called Plutarch "incomparable," and had listed him among the historians whom "a person of good sense should know." This Greek, whose heroes had once inspired princes and emperors, was read in the eighteenth century as a spokesman of liberty by the founding

INTRODUCTION

fathers of young America. At the close of the eighteenth century, Plutarch remained a predominant influence in thought and education in America; through Emerson he continued to exert great influence upon American thought and letters into the nineteenth century.

Emerson called Plutarch "spermatic" and assimilated him in the manner of Montaigne and Bacon before him. More than most writers, Emerson appreciated the poetic charm of Plutarch: the striking, memorable quality of his symbols and expressions, the occasionally oracular style and weight of his prose, his "cunning fetches of dignity and discipline." For these "lustres," Emerson found himself "raffling the pages of Plutarch." He said: "Plutarch cannot be spared from the smallest library . . . I know not where to find a book—to borrow a phrase of Ben Jonson's—'so rammed with life' . . . Nothing touches man but he feels to be his; he is tolerant even of vice, if he finds it genial; enough of a man to give even the Devil his due . . . if he had not the highest powers, he was yet a man of rare gifts. He had that universal sympathy with genius which makes all its victories his own; though he never used verse, he had many qualities of the poet in the power of his imagination, the speed of his mental associations and his sharp, objective eyes. But what specifically marks him, he is a chief example of the illumination of the intellect by the force of morals . . . Go with mean people and you think life is mean. Then read Plutarch, and the world is a proud place, peopled with men of positive quality, with heroes and demigods standing around us, who will not let us sleep . . . The lives . . . are what history has of best . . ."

In England, however, during the nineteenth century, Carlyle, Macaulay and others reacted against traditional exaggeration and idolization of Plutarch and went to the other extreme. Plutarch had never pretended to write history, or said that biography is history; he had said pointedly that he wrote "not history, but lives." Nevertheless it came as a shock to the nineteenth century, accustomed to think of Plutarch as "divine," to learn—through its new scientific school of classical history —that Plutarch was often historically inaccurate. With the rise of nationalism, the interest of historians turned from the accomplishments of individuals to the masses behind the individuals, to a collectivist interpretation of history in terms of nations and their destinies. For the first time since the Renaissance, the concept of biography as history was then generally rejected.

In literature the strong, calm, self-reliant Plutarchan hero went out of style, replaced by the superhero and the romantic hero. Even humanism found a new emphasis: upon beauty rather than ethics, and upon art rather than the deeds of heroes. The popularity of Plutarch declined. By the middle of the nineteenth century, Herodotus, Thucydides, Demosthenes, Plato and Homer had taken the place of Plutarch as the textbook of classicism. Yet literate men continued to read Plutarch; in 1864 Arthur Hugh Clough published the first of numerous editions of his revision of the so-called Dryden translation, the version most frequently encountered today. At the beginning of the twentieth century, Theodore Roosevelt quoted from the *Moralia* in correspondence with Henry Cabot Lodge. Lives of five Greeks and four Romans are included in the Harvard Classics, and the *Lives* constitute one of fifty volumes of *The Great Books of the Western World*. Although the past century has not been Plutarch's, many great men of the modern western world have been strongly influenced by the *Lives;* all of us have been influenced by the absorption of the Plutarchan tradition into education, thought and literature.

Today a new—perhaps more realistic—appraisal of Plutarch is forming. There is new appreciation of his warm, tolerant

INTRODUCTION

humanity, almost unique among the ancients. There is new interest in the broad, sunny, intimate window which he opens on the ancient world.

This new interest is a part of the current general revival of the classics, but it is more specific. The once-brave promise of collectivistic, materialistic, scientific solutions to the problems of man now appears illusory to many; the West instinctively looks again to the individual. Biography is still not history, but perhaps more nearly so than the economic historians have taught us. The superhero has been painfully and grotesquely personified for us in Hitler, Mussolini and Stalin. The tragic aspects of these figures command our attention; but the superhero as the object of admiration is increasingly confined to the comic strips. The romantic hero, never compelling, lingers on in television melodrama. The modern hero is again the ethical man of action. Plutarch portrayed him first and best.

Perhaps the greatest need of the modern world—the greatest challenge to mass education—is the production of sound leadership, ethical men of action. Albert Schweitzer said: "Example is not the *main* thing in influencing others. It is the *only* thing." The modern business or professional man or administrator can learn from Cato's patient building of a way of life. Decision-making for Caesar posed many of the same problems facing the effective modern statesman or citizen. Everyone can learn justice from Aristides, responsibility from the Gracchi, courage from Alexander, moderation from Pericles, and eloquence from Cicero. Everyone can observe vanity in Coriolanus, duplicity in Alcibiades, and weakness in Antony. Everyone can find example in the *Lives*, which Arnold J. Toynbee has applauded as "one brilliant picture after another . . ."

In their original form the *Lives* are long and contain many passages which lack interest for the modern reader. Existing full translations in English, with notable exceptions only in the instances of a scattered few of the *Lives*, are archaic and unsympathetic—Victorian, eighteenth century, seventeenth century or Elizabethan. Abridgments in print are either over-simplifications or disjointed patchworks from outmoded translations. Recognizing almost overwhelming competition for attention in today's crowded, hurried life, we present in this volume twelve lives from Plutarch, approximately half the length of the originals, written for modern Americans.

JOHN W. MC FARLAND
PLEASANT & AUDREY GRAVES

LYCURGUS

*H*istorians are not certain when Lycurgus lived; some say it was before the Olympic Games began, while others claim that it was Lycurgus who led the Greeks to stop all warfare during the Olympic Games. Some list him as a contemporary of Homer, whom perhaps Lycurgus knew personally; most men credit him with introducing the *Iliad* and the *Odyssey* into Sparta and establishing them as inspirations for courage and heroism.

Certainly Lycurgus was an early Spartan king, living probably about 800 years before Christ. He considered himself a descendant of both Heracles and Patrocles and the great-grandson of Soiis. He told a story about a time when Soiis was besieged in a dry and stony place without access to water. He and his men were about to die of thirst, and Soiis agreed with his besiegers to hand over the spoils of all his conquests provided that he himself and all his men should drink from a certain nearby spring held by his besiegers. After the usual oaths and ratifications, he assembled his soldiers and offered his kingdom as a reward to any man who would forego drinking from the spring. Their thirst was so severe that not a man was able to resist. When all the soldiers had drunk their fill, King Soiis passed the spring without swallowing one drop. Then he marched off in full view of his enemies, refusing to yield his conquests. Adhering to the letter of the covenant, he said that since he personally had not drunk from the spring, he would not carry out his part of the agreement. Thus the great-grandfather of Lycurgus relieved the thirst of his men but not his own, without having to give up his conquests.

The grandfather of Lycurgus had relaxed the discipline of the Spartan monarchy in order to seek favor and popularity among the masses. Other Spartan kings also went from one extreme to the other, either using force against the people to discipline them or relaxing their power to be popular among the people. The father of Lycurgus was stabbed with a butcher's knife while trying to quell a riot. Lycurgus' brother reigned only a short time, and the right of succession (everyone thought) rested on Lycurgus. Soon after he became king, however, it was learned that his sister-in-law, widow of the dead king, was pregnant. Lycurgus immediately announced that the crown would belong to his brother's son, if indeed a son rather than a daughter were born. In the meantime, he said he would reign as regent for the future king. The wicked widow, however, offered to destroy her own child if Lycurgus would make her his queen. Abhorring the woman's vicious and selfish plan, Lycurgus pretended to cooperate in her scheme, but he carefully guarded her health and insisted that she bring the baby to a natural birth. When she went into labor, he instructed those he could trust that if the baby were a girl, they should turn her over to nursemaids, but that if a boy were born, the baby should be brought to Lycurgus himself, wherever he might be and whatever he might be doing. Many urged Lycurgus to keep the throne himself, since they knew what a good king he had already proven himself to be; but his instructions were followed and the baby boy was brought to him as he sat at a banquet with the chief officials of Sparta. Taking the infant in his arms, Lycurgus proclaimed, "Men of

Sparta, here is a king born to us." He laid the infant in the king's place and named his nephew Charilaus (joy of the people).

Lycurgus was honored more for his wisdom, virtues, and laws than for being regent and holding the royal power. Some, however, envied him and tried to impede his growing influence while he was still young. The queen mother and her brother and friends particularly opposed and accused Lycurgus because he had thwarted her scheme for power.

Troubled at these accusations and not knowing what might evolve from them, he decided to go into voluntary exile; he traveled outside of Sparta until his nephew could marry and secure the succession by having a son. He visited Crete and studied the government and laws of that ancient kingdom. There he found Thales, a wise law-giver, and persuaded him to go to Sparta, where Thales wrote poems and songs urging peace and obedience. The rhythm and cadence of his songs had an enormous influence on the minds of the singers and listeners, who were thus inspired to order and tranquillity. Under the influence of Thales, the people tended to renounce their private feuds and jealousies and to be reunited in common loyalty to Sparta. In a way, by softening and civilizing the Spartans, Thales prepared the way for the discipline which was later introduced by Lycurgus.

In Ionia Lycurgus discovered Homer's *Iliad* and *Odyssey*. He liked their serious lessons of politics and patriotism and the stories of morality and courage in the poems, and he resolved to make Homer's poems a guide for Spartans. He compared the sober and temperate way of life in Crete to the sumptuous, delicate, and luxurious ways of the Ionians. He said he was like a physician measuring a healthy body against a diseased one. Historians say Lycurgus traveled to Egypt, and was favorably impressed there by the way the soldiers were kept separate from the rest of the people. His reported trips to Spain, Africa, and the Indies have little evidence to support them.

Many in Sparta urged Lycurgus to come home, saying that their present rulers assumed the titles of royalty but were no wiser than their subjects. They added that in Lycurgus alone did they find the true foundation for sovereignty; he had a natural ability to rule and command obedience. Lycurgus finally returned to bring order out of chaos, to change the Spartan way of life, and to build a new Sparta based on just laws. His determination to change the whole structure of Spartan life was reinforced when he went to consult the famous oracle at Delphi. There he was called "beloved of the gods, and rather a god than a man." The oracle foretold that his laws would be the best and that the people who followed them would be the most famous in the world. Lycurgus then assembled thirty of the leading Spartans, honest men of courage, to support the reforms he planned under the administration of his nephew Charilaus, one of the two Spartan kings reigning together according to the Spartan system.

Lycurgus established a Senate of twenty-eight leaders, with power equal to that of the two kings, who also sat as members of the Senate. The Senate was to be like a ballast to keep the government stable. The twenty-eight Senators supported the kings when necessary to resist democracy, but joined with the people to prevent a dictatorship by either king. Thus a balance of power was achieved.

The people met in popular assembly in an open field between two rivers. Lycurgus wanted them to meet out in the open air because he contended that ornaments, buildings and statues would divert attention from the public business. The people's assembly could propose no new law or action, but it could either accept or reject the laws and actions proposed by the kings and the Senate. In a later generation, the five ephors, elected annually by the popular assembly, were to gain so much authority that they effectively checked the power of the kings. One king who encouraged the strengthening of the authority of the ephors was criticized by his queen, who said that he would pass on to his children a power less than the power he had received from his father. "No, greater," said he, "for the power will last longer." And indeed, it seems that other kings, who were selfish about their power, were always overthrown.

With their prerogatives thus reduced within reasonable bounds, the Spartan kings were freed from further jealousies and unrealistic personal ambition. The kings avoided the pitfalls and sorrows of the neighboring rulers of Messene and Argos, who in their struggles for increasing power lost everything. Comparison between Sparta and her bordering kingdoms demonstrates the wisdom and foresight of Lycurgus. At one time Messene, Argos and Sparta had all been equal. But the disasters that later befell these other cities happened because they did not have this wise Spartan law-giver who created such an effective balance in government and in the Spartan way of life.

After establishing the Senate, Lycurgus demanded a redivision of Spartan lands. He asked the wealthy men to give up their land and to share their wealth with the poor. He said he wanted to stop arrogance and envy, luxury and crime, want and waste. He put all men on equal footing, making merit and achievement the only means to glory. The disgrace of evil and the credit of good became the only measure of difference between men.

He divided all Laconia into 30,000 equal shares of land and all Sparta into 9,000 equal shares. Each share of land was enough to produce an adequate supply of oil and wine and about eighty-two bushels of grain annually—seventy for the master of the household and twelve for his wife. Each family was to have just enough food to keep in good health. Food was for nourishment rather than for enjoyment. Observing the stacks of grain at harvest time, Lycurgus once commented that "all Laconia looks like one family estate just divided among a number of brothers."

He called in all gold and silver to be stored in the public treasury, and decreed that the coins to be used by the people would be made of iron. This money was so heavy and scarce, and of so little value, that foreign trade was discouraged. The other Greeks ridiculed Sparta's iron money, and therefore, the Spartans could not buy goods abroad. Merchants sent no ships into Spartan ports; no master of rhetoric, no itinerant fortune-teller, no jeweler, engraver, or silversmith set foot in a country without gold or silver—or even copper money. Luxury, deprived little by little of that which fed and encouraged it, gradually disappeared. In Sparta the rich had no advantage over the poor, because even with their wealth and abundance they could not travel abroad. There was also less interest in stealing the iron money or in using it as a bribe.

Lycurgus then outlawed all unnecessary and showy arts. Even the vanity of looking at or displaying riches was ruled out of order. Thus the Spartans became excellent artists in the common necessities of life. Beds, tables, and chairs were all very well made; their drinking cups were particularly admired, for the cups were colored to minimize the murky color of muddy water and were shaped so that impurities stuck to the sides, and only the clear water came to the drinker's mouth.

All Spartan citizens were required to eat at common mess halls. Thus they all ate the same food and subjected themselves to a common discipline. If a wealthy man were to eat privately at home, his fellow-citizens would know about it, because he would lack an appetite at the common table, where all were

LYCURGUS

expected to eat with enthusiasm. Lycurgus did not want the people to spend their lives at home, lying on costly couches at splendid tables, being catered to by tradesmen and cooks and becoming fat and gluttonous. He believed that overindulgence would ruin not only their bodies but their minds. He did not want them to become softened by long sleep, warm bathing, or freedom from work, or to need care and attendance as though they were continually sick. Lycurgus demanded plain, thrifty living for the Spartans.

When Lycurgus made it compulsory that all eat in the common mess halls, many wealthy men strongly protested, and one group attacked him with stones. He outran all but Alcander, who struck him on the face with his staff, putting out one eye. Lycurgus showed the wound to his fellow-citizens, who seized Alcander for punishment and took Lycurgus to his own home to treat his wounded eye. Lycurgus thanked them for their care and dismissed all but Alcander, whom he brought into his home without any bitterness and put to work as his servant. As Alcander observed Lycurgus and saw his gentleness and calmness, his hard work and sincere attitude, he became himself a reasonable, wise citizen and Lycurgus' most loyal follower. After this incident, the Spartans made a rule against carrying any weapon or even a staff to the assembly.

Lycurgus arranged for the young boys to eat in the common mess hall with the Spartan men. Here the boys learned self-control. They listened to the men's discussions of public affairs, and they learned to take part in polite conversation. They learned to joke good-naturedly and to accept teasing in good humor. To encourage the confidential nature of the fellowship of the mess hall, the oldest man in the hall would, at each meal, point to the door and say, "Through this door no words go out."

While Lycurgus ruled, men formed societies to eat together, to discuss public policy together, to develop friendships, and in general to learn to cooperate. Any man who wanted to join one of these societies had to be voted into it by the members. Each member took a soft little ball of bread and threw it into a basin. If a member disliked the candidate, or did not want him in the society, he pressed the ball of bread between his fingers to make it flat. If all the balls of bread were round, the candidate would be accepted; but if even one flat piece of bread were found, the candidate would be rejected. The purpose of this secret election was to insure that all members of each society would be acceptable to each other.

Their dinner was mainly a plain black broth which was valued so highly that the older men ate only the broth, leaving any meat for the younger men. A visitor who once complained of the bad taste of the black broth was told, "Sir, to relish this broth, you should have bathed first in the river Eurotas."

Lights were forbidden on the streets at night, so that the Spartans could become accustomed to marching boldly in the dark. All of these customs were known as *Rhetras*, and they formed the core of Spartan education. Spartan boys made these *Rhetras* integral parts of the code of life which formed their character and personality.

Lycurgus would not write down his laws, for he believed that the strength of education depended upon fixing the sense and spirit of the laws in the hearts and minds of Spartan boys. And discipline was the key to these laws.

Another restriction Lycurgus imposed was that builders could use only axes and saws as their building tools. In so limiting complicated architecture, he hoped the Spartans would live simple, disciplined lives in simple houses.

Lycurgus also prohibited Spartans from making war often or long against the same enemy, lest the Spartans train and strengthen their enemies' war-making potential by practice in defense.

II

LYCURGUS

He ordered the young Spartan girls to regularly practice wrestling, running, throwing, and dart-casting, because he wanted the future mothers of Spartan men to have strong bodies. He commanded the maidens and young men to march naked in parades, thus emphasizing the value of physical development and encouraging them to marry. Yet these appearances in parades were treated modestly and without jokes and immoral implications. The girls stressed simple, pure living and a care for good health. When someone told the wife of Leonidas that Spartan women were the only women who could rule men, she replied, "With good reason, for we are the only women who bring forth real men."

At festivals and solemn feasts, the young men and girls would dance and sing the praises of brave Spartans and their gallant victories. Thus the young were inspired to follow the courageous examples of their ancestors. At the same time they ridiculed cowardice and made fun of those who had failed or misbehaved in war.

Bachelors were disfranchised by law and were excluded from participating in the important festivals. They were frequently humiliated by the officers, and were denied the respect which younger men usually paid their elders. On one occasion an elderly commander, who was a bachelor, stood uncomfortably while a youth sat and insulted him by saying, "No child of yours will make place for me."

In Spartan marriage, the husband captured his bride and carried her off by force. In the first years of marriage they would not live together; instead the husband would remain in the army barracks while the wife stayed with her parents. They then sneaked secret meetings for love, and often they were parents before they had ever seen each other in daylight. In this way the young Spartans were taught to discipline their sentiments and to sacrifice their personal feelings.

Jealousy was forbidden, and Lycurgus made it honorable

for men to loan their wives to vigorous men to breed a healthy and strong race of men and women. Children were actually considered to be the property of the Spartan state, the parents having little claim to them, so the state wanted children to be sired by the best fathers possible. Thus the personal element in love and marriage was minimized, and marriage and parenthood served the state.

Nor did the father have the prerogative to dispose of his infant as he saw fit. Custom demanded that he bring the child before a jury of elders who would examine the infant. If the child were stout and healthy, they gave orders for his rearing and assigned him a share of land for his maintenance, but if he were unfit or lame, they ordered the infant exposed and destroyed.

The Spartans bathed their infants in wine rather than water, to test and toughen their bodies. Children were subject to strict discipline from the start, and were taught not to be afraid in the dark, not to be finicky about their food, and not to be peevish and tearful.

Lycurgus did not permit children to be taught by slaves, but he had them enrolled at the age of seven in companies or classes where they received uniform discipline and instruction. The major emphasis in their education was on perfect obedience. The old men witnessed the children's lessons and exercises and drills, and often started quarrels among the students to test which ones would be brave and which would be cowards when they later faced real dangers. The young studied only enough of reading and writing to be able to perform their civic duties. They were taught mainly to endure pain and to persevere in battle.

The children's heads were close-clipped; they usually went barefoot and frequently naked; and after they were twelve years old, they were no longer allowed to wear any underclothes. They bathed infrequently, and their bodies were tough, hard, and dry. They slept together in little bands and made their beds themselves from rushes they collected from the banks of the river Eurotas. These they broke off with their hands, without using a knife. Scarcely was there a time or place when someone was not present to remind them of their duty and to punish them if they neglected it. In addition to all this, one of the best men in the city was appointed as governor over the boys. He arranged them in companies and set over each company a temperate and bold twenty-year-old captain.

This young man was their captain when they fought and their master at home, with the authority to use them as he saw fit. He would often assign them to steal, which they had to do cunningly and boldly, using their wits to deceive and acquire. If they were caught, they were punished by being whipped and deprived of food. They were so impressed by the seriousness of not being caught that one youth, having stolen a fox and hidden it under his coat, allowed it to tear out his very bowels with its claws and teeth and died rather than betray his theft.

After supper the captain would make the boys perform—singing, demonstrating, or answering questions and solving problems. He would ask, "Who is the best man in the city? Why? What do you think of a certain law?" Thus they were trained to judge men and issues.

The young Spartans were taught to speak concisely, to say much in few words; and so by their habit of long silence, they learned to give just and wise answers. When an Athenian laughed at the Spartans' short swords, a Spartan king once replied, "They are long enough to reach our enemies." As their swords were short and sharp, so were their sayings, which came quickly to the point and held the interest of their listeners. When someone proposed setting up a democracy in Sparta, Lycurgus answered, "Begin, friend, by setting it up in your own family." When asked what exercises the Spartans practiced, he answered, "All sorts, except that in which you stretch out your hands in surrender." When he was asked how the Spartans might best oppose an invasion by their enemies, Lycurgus answered, "By each man continuing to be poor and not wishing to be greater than his neighbor." When asked about the need for a city wall, he said, "The city is well fortified that has a wall of men instead of brick." When his nephew was asked why Lycurgus had made so few laws, he answered, "Men of few words require but few laws."

Instruction in music and verse was as fully emphasized as habits of grace and good breeding in conversation. The Spartan songs had a vitality and spirit that inspired men with enthusiasm and incited them to action; their style was plain, the subjects always serious and moral—usually the songs praised heroes or derided cowards.

At one particular festival, there were three choirs: the old men singing, "We once were young, and brave and strong," the young men answering, "And we're so now, come on and try," the children singing last, "But we'll be strongest by and by."

The Spartans played instruments and sang as they marched to battle. It was both magnificent and frightening to see them march towards the deadly fight, in orderly ranks and with impassive faces, advancing calmly and cheerfully to the music of their flutes. Men in such a mood fought with the deliberate valor of hope and assurance. After they had routed their enemies, the Spartans pursued them until the victory was assured. Then they sounded a retreat, because Spartans believed it was base and unworthy of them to cut men to pieces who had already surrendered.

LYCURGUS

When they went to war, the men's exercises were generally more moderate, their food better, the discipline of their officers more friendly than at home; thus they were the only people in the world to whom war gave rest and ease.

Even in peace, the Spartans felt that their first interest was to serve their country rather than their own ends. However, Lycurgus did provide leisure time for Spartan citizens by forbidding them to participate in trade or mechanics, activities which he considered beneath their dignity.

In spite of all the discipline and sacrifice in the Spartan rule, Lycurgus himself was not unduly austere; he encouraged choral dances, hunting, and attendance at the exercise grounds. He dedicated a statue to Laughter and encouraged mirth and good humor at mealtime and after work, as a sort of dessert to accompany their strict, hard life. He did not want his citizens to live completely by themselves, but rather wanted them to unite themselves for the public good. He wished each man to be altruistic and devoted wholly to Sparta.

His system was so effective that a Spartan, who had not been chosen into the list of three hundred men for Olympic honors, returned home joyfully, proud to learn that there were in Sparta three hundred men each better than himself. A Spartan ambassador to Persia was once asked whether he had come in a public or in a private character. He replied, "In a public character, if we succeed; if not, count me as a private man." Another story is told about a Spartan mother who was being consoled after the death of her son in battle. When her son's courage was praised as being the greatest in Sparta, she answered, "Do not say so; my son was a good and brave man, but there are in Sparta many better than he."

The Senate consisted of Lycurgus' chief advisors and aides. The vacancies were filled by the ablest and most deserving men past sixty years old. Those who were chosen were judged not by who was swiftest or strongest, but on the basis of who was wisest and best and most fit to be entrusted with authority. When the election began, some officials were locked in a closed room near the place of election. This place was so contrived that these judges could neither see nor be seen, but they could hear the noise of the assembly. The election was decided by the shouts of the people. The candidates came in one after another, and the men in the closed room decided who won on the basis of the volume of applause.

The winner was declared a duly elected Senator, and he received a garland for his head. He then went in a procession to all the temples to give thanks to the gods. Young men and maidens followed him, singing verses in his honor and praising the virtue and happiness of his life. Relatives and friends would offer him food, saying, "The city honors you with this banquet." Traditionally he would reject the banquets and instead would take his regular place in the common mess hall. As Senator he received a second allowance, but he would eat only his usual portion, saving the other to give to the woman he most esteemed. She then would be honored by the other women.

Lycurgus scorned superstition and allowed the Spartans to bury their dead within the city, right around the temples. He wanted them to become accustomed to being around dead bodies. He would not allow the names of the dead to be inscribed on stones, except only for those men who fell in war or for women who died while holding a sacred office. The time for mourning was restricted to eleven days; on the twelfth the mourners were to make sacrifices to Demeter, goddess of fertility, and return to their normal activities. Thus the Spartans learned to omit all superficial activities, and even in small matters to show homage to virtue or scorn for vice.

LYCURGUS

Lycurgus tried to give the people examples of good conduct; with these constantly before all, he predicted that the people's virtue would be gradually formed and developed.

He restricted travel abroad and visitors to Sparta, because he did not want his men to learn foreign systems or standards of morality. He wanted Spartan customs to be second nature to all Spartans. His idea was that if strange people, strange ideas and words were admitted, such novelties would produce differences in thought, and thus discord might arise to destroy the harmony of the state. He was as careful to preserve his city from the infection of foreign habits as men usually are to prevent the introduction of a disease or a pestilence.

Some blame Lycurgus for the cruelty of the Spartans towards their slaves, the Helots, but it is unlikely that a man so gentle and just could have contrived a system so wicked and barbarous. The Spartans used to declare war against the Helots in order to massacre them without acting against their religion. All manual labor, agriculture and mechanical work was delegated to the Helots, who were under severe discipline, because the Spartan citizens traditionally devoted themselves only to war-making and to law-making. Sometimes they forced Helots to drink to excess and then led them in a drunken condition into the public halls, so that the children could see the evils of drunkenness. The Helots lived in dread of the Spartans, because in Sparta, he who was free was freer than any man, but a slave was the saddest slave in the world.

When Lycurgus saw that his most important institutions had become natural to his countrymen, that habit had made them familiar and easy, and that the citizens were now able to function on their own, he wanted to make his system immortal by handing it on unchanged to posterity. He called an assembly of the people and told them he thought that the harmony and virtue of the state was reasonably well established, but that one thing had yet to be done. He said he would go to Delphi to consult the oracle, and the people agreed that they would observe the laws without the least alteration until his return. Before he left, the two kings, the Senate, and the citizens all took oaths to abide by and maintain the established forms until Lycurgus returned.

Then Lycurgus went to Delphi and asked the oracle whether the laws he had established were good and sufficient for a people's happiness and virtue. The oracle answered that the laws were excellent and that the people, while they observed them, would live in the height of renown. He sent this message to the Spartans and then resolved that, in order that the Spartans might never be released from their oath, he would end his life at Delphi. He abstained from food until the end. Thus he insured the continuance of Spartan customs unchanged for many years, making his very death an act of service to the state.

A Spartan ambassador, wearing a coarse coat and carrying a common staff (around which official dispatches were rolled), gained the willing and cheerful obedience of all Greece. The Spartans suppressed unjust usurpations and despotisms in other Greek cities, arbitrated in war and peace, and quieted civil dissensions. Often it was not necessary to fight: one single Spartan deputy sent to a place could bring order. All the other Greeks would submit to him, knowing what power he represented, and thus Sparta developed a law and order which could be shared with others.

Some said the Spartans were successful not because their kings could command well, but because the people were obedient. Actually people do not obey unless their rulers know how to command, for obedience is a lesson taught by commanders. A true leader creates the obedience of his followers; it is the science of government to inspire men with a willing-

LYCURGUS

ness to obey. It is interesting that Greek cities did not usually send for Spartan ships or money or armed men, but only *for a Spartan commander*. They would then follow this Spartan's discipline and let him reorganize their forces in order to attain success. Thus many Greeks looked upon the city of Sparta itself as a model of good manners and wise government; other Greeks were the scholars and the Spartans were the masters of Greece. And indeed, when the Thebans finally defeated the Spartans at Leuctra, they acted like schoolboys who had beaten their master. In spite of all its emphasis on war, Sparta was finally defeated.

Dominion over others, however, was not what Lycurgus had intended. He thought rather that the happiness of a state, as that of a private man, consisted chiefly in the exercise of virtue and in the harmony of the inhabitants. His aim in all his laws was to make and keep the citizens free-minded, self-dependent, and temperate. All those who have written well on politics—Plato, Diogenes, Zeno—have taken Lycurgus for a model; he was the author, not in writing but in reality, of a complete philosophic state.

ARISTIDES

530–468 B.C.

"For not at seeming just, but being so
He aims, and from his depth of soil below,
Harvests of wise and prudent counsels grow."
AESCHYLUS

*W*hen these lines were recited in the theater at Athens, all eyes turned toward Aristides, who was in the audience, as if this virtue of justice belonged to him in a very special way. He had always shown such constancy, honesty and fairness in his public life that he was known as Aristides the Just. He handled large sums in the public treasury without becoming one penny richer. When he was put in charge of the spoils and prisoners after the battle of Marathon, he did not take any plunder for himself, nor would he allow others to do so.

Once when prosecuting one of his enemies in court Aristides made such a strong case that the judges refused to hear the defendant and proceeded immediately to pass judgment against him. Aristides quickly rose and urged a hearing for his opponent, because it was his right under the law.

Aristides was frequently asked to referee disputes between private parties. In one such case a man reminded Aristides that his opponent had once seriously injured Aristides himself. Aristides responded: "Tell me rather, good friend, what wrong he has done you; for it is your cause, not my own, which I now sit to judge."

Aristides was born in poverty and lived and died without riches; his two daughters did not marry for a long time because they had no dowry. But Aristides actually gloried in being poor. His wealthy cousin Callias was once criticized for not helping Aristides, whose threadbare coat suggested that he must also lack food and the other necessities of life. To relieve Callias' embarrassment Aristides quickly said that he had refused gifts from Callias. He felt it was better to be proud of his poverty than, like Callias, to be proud of wealth, since it is easy to make either a good or bad use of riches, but it is more difficult to bear poverty in a noble spirit. The only ones who should be ashamed of poverty, he said, are those who become poor against their will. Many who heard him admitted that they would rather be poor like Aristides than be rich and be like Callias.

Aristides was a friend and supporter of Clisthenes, who established the democratic constitution. He believed in self-restraint, in law and order, and in the respect for the rights and property of others. He admired Lycurgus, the Spartan law-giver, and supported the conservative and aristocratic party. He was thus the natural rival of Themistocles, who based his power on the support of the masses. It is said that the two often competed as boyhood rivals and that they even competed for the love of the same girl. Themistocles was a ready, adventurous and subtle man, willing to try any new idea, while the dignified Aristides was intent on justice, rejecting all improper or questionable actions.

Themistocles once said, "I hope I never sit on a tribunal where my friends do not have a greater privilege than strangers." But Aristides walked the lonely path of strict honor in politics; he was unwilling to go along with associates in wrongdoing. He was cautious, being convinced that the integrity of his words and actions was the only security of a good citizen.

He and Themistocles were so opposite from each other that they became involved in open debate on almost every issue.

ARISTIDES

This was painful to Aristides, who loved justice and hated prejudice. In a strong debate he was winning the day with the assembly, but, just before the vote in favor of his idea, he withdrew his motion because the opposition had convinced him, even though they had not convinced the judges, of the wisdom and justice of the other side.

He was quick to expose dishonesty, and he thus made many enemies. For revenge, Themistocles once impeached him and obtained an unjust verdict against him. Pretending now to repent of his former alertness, Aristides for a while kept quiet about dishonesty in public office, although he watched for it as carefully as before. The dishonest politicians then highly praised Aristides and nominated him for reelection as treasurer. As he was about to be reelected, Aristides taught his lesson: "When I discharged my office well and faithfully, I was insulted and abused, but now when I have kept quiet about the thieves, I am praised. I am more ashamed of the present honor than of the former sentence. Is it better to help bad men than to conserve the revenue of the public?" He then exposed the thieves who were praising him and was thanked by the most respected citizens.

When the Athenians fought the Persians at Marathon, Aristides was one of the ten generals—second in reputation only to Miltiades—and he supported Miltiades' call for an early battle. It was the custom to rotate the supreme command; each general was in command for one day. When Aristides' day came, he released the command to Miltiades, thus strengthening unity and showing that it is both noble and prudent to follow able and brave leaders. Others followed his example, giving Miltiades undivided authority. Thus the Athenians carried the day and won a crucial victory.

Strangely, his reputation for justice led to envy and jealousy. Themistocles criticized him for privately settling disputes between citizens because, he said, Aristides weakened the public courts. And in the flush of victory, the people developed envy for any man wiser than themselves.

Themistocles thus tried to ostracize Aristides. Ostracism was not a punishment for any criminal act, but was simply a popular action to eliminate or humiliate any man who had become too powerful or too great. The man whose name was written by the largest number was banned from Athens (or "ostracized") for ten years. When Aristides was being considered for ostracism, an illiterate farmer, not recognizing Aristides, asked him to write the name "Aristides" for him. On being asked if Aristides had ever done him any harm, the man replied, "None at all; neither know I the man; but I am tired of hearing him called 'the Just.'" Aristides made no reply, but wrote his own name.

As he left the city in ostracism, Aristides prayed that the Athenians might never have any occasion to remember him, hoping in vain that his city would not suffer from lack of his wise counsel and leadership.

Three years later, when Xerxes invaded with his great fleet and army, the Athenians decreed that all those in exile should return, because they particularly wanted Aristides back. Even before this, Aristides had been working to organize the other Greeks to join in a defense against Persia. In this war he assisted Themistocles both in action and counsel, and thus he helped his rival to become the most famous of men. Aristides supported Themistocles' plan to fight at Salamis. Before the big battle, Aristides led a small group of brave Athenians to clear the island of Salamis, killing or capturing all the Persians on the island. Then he placed guards all around the island, so that during the naval battle, when refugees swam ashore, his friends would be saved and his enemies captured.

After the great victory of Salamis, Themistocles wanted to

ARISTIDES

cut off Xerxes' retreat to Asia. Aristides opposed this plan and urged him instead to think of ways to help the Persians escape from Greece, and to build additional bridges to speed their retreat. Aristides argued that if the Persians were trapped, they would be forced to fight more bravely and Xerxes would use his army more wisely.

Mardonius stayed behind with a big Persian army and offered to rebuild Athens and to give the Athenians money if they would remain neutral in a new Persian war. The Spartans, learning of this, offered to help the women and children of Athens, for the city had suffered much in the war. Aristides replied that he could forgive the enemy for thinking all things were obtainable by money—since barbarians knew nothing more valuable—but he felt offended that the Spartans looked only at Athens' present poverty and did not remember her glory and valor. He told the Spartans that all the treasure on earth meant nothing to the people of Athens compared to the liberty of Greece.

Pointing to the sun, he told the Persian messengers, "As long as the sun follows its course, so long shall the citizens of Athens wage war with the Persians for the country that has been wasted and for the temples that have been profaned and burned by them."

Aristides led the Athenians at the battle of Plataea. The Greeks began to contend among themselves for places of honor: Pausanias and his Spartans claimed the right-wing position, and the Tegeatans contended with the Athenians for the left-wing place of honor. Aristides said this was no time to argue about places of honor. "Place neither takes away nor contributes courage. We shall try, by protecting the post you assign us, to reflect no dishonor on our former battle. For we are here not to differ with our friends but to fight our enemies, not to extol our ancestors but to be brave men ourselves. This battle will show how much each city, each captain, and each soldier is worth to Greece."

Throughout Greece there was suspense before the battle, especially among the wealthy Athenians whose homes and property had been burned or destroyed. Some of the aristocrats began to think of revolting or even of betraying Athens to Persia. When Aristides discovered eight of these men, he dismissed them from the army, and thus gave the opportunity to the other conspirators to repent and take courage. By bravely defending Athens, each man had a chance of showing his sincere loyalty toward the city.

In full strength the Persian cavalry attacked the Megarians, who called for help. Pausanias asked for volunteers, and Aristides sent three hundred of Athens' best soldiers to assist. They fought as though the whole war depended on their success. Brave Athenians unhorsed the Persian cavalry leader, who was so burdened with heavy armor that he could not get up from the ground. Even so, the Athenians had great difficulty killing him because of the protection of this wonderful armor. The leader's death triggered a retreat; the Persians' extreme sorrow made it clear how important his leadership had been.

Both armies delayed engaging in a major battle because an oracle had said the victory would go to those who defended rather than to those who attacked. Alexander of Macedon (an ancestor of Alexander the Great) came through the Persian lines secretly to tell Aristides that the Persians would finally fight on the next day because their provisions were low. Aristides told Pausanias, who ordered the soldiers to prepare for battle. Because of their success against the Persians, the Athenians were assigned the right flank, directly opposite the toughest Persian soldiers. The Spartans exchanged places with the Athenians so that they could fight against the Greeks who

ARISTIDES

had deserted to the Persian army. The Athenian leaders resented being moved about "like so many Helots," but Aristides urged cooperation. He reminded them that earlier they had contended with the Tegeatans for the left flank, and asked them how they could be discontented with the honor of leading the entire Greek army. He pointed to the advantage of fighting against the barbarians, who were their natural enemies, rather than against their Greek neighbors.

As they went into battle, the Athenians noticed that the Persians looked very much like the ones they had beaten at Marathon—they had the same armor, weapons, and gold-embroidered robes—and the Athenians became determined to show that they could beat Persians any time, any place.

After the transfer, the Persians again reversed their flanks, either because they were afraid of the Athenians or because they wanted to fight the Spartans. Thus they wasted the day by marching instead of fighting.

That night the Greeks decided to move to a safer location with a better water supply. Most of the Greek army moved to Plataea, but certain Spartans, considering a retreat to be cowardly, decided to stand their ground. In the morning the Persians attacked the remnant of the Spartans, and thus the battle of Plataea began. Pausanias at first ordered the Spartans not to fight until he could make sacrifices to the gods and secure a sign of good auspices, so the Spartans stoically stood the first Persian charge without defense. When Pausanias gave the signal, however, the Spartans fiercely attacked the Persians, who had surrounded them.

The Athenians had stopped their retreat to wait for the Spartans, but when they heard the noise of battle, they turned around and hurried towards the fight. On the way they met the Thebans and other Greeks who sided with Persia. Aristides called to these Greeks to forsake the Persians and come over and join the Greeks as natural allies. The Thebans and other Persian allies answered by a fierce assault, but Aristides and the Athenians soon crushed these Greeks. Then they rushed to help the Spartans capture the Persian forts and camps.

After the battle the various rival Greek tribes, who had joined in defeating their common enemy, argued as to whether the victory monuments should honor the Spartans, who claimed to have done most of the fighting. Aristides finally persuaded them that all the Greeks should vote on it. The Corinthians proposed that the honor should go to the Plataeans, on whose land the battle was won, and everyone agreed to this compromise.

When the Athenians returned to their ruined city, Aristides realized that they wanted a democracy. Since they had earned a great deal of respect by their brave fighting, Aristides made a motion that everyone should share in the government.

Then Themistocles said he had a secret idea that was most important for the security of the city, but that it could not be publicly stated. The people chose Aristides to hear it secretly and to judge the proposal for all of Athens. The proposal was to set fire to the arsenal of their Greek allies and thus to gain control of all Greece. Aristides reported to the assembly that nothing could be more advantageous than Themistocles' proposal, but also nothing could be more unjust. The assembly ordered Themistocles to abandon his plan, reflecting the strength of the love of justice felt by the men of Athens and their confidence in Aristides.

Aristides and Cimon were given a joint commission to lead the men of Athens in the allied Greek army. Aristides, noting that the allies were offended by the harshness, conceit, and imperiousness of Pausanias and the Spartan officers, was gentle and considerate towards everyone. The humble attitude of

ARISTIDES

Aristides and the calm moderation of Cimon made the allies turn to Athens, rather than Sparta, for leadership. Thus Athens gained the chief command, not by weapons, ships, or horses, but by equity and wisdom.

When the Spartans realized that their generals had been corrupted by authority, they voluntarily relinquished the chief command and withdrew, choosing to have citizens of moderation following Spartan customs rather than dominion over all Greece.

Under the Spartan leadership each city had paid a certain contribution towards the cost of the war. The allies asked Aristides to rate them city by city in due proportion, how much each should pay.

Even with such vast power and opportunity for enrichment, Aristides went out poor and returned poorer. He determined the tax justly and to the satisfaction of all. The allies called Aristides' time of command "the happy time of Greece."

Themistocles belittled Aristides' reputation for justice in dealing with the allies, saying he was a moneybag rather than a man. Themistocles said the highest virtue of a general was to understand and predict the measures the enemy would try. Aristides replied, "This is indeed necessary, but the best thing a general can do is to keep his hands from taking money."

At this time Aristides took an oath, with the other allied leaders, to keep the treaty and to be cursed if Athens left the League. Later when the situation called for Athens to take a more independent stand, Aristides told the Athenian people to place upon him the burden of perjury and to negotiate in the best interests of the city of Athens.

Although he was rigorously just in his own private business and in the affairs of his neighbors, he still acted according to Athenian interests in public matters—which sometimes included a bit of injustice. For example, in the debate about moving the treasury of the League from Delos to Athens, he argued that the proposal, though not just, was expedient because it would make Athens stronger.

But when Cimon and many others proposed ostracism for Themistocles, Aristides neither did nor said anything against his old rival. Thus he showed his moderation and disdain for revenge. He no more triumphed over his enemy in adversity than he had envied him in his prosperity.

Little is known about the death and old age of Aristides, although it is known that he died in poverty. His children and grandchildren also suffered from poverty, and there was not even money for his funeral expenses. The city of Athens erected a monument to his honor, but his true monument was his reputation in the hearts of the men of Athens for his justice, his moderation, his loyalty, and his honesty.

CIMON

507–449 B.C.

*W*hen Cimon was ready to begin his political career, the people welcomed him. Cimon was frank and even-tempered; both qualities appealed strongly to the Athenians, who were weary of the cunning ways of Themistocles.

Cimon, an Athenian, was the son of Miltiades, the hero of Marathon. While Cimon was still a young man, his father was thrown into prison for not being able to pay a large fine imposed by the Athenians. Miltiades died there, leaving Cimon and his young unmarried sister Elpinice orphans.

In his youth Cimon had a reputation for being disorderly and fond of drinking. Some said he resembled his grandfather, who was known as Cimon the Simpleton. He had very little knowledge of music or the other liberal arts and accomplishments that were then common among the Greeks. He showed none of the quickness and eloquence of his countrymen of Attica, and in some ways, he was more like a Spartan than an Athenian. But, to borrow Euripides' description of Heracles, Cimon was "rude and unrefined, for great things well endowed."

Despite the fact that in his youth there was gossip about his relationship with his sister, all other facets of Cimon's character were considered noble and good. Aristides recognized his potential ability and sponsored him as a counterpart to the craft and boldness of Themistocles. Cimon was as daring as his father, comparable with Themistocles in judgment, and more just and honest than either of them. He was fully their equal in military virtues; and in the ordinary duties of a citizen at home, he was immeasurably their superior.

When Themistocles, facing the Persian invasion, advised the Athenians to abandon Athens and to fight the enemy by sea, in the straits of Salamis, all the people were amazed at the rashness of his proposal. However Cimon, still very young, was the first to be seen striding cheerfully with his companions to the citadel, carrying a bridle to offer to the goddess, intimating that his country did not need horsemen, but mariners. After paying his devotions and offering his bridle, he took one of the bucklers that hung upon the walls of the temple and went down to the port. Inspired by Cimon's example, many of the Athenian citizens regained confidence. And when he fought with extraordinary gallantry in the battle of Salamis the Athenians regarded him with affection as well as admiration. Many encouraged him to aspire to deeds as glorious as those of his father at the battle of Marathon.

When the Medes had been driven out of Greece, Cimon was appointed admiral of the Athenian ships, which were under the fleet command of Pausanias, the Spartan. Under Cimon's leadership the Athenians distinguished themselves both by excellent discipline and extraordinary zeal. Pausanias, who was haughty and arrogant of his own authority and success, treated his allies arrogantly, but Cimon was kind and humane to them. When he discovered that Pausanias was secretly communicating with the enemy and planning with the king of Persia to betray Greece, he swayed most of the allies to follow his and Aristides' command. Thus before most people were aware of what had happened, Cimon emerged the

CIMON

true leader—not by force but by his character and persuasiveness.

Now, strengthened by allies, he went as general into Thrace. He had been told that some Persians—kinsmen of the King—controlled the city of Eion, and that the Thracians were supplying them with provisions. Cimon attacked Eion and imprisoned the Persians within the city walls. He then routed the Thracians from the countryside and claimed the land. He reduced the Persians to such straits that their commander set fire to the city of Eion and burned himself, his relations, and his property in one common flame. Though by his conquest Cimon gained only the charred remains of the city, he gave the surrounding countryside to the Athenians for a colony.

Cimon was then permitted by the people to erect three statues of Hermes. The inscriptions, though they do not mention the name of Cimon, pay him the highest honors—greater than Miltiades and Themistocles ever received. One of them reads:

> *The Athenians to their leaders this reward*
> *For great and useful service did accord;*
> *Others hereafter shall, from their applause,*
> *Learn to be valiant in their country's cause.*

One wonders why the Athenians so particularly honored Cimon. Perhaps it was that with other commanders they had always stood on the defensive, while under his leadership they had invaded enemy countries and acquired new territories. One such territory was the isle of Scyros whose inhabitants, the Dolopians, had for generations forsaken the soil in favor of piracy. Heartened by their successes, these pirates had begun to plunder the ships of foreigners who brought merchandise into their ports. Once some of the Dolopians had not only stolen the cargo of a Thessalian ship but had also imprisoned the merchants who were aboard. The men, escaping from prison, obtained a judgment against Scyros. The Scyrian people refused to make restitution out of the public funds and demanded that the individuals who had the plunder return it to the merchants. The thieves, in desperation, sent word to Cimon, declaring that they were ready to deliver the town into his hands if he would rescue them. Cimon accepted their offer and took the town, but he expelled the Dolopian pirates and so opened up the Aegean Sea to traffic.

While at Scyros, Cimon was determined to find the burial place of the Athenian hero, Theseus. According to legend, when Theseus fled Athens 400 years earlier he had taken refuge on this island, where he was eventually slain. An oracle had once commanded the Athenians to bring home his ashes and to pay him all honors due a hero, but the people of Scyros had refused to acknowledge the burial or to allow a search for the tomb. Cimon undertook the search enthusiastically and after some difficulty discovered the tomb. He had the remains put aboard his ship and brought them back to Athens with great pomp and ceremony. This, more than any other accomplishment of Cimon's, made him loved by the people.

One story is told by a poet who dined with Cimon and his friends. After supper, when they had poured out wine to honor the gods, Cimon was asked to give them a song. He performed so skillfully that everyone applauded him, and remarked on his superiority to Themistocles, who on a similar occasion had said, "I have never learned to sing, nor to play a musical instrument, and only know how to make a city rich and powerful." They then discussed Cimon's most impressive accomplishments, but he told them that they had omitted the one he valued most, which he proceeded to recount:

CIMON

"When the allies had taken a great number of barbarian prisoners in Sestos and Byzantium, they allowed me to divide the booty. I accordingly put the prisoners in one lot, and the spoils and jewels in the other, but the allies complained that this was an unequal division. I gave them their choice, saying that the Athenians would be content with what they refused. They took the ornaments for their share and left the slaves for the Athenians. I went away, and everyone laughed at me for this ridiculous division. The allies carried away the golden bracelets, armlets, collars, and purple robes, while we Athenians had only the naked bodies of the captives. But later, the friends and kinsmen of the prisoners came to redeem every one of their relations at a high ransom. We got so much treasure that I maintained our whole fleet for four months with the money, and there was even some left over to put in the treasury of Athens."

With all his victories, Cimon grew rich; but what he gained from the barbarians with honor, he spent even more honorably upon the citizens of Athens. He pulled down all the fences around his gardens and grounds so that strangers and the needy citizens could gather food when they wished. At home he kept a table, plain but with sufficient food for a considerable number, to which any poor townsman had free access. Besides this charity, he was always attended by two or three well-dressed young companions who, upon meeting a poorly clothed elderly citizen, would change clothes with the elder. He also told his companions to carry a large quantity of coins, which were given silently to the better class of poor men that stood in the marketplace. He got riches in order that he might use them, and he used them that he might get honor by them. Cimon's noble generosity outdid all the old Athenian hospitality and good nature.

During his entire time in power, Cimon never profited by the public money but kept his hands clean and untainted: he never acted or spoke for his own private gain. It is said that a Persian, who had revolted from his king, fled to Athens, where he was harassed. He went to Cimon, and to gain his favor, he placed in his doorway two cups, one full of gold and the other of silver. Cimon smiled and asked him whether he wished to have Cimon's hired service or his friendship. The Persian replied, "Your friendship." "If so," said Cimon, "take away these pieces, for being your friend, when I shall have occasion for them I will send and ask for them."

The enemies of the Greeks had been driven out of the country. The allies of the Athenians were becoming tired of war and wanted to remain at home and attend to their businesses. They still paid the tax they were assessed, but were no longer willing to send men and galleys as they had before. Other Athenian generals attempted through Greek courts to require both men and galleys, and as a result, relations became strained and the authority of Athens unpopular. Cimon, however, forced no man to go to war who was not willing—instead of service, he accepted money and unmanned vessels.

Those Greeks allied with Athens who chose to stay home soon lost their military discipline and through their own folly were transformed into unwarlike men. But Cimon continued to discipline large numbers of Athenians on military maneuvers at sea. The softened allies unwittingly became tributaries and subjects of the armed Athenians they maintained.

No man ever did more than Cimon to humble the pride of the Persian king. Not content to merely force the Persians out of Greece, he followed close at their heels, without giving them time to breathe, until he had cleared Asia Minor of Persian soldiers. At one point word was brought him that the royal commanders of Persia were waiting at the coast with a large land army and a large fleet. He was determined to make the whole sea on his side of the Chelidonian Islands so

CIMON

well protected that the Persians would not dare to show themselves in it, and so he set out from Cnidos with two hundred galleys. These particular galleys had been built originally for their speed by Themistocles. Cimon had them rebuilt so that the ships were wider and the decks roomier to allow a great number of fully armed soldiers to fight directly from the decks. His first attack was on the town of Phaselis, which, though it was inhabited by the Greeks, was still allied with the Persians. Among the allies fighting loyally under him were men of Chios, who were old friends of the Phaselites. Trying at the same time to dissuade Cimon from attacking and to warn their threatened friends, they shot into the town arrows which had messages attached for the Phaselites. Finally, Cimon made peace with the Phaselites upon condition they would pay ten talents and follow him against the barbarians.

The Persian forces now lay with their whole fleet at the mouth of the river Eurymedon, waiting for reinforcements from eighty Phoenician ships on their way from Cyprus. They had no intention of fighting until the reinforcements arrived, but Cimon decided to force them into battle. Realizing this, the Persians moved into the mouth of the river to avoid being attacked, but Cimon continued to provoke them. The hundreds of Persian ships which finally met the attack fought with little enthusiasm and were soon turned toward shore. Those who landed fled to join the army; the rest perished with their ships or were taken. In this one battle two hundred galleys were won by the Athenians.

At this point, Cimon was uncertain whether he should try to force his way ashore. His Greeks were tired; on land, they would be fighting against all fresh men, many times their number. But seeing that his men were flushed with victory, he encouraged them on, and as soon as they touched ground, they set up a shout and charged the enemy. The fight was a hard one and some of the most outstanding men of Athens were killed. However, the Athenians fought with such spirit that they routed the barbarians, took some prisoners, and looted all their tents and pavilions, which were filled with riches.

Cimon, like a skilled athlete at the games who had won two victories in one day, was encouraged to try for yet another. Hearing that the eighty Phoenician ships had come into sight at Hydrum, he quickly set off to surprise them and succeeded in destroying most of their vessels. His success so daunted the king of Persia that he soon made a celebrated peace. In this peace he agreed that his armies would come no nearer the Grecian sea than the length of a horse's course, and that none of his galleys or vessels of war would appear between the Cyanean and Chelidonian isles.

Out of proceeds from the public sale of Cimon's war spoils, Athens was able to build the southern wall of the Acropolis and sink great weights of stone and rubble into the marsh to form the foundations known as the "legs," of the Long Walls, which were completed in a later age. It was Cimon also who first beautified the upper city of Athens with handsome public buildings for meetings and exercise. He planted plane trees around the marketplace and transformed the Academy from a barren place into a well-watered grove with shady paths and open courses for races.

The Persians despised Cimon because of the relatively small forces with which he almost conquered them; and so with the aid of the people of the interior of Thrace, they again planned to attack. This time Cimon attacked them with only four of his own galleys and took thirteen of theirs. After driving out the Persians and subduing the Thracians, he made the whole Chersonese the property of Athens. He then attacked the people of Thasos, who had revolted against Athens. He defeated them at sea, captured thirty-three of their ships, took their

CIMON

town by siege, and acquired for Athens the gold mines on the opposite coast as well as all the territory dependent upon Thasos.

This victory opened the passage into Macedon. Some Athenians believed that Cimon could have acquired a good portion of that country too, but he neglected to do so; they suspected that he had been bribed by King Alexander. His adversaries joined in Athens to accuse him of being false to his country. At his trial, Cimon contended that he had not sought riches for himself in his conquests but that his conquests had always enriched the citizens of his country. Because of his temperance and goodness and the glories of his victories, he was acquitted.

After this, Cimon attempted to control and restrain the common people, who wanted to claim all the power and sovereignty of the nobility for themselves. When he once again left Athens to wage war, the people overthrew the ancient laws and customs and tried, with the help of Pericles, to substitute a strongly democratic form of government.

When Cimon returned, he was troubled. He attempted to restore the power of the courts of law which Pericles had weakened and to revive the old aristocracy. The new democratic leaders inveighed against him, circulating once more the old rumors of his misbehavior, and accusing him of disloyally favoring the Spartans.

An Athenian poet commented:

> *He was as good as others that one sees,*
> *But he was fond of drinking and of ease;*
> *And would at nights to Sparta often roam,*
> *Leaving his sister desolate at home.*

If, indeed, Cimon was as his enemies pictured him, lazy and dissolute, then had he been by nature more diligent and temperate, surely no Greek commander before or after him could have surpassed his exploits of war. He had always shown his affection for Sparta, and on occasions had said to his fellow Athenians, "But that is not what the Spartans would do." At one time this attitude had appealed to the Athenians, who sought an alliance with their neighboring city-state; but now that the Athenians had grown more powerful and had little need for Sparta's aid, Cimon's devotion to the Spartans made them angry.

Their relationship with the Spartans had become further strained when Sparta, shattered by an earthquake, had been attacked by an enemy tribe wanting to overpower those the earthquake had spared. Some Athenians argued against sending aid to Sparta, saying that since their rival was down, it was best to keep her so. But Cimon had persuaded the people: "We should not allow Greece to be lamed, nor our own city to be deprived of her yoke-fellow." And thus, with a large Athenian army, he had gone to the aid of Sparta. Not long after Sparta again had called for help. This time, when the Athenians arrived, the Spartans, now fearing their power, dismissed only the Athenians from among their allies, claiming they came for selfish reasons. The Athenians, enraged, returned home and took their revenge on all Spartan sympathizers, and especially on Cimon, who was ostracized from Athens for ten years.

In the meantime, the Spartans, on their return from freeing Delphi, had encamped their army at Tanagra. Cimon, in exile, learned that the Athenians were going to attack them, and so he came armed to fight with his own tribe against the Spartans. His old enemies argued that he would first disrupt the Athenian army and then lead the Spartans against Athens. The Athenian Council of Five Hundred was frightened and ordered its officers to reject Cimon's aid. However, before leaving the Athenian army, Cimon convinced his friends, who were also suspected of favoring the Spartans, that they should take this opportunity to prove their innocence to their countrymen. Making a separate company by themselves, one hundred of his friends took up Cimon's armor and standards and fought so desperately that all were killed. When the Athenians realized what had happened they grieved at the loss of those brave men and regretted having suspected them unjustly.

Cimon was then recalled to Athens, partly in appreciation of his former services and partly because the Athenians were afraid the Peloponnesians would attack them soon. Pericles, who for a long time had resisted Cimon's influence, was himself the author of the decree which recalled him. His action illustrates how extraordinarily reasonable the Athenians were, and how moderate their anger was, that they gave way to the public good. Even ambition, the least governable of all human passions, could yield to the necessities of the state.

Cimon, as soon as he returned, put an end to the war and reconciled the Athenians to the Spartans. With internal strife removed, he sought to direct the energies of the restless Athenians away from fighting other Greeks, and so he equipped two hundred galleys and planned to attack Egypt and Cyprus. He hoped to use this campaign to train the Athenians to fight against the Persians and to enrich themselves at the expense of Greece's natural enemies. As the army was ready to embark, Cimon had a dream. In it a furious dog was barking at him, and mixed with the barking, a kind of human voice uttering these words:

> *Come on, for thou shalt shortly be,*
> *a pleasure to my whelps and me.*

An intimate friend told Cimon that the dream foretold his death. He explained it this way: a dog is enemy to him he barks at; and Cimon's death was his enemies' goal. It was impossible for Cimon to call off the attack, and so he set sail. He sent sixty of his ships toward Egypt. With the rest of his fleet he defeated the king of Persia and secured the allegiance of the cities in the Cyprus area. Seeking the complete ruin of the Persian empire, Cimon next planned to attack Egypt.

In an attempt to execute his great designs, Cimon kept his navy near the isle of Cyprus and sent messengers to consult the oracle for his guidance. The god would give them no answer to their secret request but commanded them to return, saying that Cimon was already with him. Hearing this they returned to sea, and as soon as they reached the Greek army, which was then near Egypt, they were told that Cimon was dead!

Some say he died of sickness while besieging Citium, while others say he died of wounds he received in a skirmish with the Persians. But before he died, he commanded his men to return to Athens without letting anyone along the way know of his death. This they did with such secrecy that they had all returned safely home before either their allies or their enemies knew that Cimon was dead.

Although Cimon had carried the scene of war far from his own country, had won famous victories and had brought his enemies near ruin, he had failed to conquer them. After his death, popular Greek leaders stirred their people against one another instead of uniting the Greeks against their common enemies. They ruined the power of Greece by giving the Persians time to recover and repair all their losses. Thus, the Persians were soon able to impose whatever tribute they pleased on the Greek cities in Asia, the confederates and the allies of Sparta. But in the time of Cimon not so much as a Persian letter-carrier or a single Persian horseman was ever seen to come within four hundred furlongs of the sea.

Such was the Greek commander!

PERICLES

495–429 B.C.

*A*s a young man of Athens, Pericles was wary of the people. Because of his wealth, his distinguished family and influential friends, and his striking resemblance to a tyrant of the past, he feared he might be considered a dangerous person and subsequently ostracized. But when Aristides was dead, Themistocles driven out, and Cimon usually abroad on expeditions, Pericles became the spokesman for the common people rather than for the aristocrats. By nature he was far from democratic; actually he chose the party of the people to protect himself from any suspicion that he wanted arbitrary power. Also, the people's party seemed the most likely source of support in his political contest with Cimon, who had great power with the aristocracy.

Pericles was himself of the noblest birth. His father, Xanthippus, had defeated the Persians at Mycale. His mother was a relative of Clisthenes, who had ended the tyranny of the Pisistrati and established a model government which promoted harmony among the people. Shortly before the birth of Pericles, his mother dreamed that she gave birth to a lion. A few days later her son was born, perfectly formed except that his head was somewhat long and out of proportion. The poets of Athens eventually named him "Schinocephalos," or squillhead, after the sea creature, and made fun of him as "fainting under the load of his own head." Sculptors preferred to portray him wearing a helmet which concealed that peculiarity.

Under the pretense of teaching him only music, the sophist Damon (who was later ostracized for supporting tyranny) trained Pericles to be a young athlete of politics. Zeno the Eleatic, who taught natural philosophy with a tongue like a double-edged weapon, instructed Pericles in the art of silencing opponents in argument, no matter which side he might take. But it was Anaxagoras, the tutor who saw the most of Pericles, who inspired him to nobility of purpose and character. Anaxagoras was the first philosopher to teach that the order of the world was the work of a conscious intelligence rather than the result of chance. Pericles held Anaxagoras in high esteem; he filled himself with his tutor's lofty thought. He developed, under the influence of Anaxagoras, a sustained, even tone of voice which was extremely effective. More importantly, Anaxagoras inspired in the young Pericles a composure, serenity, and majestic dignity which nothing could disturb.

Consciously changing his entire way of life, Pericles carefully reserved the effectiveness of his own appearances for great occasions, just as the Athenians reserved their sacred state galley *Salaminia*. He did not speak on every occasion, nor did he attend the assembly at each meeting. Matters of lesser importance were taken care of by friends or other speakers. He was never seen walking in public except when he went to the marketplace or the council hall. He declined all invitations to supper, all friendly visits and indeed any intimate association which might weaken the public impression of his superiority and gravity. He knew well that dignity is not easy to preserve in the familiarity of comradeship or drinking.

Pericles was very careful of what and how he would speak —so much so that before he addressed the people he prayed to

PERICLES

the gods that no word might slip unawares from his lips which might be unsuitable to the occasion. When he did appear to harangue them, they spoke of his "thunder and lightning" and the "dreadful thunderbolt in his tongue." And concerning the dexterity of his speaking skill Thucydides, his greatest opponent, once said: "When I have thrown him in wrestling and given him a fair fall, he, by persisting that he had no fall, gets the better of me, and makes the bystanders, in spite of their own eyes, believe him!" But it was his study of philosophy which gave his eloquence what Plato calls "that all-commanding power." With this quality he surpassed all other orators of his time, and earned his nickname, "The Olympian." The poet Ion criticized Pericles for being haughty and arrogant; but Zeno urged those who sneered at his gravity to affect the same sort of pride themselves, saying that by imitating it they might in time come to possess it naturally.

When Pericles first decided to challenge Cimon's authority, he realized he must win the favor of the people. Cimon spent his own money lavishly on feeding, clothing and caring for the needy citizens of Athens. Pericles did not have Cimon's wealth. Outmatched in that contest for popularity, Pericles turned to the distribution of public funds. With the moneys allowed for public entertainments and for service on juries, and with other forms of pay and largess, Pericles soon bought the people over as supporters. At the beginning of his climb to power, he turned the people against the council of Areopagus, to which he did not belong. He succeeded in removing from its jurisdiction most of the cases formerly tried by that court. The power which Pericles had gained from the populace also allowed him to bring about the ostracism of Cimon. Although Cimon had won brilliant victories over the Persians and had filled Athens with money and spoils of war, Pericles was able to persuade the people that Cimon disloyally favored Sparta and was therefore dangerous to Athenian security. Some years before, when Cimon was tried for his life, Pericles had been one of the prosecutors appointed by the people. When Cimon's sister Elpinice had tried to influence Pericles, he told her with a smile, "Elpinice, you are too old for such business as this!" Pericles, however, spoke only once against Cimon at that time, merely to discharge his obligation, and left the assembly, having hurt Cimon less than any of his accusers.

Before the end of Cimon's ten-year period of exile, he returned to command members of his own tribe and assist the Athenians in battle against the Spartans. He hoped that by risking his life with his countrymen he would disprove the suspicion that he had favored Sparta. But friends of Pericles forced Cimon to withdraw from the battle, insisting he had no right to participate while still under sentence of ostracism. Pericles then fought more vigorously than in any other battle and was conspicuous above all others for exposing himself to danger. Nevertheless, the Athenians were defeated on their own frontiers. Expecting a new attack, the Athenians began to regret the absence of Cimon. Pericles, aware of their feelings, proposed that they recall Cimon. It is not certain whether Elpinice negotiated this agreement, but when Cimon returned, he immediately went to sea with a fleet of two hundred ships as commander-in-chief abroad while Pericles retained power at home.

As leader of the people, Pericles was soon the most powerful man in Athens. The aristocrats wanted someone to oppose him, a foil to blunt and weaken his power, so they put forward Thucydides, a sensible kinsman of Cimon. Thucydides was a talented speaker and politician, who was not content to allow superior men to avoid responsibility for public affairs, wasting their value to Athens in obscure private life among the masses. By uniting these men of distinction in one body, he

PERICLES

was able to effectively oppose the popular party. From the beginning there had been a concealed rift in the public life of Athens, dividing the tendencies of the aristocracy from those of the masses. Open rivalry and contention between Pericles and Thucydides made a deep gash and severed the city into two parties of equal power, the party of the people and the party of the few.

More than at any other time, Pericles made it his policy to gratify the desires of the people. He arranged to always have some great public show, banquet, or procession in town to please them—coaxing and managing his countrymen like children with such delights. Many have said that Pericles encouraged and led the people to bad habits; that by his public indulgences he changed the Athenians from a sober, thrifty people, who were self-sufficient, into lovers of expense, intemperance and license. On the other hand, Thucydides described the rule of Pericles as an aristocratical government which, though it was called a democracy, was in fact the supremacy of a single great man. Every year Pericles sent out sixty galleys, each carrying many citizens who were paid for eight months while they learned the art of seamanship. To further ease the city of an idle, restless crowd, he sent a thousand citizens into the Chersonese as planters—dividing the land among them, five hundred more to the isle of Naxos, a thousand into Thrace, and others to Andros and Italy. In this way he both met the needs of poor Athenians and intimidated their allies by, in effect, posting garrisons in the midst of them.

But it was the construction of public and sacred buildings which Pericles ordered that gave the most pleasure to the Athenians and astonished all strangers. Indeed, these are now Greece's only physical historical evidence of her ancient power and wealth. Yet this was the policy for which Pericles was most criticized. His enemies denounced him: "Our Greek allies cannot but resent it as an insufferable affront, if not open tyranny, when they see the treasure they contributed for the Persian war wantonly lavished by us upon our own city. We use their money to gild Athens and adorn her like some vain woman bedecked with precious stones, to sculpt figures and temples which cost a thousand talents!"

But Pericles informed the men of Athens that so long as they maintained the defense of their Greek allies and kept the Persians from attacking, Athens was in no way obliged to make any accounting. "Those we defend do not supply so much as one horse or man or ship, but only money. If we uphold our side of the agreements," he said, "that money is not theirs who give it, but ours who receive it." Pericles wanted not only eternal glory for Athens, but also work and immediate prosperity for the undisciplined multitude of workers who stayed at home while those who were eligible earned public pay in military service. With the variety of workmanship needed to erect these great works of Athens, almost everyone in the city, either directly or indirectly, was on the public payroll; and thus the wealth of Athens was distributed into every home.

Marble and stone, brass, ivory, ebony and cypress woods, were all used in the construction; and so carpenters, modelers, blacksmiths and braziers, coppersmiths, stonemasons, dyers, goldsmiths, ivory workers, painters, embroiderers, and engravers were all employed. Others who helped in the work were those who transported materials—merchants and sailors and shipmasters by sea, and wagonmakers and trail drivers by land, as well as cattle breeders, ropemakers, flax workers, shoemakers and leather workers, road builders and miners. Each trade had its own hired company of unskilled laborers who were banded together for a unique service.

Phidias, who created the gigantic golden statue of Athena,

PERICLES

directed and supervised all the construction, though other great masters and workmen were also employed. Callicrates and Ictinus built the Parthenon. The chapel at Eleusis, where the mysteries were celebrated, was begun by Coroebus, who erected the pillars that stand upon the pavement; after his death Metagenes added the frieze and the upper line of columns. Xenocles roofed the tower on the top of the temple of Castor and Pollux. The long wall, which Socrates says he himself heard Pericles propose to the people, was undertaken by Callicrates. The Odeum, or music hall, was filled with seats and ranges of pillars and was covered with a conical roof made to slope from a single point at its top, constructed in imitation of the pavilion of the king of Persia.

As these stately and exquisite buildings progressed, the workmen sought to outdo each other in the materials, designs, and beauty of their workmanship. Hearing Agatharchus the painter boast of the speed and ease with which he completed his work, Zeuxis, another artist, replied, "Mine cost me a great deal of time." Ease and speed in doing a thing do not necessarily give a work permanent beauty; and the time and pains spent in preparation for the production of work is repaid with interest by the lasting quality of the work produced. Pericles' works are especially admired as having been made to last long, though made quickly. Every piece of his work had immediately the beauty and elegance of things antique, yet in its vigor and freshness it always seems to have just been executed. There is a sort of bloom of newness upon them which preserves them from the touch of time, as if they had some perennial spirit and undying vitality mingled within their very composition. Yet the most extraordinary thing about them was the rapidity of their execution. Buildings, any one of which might have taken several generations to complete, were all accomplished in the height and prime of one man's political service.

When the orators who sided with Thucydides and his party denounced Pericles for squandering the public money, Pericles rose in open assembly and put the question to the people whether they thought he had spent too much. They answered, "Too much, a great deal!" "Then," he said, "since it is so, let the cost be charged not to your account, but to mine; and let the inscriptions upon the buildings carry my name." When they heard this, whether from surprise at his generosity or from a determination to share in the glory, they cried aloud, urging him to spend what he thought fit from the public purse, and to spare no cost till all work was finished.

When they came to a final contest as to who should be ostracized, Pericles threw Thucydides out of Athens and broke up the party which had been organized to oppose him. With the people no longer divided, he got all of Athens and all affairs that pertained to the Athenians into his own hands. He controlled their tributes, their armies, their galleys, the islands, the sea, and the far-flung power and leadership they exercised over other Greeks as well as barbarians.

After Pericles had consolidated all political power, he was no longer the same man he had been before—he was not so tame, gentle and familiar with the people, nor so ready to comply with their wild and capricious desires. He turned from indulgence in courting their support to the austerity of aristocratic and regal rule. By being honorable, firm, and consistent in the city's best interest, he was able to lead the people along and show them what should be done. Sometimes, though, he had to urge them forward and force them against their will to do what was for their best advantage.

It was only natural that, from time to time, there arose all kinds of controversies among a people with such vast power over so wide an area. Pericles alone knew how to deal wisely with each. Using the fears and hopes of the people as his two chief rudders, with the one he checked the growth of their confidence, with the other encouraged them when they were discouraged. His success gave substance to Plato's statement that rhetoric is the art of using words to govern the minds of men, and that the chief business of public speaking is to play upon the affections and passions—those strings and keys to the soul which require such a skilful touch.

Actually, Pericles' influence was due not only to his eloquence but also, as Thucydides admitted, to the whole fabric and reputation of his life, the confidence felt in his character, his manifest freedom from every kind of corruption, and his superiority to all considerations of money. He made the city of Athens, which was already great, stronger and richer than it ever had been. In power he was more than equal to many kings and absolute rulers. Nor did greatness come to Pericles as the lucky windfall of some happy chance of fate, nor as the brief bloom of a policy that flourished for a season only. For forty years he was first among statesmen, and after the banishment of Thucydides, for fifteen more years he held continuous command in the office of general. During this entire period he preserved his integrity unspotted.

Yet Pericles was not indifferent to earning money. Indeed, he was neither idle nor careless in looking after the property he inherited from his father, but managed his business so it would not absorb his time and attention, yet not suffer from neglect. Each year's produce he sold in a single sale. From the proceeds, he supplied everything needed for his family until the next year's sale. Every expenditure was ordered and set down from day to day with great exactness; no money was spent except from profits already in hand. His sons and their wives objected to scanty allowances and minute calculation of daily expenditures; and claimed they should be able to enjoy some of the luxury customary to so great a family with such a large estate.

This tight, parsimonious personal economy of Pericles was

very unlike the conduct of his philosopher-tutor Anaxagoras, who, in contempt of wealth, left his house and his fields untended, insisting that one employed in purely intellectual contemplation should be independent of external and material things. Pericles, however, dedicating himself to the service of society and the business of life, found use for material wealth in helping the poor. To him, therefore, wealth was not only useful but also honorable and good. It is said that in the involvement of public business Pericles forgot Anaxagoras, who finding himself neglected and deserted in his old age, wrapped himself up, intending to starve. Pericles, hearing this, ran immediately to him and earnestly entreated him to give up his purpose, if not for his own sake, then so that Pericles and Athens would not be deprived of such a faithful and able counselor. Unfolding his robes, Anaxagoras replied, "Ah, Pericles! Those who have need of a lamp take care to supply it with oil!"

As a military leader, Pericles gained a great reputation for prudence. He would not willingly engage in any fight which he believed was unduly risky. He did not envy the glory of generals whose rash adventures were by chance crowned with success. Pericles preferred the path of caution so that, so far as it was in his power, his fellow-citizens could expect to live forever. When a rash young Athenian warrior sought volunteers for an untimely attack upon the Boeotians in their own territory, Pericles attempted to prevent the disaster which followed. Speaking in the assembly he urged the younger man, "If you do not value the advice of Pericles, at least wait till time, that wisest counselor of all, shall advise you."

Pericles did send a popular expedition to the Chersonese to protect the Greeks living there from the Thracians and their barbarous neighbors. He was admired abroad for sailing around the Peloponnesus with a hundred galleys, pillaging the

PERICLES

seacoast and advancing with his soldiers far into the mainland. He also won other victories against other tribes and cities on both continents. When he started for home, he had shown himself to be formidable to his enemies, yet both sound and bold to his fellow-citizens; for not a single Athenian was lost on the whole voyage. Entering the Black Sea with a large and well-equipped fleet, he secured for the Greek cities there new commercial arrangements they wanted and established friendly relations with them. To the barbarous nations, and kings and chiefs around about them, Pericles showed the power of the Athenians to sail wherever they wished and to bring the whole sea under their own control.

The wisdom of Pericles in confining the Athenian military exploits within Greece itself soon became apparent. The Euboeans revolted, and, immediately after, the Megarians turned against Athens. They marched their army to the borders of Attica under the leadership of the king of the Spartans. Pericles hurried back from Euboea with his army to meet the war which threatened at home. But he did not want to fight such a large and brave army.

He knew that the leader of his adversaries was a very young man, governed by the counsel of Cleandrides, whom the Spartan elders had appointed as a sort of guardian. Pericles privately tested this man's integrity. He soon corrupted Cleandrides with money and persuaded him to withdraw the Peloponnesians out of Attica. When they learned of this, the Spartans angrily passed sentence of death upon Cleandrides, who fled. They fined their king so large a sum of money that, when he was unable to pay it, he left his country. Pericles immediately returned to the island of Euboea with fifty ships and five thousand men in arms. He captured a number of cities and drove the Histiaeans out of their country, replacing them with Athenians. His treatment of the Histiaeans was his one example of severe punishment for a defeated enemy, ordered because the Histiaeans had captured an Attic ship and killed all on board.

When Pericles and his first wife no longer agreed nor liked to live together, they parted by mutual consent, and she married another man. She had borne Pericles two sons, Xanthippus and Paralus. Pericles then took himself Aspasia, a woman who captivated the greatest statesmen and provoked much comment from the philosophers. Some say Pericles visited Aspasia on account of her knowledge and skill in politics. She had the reputation for being interested in only the most powerful men, and having taught public speaking to many famous Athenians; even Socrates sometimes went to visit her. Her occupation had been anything but creditable; her house was a home for young courtesans. She was not an Athenian, but a Milesian by birth, who became famous throughout the Mediterranean world. Pericles loved her very much, and every day as he left and returned from the marketplace he greeted and kissed her. She bore him a son, who lacked full Athenian citizenship because of his mother's foreign birth.

Aspasia is credited with influencing Pericles to undertake his expedition against the isle of Samos. The Samians were at war with Aspasia's people, the Milesians; and the Samians, who were winning, refused to stop fighting and allow the Athenians to arbitrate the controversy. So Pericles sailed to Samos and broke up its oligarchical government. He sent fifty leading citizens and their children as hostages to the isle of Lemnos. Many of these individuals, and even a Persian satrap who favored the Samians, offered Pericles personally great sums of gold for their release, but he would accept none of it. After taking the course he thought wise, and setting up a democratic form of government in Samos, he sailed back to Athens.

PERICLES

The Samians revolted immediately and resolved to gain control of the sea. Pericles came out with his fleet a second time, and in a sharp sea fight obtained a decisive victory, routing the enemy's seventy ships with his own fleet of forty-four. Now master of their harbor, Pericles laid siege to the city of Samos itself. He then sailed out into the main sea with a greater fleet which had arrived from Athens and intercepted a squadron of Phoenician ships coming to help the Samians. On his departure, the Samians attacked the Athenian army at their gates and won the battle. They disabled several Athenian ships and brought necessary supplies into Samos. In order to even the score for a previous affront, they branded the Athenian prisoners upon their foreheads with the figure of an owl. Before this the Athenians had marked captured Samians with a brand in the shape of a Samaena, which is a kind of low, flat-prowed ship first seen at Samos.

When Pericles learned of this disaster, he hurried to help his men, hemming in the Samians by building a wall around their city. He resolved to conquer them and take their town by this slow, costly method rather than with the wounds and lives of his soldiers. In this siege he used battering rams, a new invention. However, it was hard to keep back the Athenians, who were irritated by the delay and eager to fight. In an effort to calm them, Pericles divided the whole Athenian force into eight divisions and arranged that each day the divisions would draw lots and the one which drew the white bean would leave the battle to feast while the other seven were fighting. The day spent in feasting and merriment was called a white day. In the ninth month of the siege the Samians surrendered. Pericles pulled down their walls, seized their ships, and fined them severely.

On his return to Athens, Pericles delivered a brilliant funeral oration for those who had died in the war; the women

clasped his hand and crowned him with garlands like a victorious athlete. Elpinice, however, drew near him and said, "Glorious deeds, Pericles! We give you garlands for sacrificing the
lives of many brave Athenians, not in a war against our enemies such as my brother Cimon fought, but in one against an
allied and kindred city!" As Elpinice spoke, Pericles only
smiled, and quoted the verse, "Old women should not seek
to be perfumed. . . ." Pericles was extremely elated over his
success against the Samians; and understandably so, as Thucydides wrote that the Samians were close to wresting control
of the sea away from the Athenians.

Although Pericles had negotiated a thirty-year truce with
Sparta, the Peloponnesian War was about to break out in full
tide. Pericles advised the Athenians to ally themselves with an
island power which had great naval resources, since the Peloponnesians were so close to declaring war. For this reason he
decided to send help to the island of Corcyra, which was
under attack from the Corinthians; and he chose Lacedaemonius, son of Cimon, to lead the force.

While he was building his own power, Pericles had been constantly on guard against Cimon's sons rising to prominence in
Athens. He often said they should not be considered native
Athenians, since even their names indicated a foreign origin,
one being named Thessalus, another Eleus, and Lacedaemonius being named in honor of the people of Sparta. In sending
Lacedaemonius with only ten ships, not enough to gain a real
victory, Pericles appeared to insult Lacedaemonius, or to hope
that his failure to achieve any notable success would give rise
to suspicion Lacedaemonius favored the Spartan interests.
When he was criticized, Pericles sent a larger fleet to reinforce
Lacedaemonius.

The Corinthians, angry and indignant, accused the Athenians publicly at Sparta. The Megarians joined them, complain-

PERICLES

ing that they were, contrary to common right and the articles of peace sworn to among the Greeks, driven away by decree of Pericles from all ports under control of Athenians. The Spartans then sent ambassadors to press these complaints of their fellow Greeks at Athens. Pericles rejected their efforts, accusing the Megarians of seizing sacred land on the frontier. He sent a herald to Megara with instructions to continue to Sparta to state this charge against the Megarians. The herald was killed on his mission, presumably at the hands of the Megarians. The men of Athens then decreed eternal enmity between the two cities; they declared that if any Megarian set foot in Attica, he would be put to death; and that thereafter all Greek commanders taking their oaths of office should swear to invade Megarian territory twice each year.

War might have been avoided if the Athenians could have been prevailed upon to repeal the ban against the Megarians and to make a truce. Since it was Pericles who mainly opposed repealing the ordinance and urged the people to persist in their disputes with the Megarians, he was regarded as the sole cause of the war. Some say that, thinking that war was in the best interest of Athens, he acted out of high purpose. They said that Sparta's support of the Megarian cause was designed to test Athens, and that any concession would be taken as a confession of weakness. Others say that Pericles was stubborn and arrogant, and eager to show his own strength.

At that time Pericles undoubtedly was having political problems. His wife Aspasia had been indicted for impiety; his old tutor Anaxagoras was under attack for teaching new doctrines about the heavens; and Pericles himself was afraid of impeachment, because he was under command to account for moneys he had spent. Phidias, his sculptor friend and favorite, had been prosecuted in the assembly by enemies seeking to reach Pericles himself.

The charges brought against Phidias—that he stole gold while constructing the golden statue of Athena—were disproved. From the beginning of its design, on the advice of Pericles, Phidias had wrought and wrapped the gold used in the work around the statue in such a way that he could then remove and weigh it all. This was the way he proved that he had used in the sculpture every ounce of gold allotted to him. But he was sent to prison anyway, convicted of impiety because he had wrought likenesses of himself and of Pericles upon the shield of the goddess. Aspasia was acquitted through the tears and entreaties of Pericles. Anaxagoras he personally escorted from the city, rather than allow him to stand trial.

Most witnesses confirmed that Pericles' principal motive in continuing the dispute with the Megarians was to kindle the war, which had up to that time lingered and smoldered, and to blow it up into a flame, hoping in that way to disperse the remaining complaints and charges against himself. Pericles knew that in times of public danger, the city habitually threw itself upon him alone, trusting him because of his authority and prestige.

The Spartans believed that if Pericles was out of power they would be able to make whatever terms they pleased with the Athenians. They insisted that Athens expel the "pollution," the term they applied to Pericles. Instead of bringing him under suspicion and reproach, this demand made him more popular with the Athenians as the man their enemies most hated and feared. At last the Spartans and their allies invaded Athenian territories with a great army. Destroying everything in their path, they marched on as far as Acharnae, and there they pitched camp. They expected the Athenians would not endure their presence so close to Athens, and would come out and fight for the sake of their country and their honor.

PERICLES

But Pericles was determined to restrain those among the Athenians anxious to fight, thinking it was dangerous to engage in battle against sixty thousand men at the risk of the city itself. He avoided convening the people into assembly for fear they might force him to act against his judgment. Like the captain of a ship who, in a sudden squall at sea, sees that all is tight and fast and then follows the dictates of his own skill, ignoring the tears and entreaties of seasick and fearful passengers, so Pericles closed the city gates and placed security guards at all posts, following his own judgment and ignoring those who cried out against him and his plan. To those who opposed him he said: "Trees, when they are lopped and cut, grow up again in a short time, but men, being once lost, cannot be easily recovered."

Pericles then sent out a fleet of a hundred galleys to Peloponnesus. He did not sail with it, but stayed at home to watch and keep the city under his own control. To soothe the common people he distributed public money and ordered new divisions of conquered lands. The men of Athens received some comfort also from the misery their enemies were then enduring. For the Athenian fleet, sailing around the Peloponnesus, ravaged a great deal of the country, pillaging and plundering the towns and smaller cities. Though the Peloponnesians had inflicted great damage on the Athenians by land, they suffered as much themselves by sea.

Without the intervention of some divine power which crossed human purposes, the Peloponnesians would not have protracted the war so long but would quickly have given it up as Pericles predicted. But a plague seized Athens and destroyed its youth and strength. The people, affected in spirit as well as body, began to rave against Pericles. Like delirious patients, they turned on the man to whom they looked as their physician and father. Enemies of Pericles encouraged the belief that the plague was caused by his crowding together into Athens great numbers of country people accustomed to living in pure open air.

To stop this dissension and inflict some damage on the enemy, Pericles readied one hundred and fifty galleys. The Athenians took hope; their enemies were alarmed. When the fleet was prepared to sail, and Pericles had gone aboard his own galley, an eclipse of the sun occurred. As it suddenly grew dark, the men became frightened by the omen. Pericles, seeing his helmsman seized with fear, took his cloak and held it up before the man's face. Screening him with it so he could not see, Pericles asked the helmsman whether he imagined there was any harm or sign of any harm in this. When the man replied, "No," Pericles asked, "How does that darkness differ from this, except that it is caused by something larger than a cloak?" This is a story which philosophers have repeated over and over again to their scholars. Pericles was unable, however, to make effective use of his fleet. His siege of the holy city of Epidaurus failed; his men were laid low by the plague, which not only gripped the Athenians but all others who came in contact with their army.

Athens then lost confidence in Pericles, who tried in vain to comfort them and patiently bore their abuse. Once after having been reviled and criticized all day long as he calmly went about the city's business in the marketplace, Pericles was followed home by one of his critics, who continued to heap abuse upon him while Pericles walked on in silent composure. Since it had grown dark when they arrived at Pericles' home, he stepped inside and quietly instructed one of his servants to take a torch and attend his critic safely to his own home.

Pericles tried to appease the anger of his fellow-citizens and to rally their spirits, but he was unable to move them before they had voted against him, relieving him of his power and

PERICLES

command, and fining him. He patiently submitted in silence to ill will and disgrace, although soon all public troubles were to leave him unmolested; the people seemed to have discharged their anger in their stroke, and to have left their stings in the wound.

However, his private affairs were unhappy. His family had long since been in a kind of mutiny against him. Xanthippus, eldest of his lawful sons, resenting the meager allowance his father gave him, had borrowed money in his father's name. When Pericles refused to repay it, the son ridiculed and reviled his father; the breach between them was never healed. Xanthippus died in the plague, and Pericles lost also his sister and most of his relations and friends, as well as those who had been most useful and helpful to him in managing the affairs of state. Through all these misfortunes Pericles kept his noble spirit and great mind. He was not even seen to mourn until, at last, he lost his only remaining legitimate son. Subdued by this loss, yet striving still to maintain the principles of his life, he was overcome by emotion when he came to perform the ceremony of putting a garland of flowers upon the head of the corpse and burst into tears—a thing he had never done before.

Athens tried other generals to command the armies and other statesmen to run the business of the city; but they found none with sufficient authority and strength for such responsibilities. They regretted their rejection of Pericles, and so they asked him to address and advise them again. At that time he had retired in dejection and mourning, but he was persuaded by Alcibiades and others to appear before the people. When he did so they applauded him and apologized for their treatment of him; so he undertook public affairs once more. Pericles soon requested that the law concerning baseborn children be suspended, because he was afraid that the name of his family would be extinguished for want of a lawful heir. Long before, at the height of his power, with children born of an Athenian mother, Pericles had proposed the law which provided that only those who were born of parents who were both Athenians could be considered true citizens of Athens.

Under this law, almost five thousand people had been convicted and sold as slaves. It seemed strange that a law which had been harshly enforced against so many should be waived for the same man who had made it. Yet the Athenians pitied him because his personal losses had sufficiently punished him for his former presumptions. They felt his request was fitting for a man to ask and for men to grant. They gave him permission to enroll his son by Aspasia in the register of legitimate Athenian citizens and to give him his own name.

At about the time his son was enrolled, Pericles was seized with the plague and had a dull, lingering fever, so that little by little the strength of his body and mind wasted away. Theophrastus, in his *Ethics*, discusses whether men's characters change with their circumstances and whether their virtues are destroyed by the suffering of their bodies. He recounts that Pericles, when he lay sick, showed one of his friends an amulet or charm the women had hung around his neck, as if to say he must be very sick indeed to permit such foolishness. When Pericles was near death some of the leading citizens of Athens as well as his friends sat near him, talking as though he were unconscious and unable to understand what they said. They spoke of his merit and power, his famous deeds and the nine great military victories he had won. Pericles, however, had listened all the while. Suddenly he spoke out, saying that he wondered why they commended things which were due as much to good fortune as to anything else, without mentioning his greatest accomplishment: "No Athenian because of me ever wore mourning."

Pericles was a man to be admired for his kind, just, dispas-

PERICLES

sionate nature and the patience with which he accepted the conflicting humors of the Athenians, while persevering in working for Athens. Though his power was nearly absolute, he never used it to gratify himself nor did he ever treat an enemy as if he were irreconcilable. His unblemished integrity and irreproachable conduct during his whole administration made that otherwise absurd and arrogant title "Olympian" fitting and becoming. His nature, which was so dispassionate, and his life, which was so uncorrupted even at the pinnacle of power, lent support to the idea that the gods were the cause of all good but of nothing evil.

The events that followed his death made the Athenians sharply aware of the loss of Pericles. Those who, while he lived, resented his great authority because it overshadowed their own, were soon disillusioned with other orators and statesmen. They soon began to acknowledge that for all his majestic power, no man had ever been more moderate, and that none had ever given to moderation such impressive authority. Corruption and vice, which Pericles had kept under control, grew, through licentious impunity, to become a flood of wrongdoing. Only then was the wisdom and restraint with which Pericles had exercised his great power recognized as having been the chief bulwark of Athenian democracy.

Following is a portion of Thucydides' account of the oration Pericles made in Athens honoring those who died in the battle of Samos. It is from Thucydides' The History of the Peloponnesian War, *and it illustrates the richness and power of his eloquence and contains his appraisal of Athens' distinctions in the Periclean age:*

LIVES FROM PLUTARCH

"I shall begin with our ancestors: it is both just and proper that they should have the honour of the first mention on such an occasion as the present. They dwelt in the country from generation to generation, and through their valor handed the land down in freedom to the present generation. And if our more remote ancestors deserve praise, much more do our own fathers, who added to their inheritance the empire which we now possess, and spared no pains to be able to leave their acquisitions to us of the present generation. Lastly, almost all of our dominions have been augmented by those of us here, who are still more or less in the vigor of life; and at the same time we have furnished our mother country with everything that can enable her to depend on her own resources, whether for war or for peace. That part of our history which tells of the military achievements that gave us our several possessions, or of the ready valor with which either we or our fathers stemmed the tide of Hellenic or foreign aggression, is a theme too familiar to my hearers for me to elaborate on, and I shall therefore pass it by. But what was the road by which our greatness grew, what the national habits out of which it sprang; these are questions which I may try to solve before I proceed, since I think this is a subject upon which, on the present occasion, a speaker may properly dwell, and to which the whole assemblage, whether citizens or foreigners, may listen with advantage.

"Our constitution does not copy the laws of neighbouring states; we are rather a pattern to others than imitators ourselves. Its administration favors the many instead of the few; this is why it is called a democracy. If we look to the laws, they afford equal justice to all; even if a man has no social standing, advancement in public life comes from his reputation for capacity, and class considerations are not allowed to interfere with merit; nor again does poverty bar the way; if a man is able to serve the state, he is not hindered by the obscurity of his condition. The freedom which we enjoy in our government extends also to our

PERICLES

ordinary life. There, far from exercising a jealous surveillance over each other, we do not feel it necessary to be angry with our neighbour for doing what he likes, or even to look askance, for those injurious looks cannot fail to be offensive even though they inflict no positive penalty. But all of this ease in our private relations does not make us lawless as citizens. Our fear of lawlessness is our chief safeguard, teaching us to obey the magistrates and the laws, particularly those which concern the protection of the injured—whether they are actually on the statute book or belong to that code which, although unwritten, cannot be broken without acknowledged disgrace.

"Further, we provide plenty of means to refresh our minds when away from business. We celebrate games and sacrifices all the year round, and the elegance of our private establishments forms a daily source of pleasure and helps to banish ill temper. Since the magnitude of our city draws the produce of the world into our harbor, the fruits of other countries are as familiar a luxury for the Athenian as those of his own land.

"If we turn to our military policy, there also we differ from our antagonists. We open our city to the world, and never by alien acts exclude foreigners from any opportunity of learning or observing, although the eyes of an enemy may occasionally profit by our liberality; we trust less in system and policy than in the native spirit of our citizens. While in education, where our rivals begin to seek manliness from their very cradles by painful discipline, at Athens we live exactly as we please, and yet are just as ready to encounter every legitimate danger. In proof of this it may be noticed that the Lacedaemonians are not alone when they invade our country, but bring with them all their confederates; while we Athenians advance unsupported into the territory of a neighbour, and fighting upon a foreign soil usually vanquish easily men who are defending their homes. Our united force was never yet encountered by any enemy, because we have at once to attend to the sea and to dispatch our citizens by land upon a hundred different services; so that, wherever they engage, with but a fraction of our strength, a success against a small detachment of our many forces is magnified into a victory over our entire nation and a defeat suffered by our entire people. And yet if with habits not of labor but of ease, and courage not of art but of nature, we are still willing to encounter danger, we have the double advantage of escaping the experience of anticipating hardships and of facing them in the hour of need as fearlessly as those who are never free from them.

"Nor are these the only points in which our city is worthy of admiration. We cultivate refinement without extravagance and knowledge without effeminancy; wealth we employ more for use than for show, and place the real disgrace of poverty not in the fact but in declining the struggle against it. Our statesmen have their private affairs to attend to, and our ordinary citizens, though occupied with the pursuits of industry, are still fair judges of public matters; for, unlike any other nation we Athenians are able to judge at all events if we cannot originate them, and, instead of looking on discussion as a stumbling-block in the way of action, we think it an indispensable preliminary to any wise action at all. Again, in our enterprises we present the singular spectacle of daring and deliberation, each carried to its highest point, and both united in the same persons; although usually decision is the fruit of ignorance, hesitation of reflection. But the palm of courage will surely be adjudged most justly to those who best know the difference between hardship and pleasure and yet are never tempted to shrink from danger. In generosity we are singular, acquiring our friends by conferring favors rather than by receiving them. Yet, of course, the doer of the favour is the firmer friend of the two, for by continued kindness he keeps the recipient in his debt; while the debtor feels less keenly from the very consciousness that his return will be a payment, not a free gift. And it is only

PERICLES

the Athenians, who, fearless of consequences, confer their benefits not from calculations of expediency, but in the confidence of liberality.

"In short, I say that as a city we are the school of Hellas; while I doubt if the world can produce a man who, when he has only himself to depend upon, is equal to so many emergencies, and graced by so happy a versatility, as the Athenian. And that this is no mere boast thrown out for the occasion, but a plain matter of fact; it is proved by the power which our state has acquired by these habits. For of her contemporaries Athens alone has shown when tested that she is greater than her reputation; and she alone gives no occasion to her assailants to blush when they have been worsted, or to her subjects to question her title by merit to rule. Rather, the admiration of the present and succeeding ages will be ours, since we have not left our power without witness, but have clearly demonstrated it; and far from needing a Homer for our panegyrist, or other of his craft whose verses might charm for the moment, we have forced every sea and land to be the highway of our daring, and everywhere, whether for evil or for good, have left imperishable monuments behind us. Such is the Athens for which these men, in the assertion of their resolve not to lose her, nobly fought and died; and well may every one of their survivors be ready to suffer in her cause."

ALCIBIADES

450–404 B.C.

"*But* gentlemen of the assembly of Athens," said Alcibiades, "it is monstrous to be sent with such an important command when I face such accusations. I deserve to die if I cannot clear myself of the crimes of which I am accused. When I have proved my innocence, I will cheerfully go to war."

His command included 140 triremes (galleys), 5,100 men at arms, and about 1,300 archers, slingers, and light-armed men who were supposed to capture Sicily in the name of Athens. Alcibiades was one of the three generals chosen to lead them.

The Athenians had often looked longingly toward Sicily, but it was Alcibiades who inflamed their desire for conquest and persuaded them to wait no longer. Alcibiades himself thought of the conquest of Sicily as little more than a stepping-stone to the conquest of Carthage and Libya and, eventually, all of Italy and Peloponnesus. Nicias, one of the other generals, tried to stop this expedition, saying that it was impractical and extremely difficult. But Alcibiades, with his eloquence, had already convinced the people that they should sail out immediately with a large fleet and become the masters of Sicily. The Athenians knew Alcibiades well enough to know he needed restraint; and so they had chosen two other generals, Nicias and Lamachus, to aid in the campaign.

On the eve of the soldiers' departure, a crime was committed which frightened the people of Athens. All but one of the statues of Hermes that stood before public buildings and private homes were mutilated. It happened during the feast of Adonis—a time when the women of the city displayed images of dead men being carried to their burial and acted out funeral rites, moaning mournful songs. The Athenians seemed ready to forsake their Sicilian campaign so that they could punish the accused men and thereby appease the gods.

There were several theories as to who the vandals were: some believed the Corinthians destroyed the statues because they wanted to discourage the Athenian attack on Syracuse, their Sicilian colony; others believed some wild young men were the culprits. The council and the assembly examined both the theories—and also a third. Androcles, an unprincipled politician who was skilled in arousing the people, produced certain slaves and foreigners who accused Alcibiades and some of his friends of once defacing other statues in the same manner. It was argued that if Alcibiades and his friends had done the same thing before, they were not above suspicion. The people, who were aware of these antics of Alcibiades, were exasperated with him and were ready to put him to trial immediately.

However, the seamen and the soldiers under Alcibiades' command did not believe in the accusations. They swore that if their general were abused, they would go home, abandoning the attack on Sicily.

Alcibiades realized it would be to his advantage to be tried immediately and so he requested that the trial proceed at once. His enemies were dismayed. They knew that the people, needing Alcibiades for the attack on Sicily, would be gentle in any sentence rendered before his departure. So his enemies cried: "Let him sail at once and may good fortune attend him!

ALCIBIADES

When the war is over, we will recall Alcibiades and allow him to make his defense according to the laws."

The Athenians were so eager for the glories of conquest that they now turned deaf ears on the eloquence with which Alcibiades sought justice for himself. Sicily must be captured! The decision was made; Alcibiades sailed with the army, sharing his command with his rival Nicias, and with Lamachus. His enemies had won a great victory!

The invaders arrived on the coast of Italy and landed at Rhegium. There Alcibiades plotted the course he felt should be followed. He was opposed by Nicias, but Lamachus agreed, and so they immediately sailed for Sicily and took Catana. The aggression was under way; the Athenians had tasted victory.

At home, however, the enemies of Alcibiades attacked him more violently. In his absence they led the people to believe that the disfigurement of the statues of Hermes was a part of some sort of conspiracy led by Alcibiades for changing the government. The people proceeded to imprison all who were accused, without distinction and without hearing them. They began to regret that they had not brought Alcibiades to trial immediately. But the truth is there was no evidence of such a conspiracy. One of the witnesses who was reported to have recognized the vandals said that he had seen them by the light of the moon. Wiser men protested this statement, since it was known that the vandalism occurred when the moon was new.

Among the accused was Andocides, an Athenian who was supposed to hate popular government and support oligarchy. He was particularly suspect because the Hermes which stood near his house was almost the only significant one which had not been defaced. Andocides was convinced that it would be best to name offenders and save his own life for aiding the state. Everyone named by him, including slaves, was put to death. But the people's anger was still not appeased; they continued to rage against Alcibiades.

The great state galley, *Saaminia,* was sent to recall him from Sicily. Those aboard were told to use no violence, but to present themselves to him in the mildest terms, saying that he was needed in Athens to stand trial and clear himself. The people feared that if he were mistreated, their army in Sicily might mutiny. Indeed, the soldiers were already dispirited, for they knew that under Nicias the war would only drag on inconclusively.

Before he left, Alcibiades gave information to some friends of the Sicilian armies so that the Athenians would be defeated. He left his command and began the trip home.

When the ship arrived at Thurii, he went ashore and escaped. Someone who knew him asked if he did not trust his own country. To this, Alcibiades answered, "In everything else, yes, but in the matter of my own life, I would not even trust my own mother. She might by mistake throw in the black ball instead of the white."

His property in Athens was confiscated and it was decreed that all the priests and priestesses should solemnly curse him. One refused, insisting that her holy office obliged her to pray, not to curse. In his absence, Alcibiades was convicted by default. Later, when he was told that the assembly had pronounced the judgment of death, all he said was, "I will make them feel that I am alive."

The Athenian people had always been extremely aware of the lively spirit of Alcibiades. He was born an Athenian but was orphaned when his father, Clinias, lost his life in a sea fight. After his father's death he lived with Pericles, a relative who became his guardian.

ALCIBIADES

From childhood, Alcibiades' behavior completely unnerved the citizens of Athens. Aristophanes expressed perfectly the people's feeling toward him: "They love, and hate, and cannot do without him."

Again, using figurative language to describe him, Aristophanes said:

> Best rear no lion in your state, 'tis true;
> But treat him like a lion if you do.

Many incidents reflect his strongest passion, the desire for superiority. Once when he was wrestling, and was about to be thrown, he got his opponent's hand in his mouth, and bit it with all his force. When the other loosened his hold, he said, "You bite, Alcibiades, like a woman." "No," he replied, "like a lion!"

He made his likes and dislikes so well known that they influenced many customs in Athens. He refused to learn to play upon the flute, saying it disfigured a man's face and kept him from talking. "Therefore," he said, "flutes are for Theban youths, who do not know how to speak, but we Athenians, as our ancestors have told us, have Athena for our patroness, and Apollo for our protector. Athena threw away the flute, and Apollo stripped the flute player of his skin."

The other young boys soon began to talk about how Alcibiades despised playing the flute and ridiculed those who studied it. Consequently, the art of playing the flute became generally neglected in Athens.

Alcibiades was a handsome man, possessing the kind of beauty which he never lost. In infancy, youth and manhood he had a grace and charm, a natural vigor of body which captivated his fellow Athenians. People said that he lisped, but his lisp was very becoming and it gave a certain grace and persuasiveness to his rapid speech.

LIVES FROM PLUTARCH

Many aristocrats sought the company of Alcibiades, most being attracted by his brilliant and extraordinary beauty. But Alcibiades believed that his power with the people rested solely on his own ability in the art of speaking.

On many occasions he had shown the Athenians his superiority, his brilliance, his aggressiveness, and his natural gifts. Some Athenians held him in awe; some were jealous of his hold on the people. But there was one among them, Socrates, whose affection for the young man was evidence of the philosopher's appreciation of Alcibiades' natural noble qualities and good disposition. Alcibiades' life was much enriched by his association with Socrates, who had resolved to preserve, if possible, such a hopeful plant from perishing before its fruit came to perfection. It was said that on specific occasions each had been willing to sacrifice his life for the other, and that when Socrates saw Alcibiades being corrupted, he pursued him as he would a fugitive slave. When Alcibiades was misled by luxury or pride, Socrates would tell him how far he was from perfection and how many virtues he lacked. Still, as some said, Socrates' only hold on Alcibiades was by his ears.

On one occasion, Alcibiades gave a box on the ear to Hipponicus, a very influential person. This he did only in fun, because he had agreed with his companions to do it. Early the next morning, Alcibiades went to the house of Hipponicus, took off his outer garment, and presented his naked body to be punished as Hipponicus saw fit. Hipponicus forgot his resentment, pardoned him, and soon after gave him his daughter, Hipparete, in marriage.

With Hipparete went a large dowry, which enabled Alcibiades to live in a grand manner. Hipparete was a virtuous and dutiful wife, but she soon grew impatient of her husband's outrageous conduct. She left him and returned to her brother's house. When she went to court to claim a divorce, Alcibi-

ALCIBIADES

ades came in, picked her up and carried her home through the marketplace. No one dared to oppose him by taking her away from him. Hipparete stayed with her husband until her death, which occurred soon after her return.

Alcibiades was still young when he felt ready to enter public life, but his noble birth, his riches, and the personal courage he had shown in many battles made his friends and dependents ready to accept him. By his wits he quickly eclipsed all the Athenian leaders, except Phaeax and Nicias, an older, successful general.

Even though Alcibiades was the Athenian appointed to look after the interests of Spartans captured at Pylos, the Spartans credited Nicias with the humane peace terms and the return of their prisoners. It was generally accepted that Pericles had started the war, but Nicias had ended it, and the peace was commonly called the Peace of Nicias. Alcibiades was jealous of Nicias and began to plot the destruction of the treaty, saying that the Athenians regretted it and would soon abandon it.

Alcibiades seized every opportunity to incite the Athenians against Sparta. With half-truths he accused Nicias of intentionally refusing to capture the enemy's troops, and then, after others had captured them, of setting them free; thus enhancing his position in Sparta. He said that Nicias encouraged Sparta to make separate alliances with Thebes and Corinth, but when any Greek state sought alliance with Athens, Nicias tried to prevent it if the Spartans objected.

Nicias was in disgrace because of these accusations, when a delegation arrived from Sparta with full powers to compromise. The council welcomed them; the assembly was to receive them the following day. But Alcibiades arranged a secret conference. He said to them, "Surely you know the council always behaves reasonably and courteously to anybody who appears before it, but the assembly stands on its dignity and expects important concessions. If you tell them that you have come here with unlimited powers, they will have no scruples in putting pressure on you and trying to dictate conditions. You really must not be so naïve. If you want to get moderate terms from the Athenians, and not be forced into going further than you are prepared, you should discuss what would be a fair settlement in principle, but not let them know that you have full powers to accept it. You can count on my full support as a friend of Sparta."

He gave them his oath, persuading them to rely upon him instead of Nicias. The next day, when the assembly met, the Spartans announced that they had not come with full powers. Alcibiades turned upon them as if he were outraged, and in a loud voice, he proceeded to call them liars with no genuine mission in Athens at all. The council was indignant; the assembly was furious with the Spartans. Nicias, who knew nothing of Alcibiades' deceit, was dumfounded and put to shame by the ambassadors' change of position. The Spartan ambassadors were rejected, and Alcibiades was made a general.

No one approved of the deceit which Alcibiades had used, yet he had accomplished a great political feat, shaking almost all the Peloponnesus and combining many men in arms against the Spartans. The possibility of war was so far removed from the Athenian frontiers that even if the Spartans conquered, they gained little, but if they lost, Sparta itself was hardly safe. Alcibiades persuaded the other Greek cities to become dependent upon Athens' sea power, but he cautioned the Athenians not to neglect their army. He reminded them of the oath young soldiers took, swearing to recognize the presence of barley, wheat, the vine, and the olive as the only valid boundaries of Attica. In this way, the Athenians were taught to claim for themselves as much of the earth as might be productive.

ALCIBIADES

Despite all his eloquent words and deeds, Alcibiades lived a life of luxury, drunkenness and insolence. He wore long purple robes, like a woman, which dragged after him as he went through the marketplace. Not satisfied with the simple, traditional shield which most Athenians carried to war, Alcibiades had his gilded and ornamented with the figure of Eros, the god of love, carrying a thunderbolt. He kept a fine, expensive dog, but cut off its tail, which had been the dog's most distinctive feature. When told that all Athens was angry and felt sorry for the dog, Alcibiades laughed and said, "That is just what I intended. I have given them something to talk about, so that they will say nothing worse about me!" Some, indeed, gave the mildest names to his faults, excusing his excesses because of his youth. But reputable people feared that his free living and his contempt for law revealed the temper of a tyrant. They were glad that there was only one Alcibiades, for Greece could certainly not endure a second.

Now these same Athenians, who stood to gain much from the conniving of Alcibiades, had sentenced him to death for the destruction of the statues of Hermes. He was forced to save his life as best he could, and so he traveled across Peloponnesus and stayed for a while at Argos. While there, he realized he could never return to Athens and would always have to be on guard against his own people. He sent word immediately to Sparta offering his services. He assured the Spartans he would in the future make amends for all the damage he had done to their country as an Athenian. The Spartans welcomed him.

He went eagerly to Sparta, with three plans in mind. His first plan was to send aid to the Syracusans and so crush the Athenian efforts in Sicily. This accomplished, he next suggested renewing war on the Athenians at home. He then proposed that Sparta should fortify Decelea, which above all else, reduced and wasted the resources of the Athenians by forcing them to be constantly alert against the fortress. By this time, the Athenians were beginning to feel that Alcibiades was, indeed, very much alive.

In Sparta the fame he earned for his public services was equalled by the admiration for his private life. People were captivated by his conformity to Spartan customs. Quite unlike the Alcibiades of Athens, while in Sparta, he wore his hair close cut, bathed in cold water, ate coarse meal, and dined on black broth.

He had a talent for gaining men's affections; and he could adapt to their ways of life and change faster than a chameleon. There is one color they say a chameleon cannot assume: it cannot make itself appear to be white.

But Alcibiades, whether with good men or with bad, could wear the appearance of virtue or vice. When he sensed that the things he liked to do offended those with whom he was dealing, he adopted a manner that he thought was agreeable to them. At Sparta he was devoted to athletics, was frugal and reserved; in Ionia, luxuriously gay and indolent; in Thrace, always drinking; in Thessaly forever on horseback; and when he lived with the Persians he outdid the Persians themselves in magnificence and pomp.

The Spartan campaigns continued to be a great success. Alcibiades himself went to sea. He persuaded almost all of Ionia to revolt, and cooperating with the Spartan general, made life miserable for the Athenians.

But Agis, the king of Sparta, hated Alcibiades because he had dishonored the king's wife. Other Spartan generals were jealous of his successes, and soon orders were sent from Sparta to Ionia that Alcibiades should be killed. Informed of this, Alcibiades knew he could no longer trust the Spartans, and so he fled into Persia to join Tisaphernes, the Persian satrap. Once

ALCIBIADES

again, Alcibiades had to use his ability to change his appearance in order to gain favor. He immediately became the most influential person about Tisaphernes, for this barbarian loved cleverness and guile.

Alcibiades convinced Tisaphernes that they could encourage the Athenians and the Spartans to exhaust their strength by fighting each other. Then, he reasoned, they would both be ready to submit to the Persians.

The Athenians, because things were going badly, regretted their severe sentence against Alcibiades. But he, too, was becoming worried about them, for he realized that if the Athenian commonwealth were destroyed, he might fall into the hands of the Spartans, who would show him no mercy.

He learned that the entire Athenian fleet waited at Samos, thinking that Tisaphernes' one hundred fifty galleys had already set sail to attack them. Secretly Alcibiades sent word to the Athenian leaders at Samos, offering them an alliance with Tisaphernes if they would overthrow democracy in Athens. Most of the aristocrats were inclined to act on this plan, although Phrynichus, one of their generals, argued that Alcibiades was less interested in restoring the government of Athens to the aristocrats than in preparing the way for his own return to Athens. Phrynichus quickly discovered that by saying this he had not only lost favor with his own party, but had also become a declared enemy of Alcibiades.

In an effort to redeem his position, Phrynichus alerted an enemy admiral to beware of Alcibiades and seize him as a double-dealer. But Phrynichus had met his match in intrigue. The Spartan admiral was eager, above all else, to please the Persian king, Tisaphernes. Knowing that Alcibiades was a favorite of Tisaphernes, the admiral decided not to seize Alcibiades, but to inform him.

In Samos, messengers from Alcibiades immediately denounced Phrynichus to the outraged Athenian commanders. Seeking to save himself, Phrynichus again sent a message to the enemy admiral, reproaching him for betraying him, but offering to deliver into his hands both the army and the navy of the Athenians. But Phrynichus, now deep in treachery, had learned at least one lesson. Guarding against a second denunciation from Alcibiades, Phrynichus told the Athenians that the enemy would make a surprise attack, and he urged them to fortify their camps and be ready to sail.

When, indeed, a second letter from Alcibiades arrived, detailing the treachery of Phrynichus, the Athenians ignored it. Although Phrynichus had saved his own skin temporarily, Alcibiades' friends kept control at Samos. Still promising an alliance with the Persians, these Athenians persuaded the people of Athens to give the control of the government to the nobility, called the Five Thousand (though they numbered only four hundred).

Once in power, the Five Thousand ignored Alcibiades and continued the war with less interest. At this point they could not yet trust the citizens who belonged to the popular party. They rationalized that since Athens was now governed by an oligarchy, as was Sparta, Athens might now gain more favorable terms for ending their conflict. The people of Athens were forced to submit, and those who openly opposed the new leaders were put to death.

The Athenians who were still fighting in Samos became indignant at what had happened at home; they sent for Alcibiades and declared him their general. They insisted that he lead them immediately back to Athens to put down the tyrants and return the government to the people. Suddenly raised from a fugitive in exile to a great command, Alcibiades resisted the natural inclination to grant their wishes, which he thought would lead them toward catastrophe. He told them that if they sailed to Athens, all Ionia would easily fall into the hands of the enemy, while at the same time the Athenians would lose everything fighting each other within their own walls. By a mixture of persuasion and force, Alcibiades prevented what would otherwise have been a great disaster for Athens.

Alcibiades and his friends in Athens soon drove out the four hundred in power. The people then commanded the return of Alcibiades from exile. But he did not want to return until he could return with glory. When he received information that the Spartan and Athenian armies were about to fight in the Hellespont, he hurried there with eighteen galleys. When he arrived, the Spartan and Athenian fleets were already engaged in a long, equal battle, with the outcome still undecided. Both fleets were misled when the ships of Alcibiades were sighted— the Spartans were encouraged, the Athenians terrified. But Alcibiades raised the Athenian flag. With his help, the Athenians took thirty of the enemy's ships and recovered all of their own.

After such a victory, Alcibiades' vanity made him eager to appear at the court of Tisaphernes. He expected to be welcomed as a victor, but his timing was wrong. Tisaphernes was worried about his relationship with the Spartans; so he seized Alcibiades and sent him as a prisoner to Sardis. Thirty days later Alcibiades made his escape, claiming in revenge that Tisaphernes had helped him. He sailed to the Athenian camp.

Learning that the Spartans and the Persians were together at Cyzicus, Alcibiades made a speech to his soldiers, saying: "You must fight on the sea, on the land and against fortified cities, too. For unless you conquer everywhere, there will be no money for you!"

The soldiers proceeded to board the ships, and then seized all of the small vessels they met, guarding them safely within the fleet so that the enemy would not learn of their approach.

A great thunderstorm contributed to the surprise of the Athenian attack.

When light came again, the Peloponnesian fleet could be seen off the coast of Cyzicus. Alcibiades was afraid that if the Spartans knew how many ships he had, they might abandon their ships for safety ashore. He commanded part of his fleet to slacken, while forty ships advanced and drew the enemy into battle. As soon as the fight had begun, the Spartans saw the other part of the Athenian fleet bearing down upon them. They became so terrified that they quickly retreated toward shore. Alcibiades broke through them with twenty of his best ships. He hastened to shore, disembarked, and slaughtered those who were retreating.

The Spartan losses were great; the Athenians won rich spoils and took all of the enemy ships. They became masters of Cyzicus, destroying its Peloponnesian garrison and securing control of the Hellespont. Most important, the Athenians drove the Spartans from the sea.

And so the battles went. Alcibiades took Chalcedonia; he then sailed into the Hellespont to raise money for supplies and took the city of Selymbria; then he captured Byzantium. At last Alcibiades was ready to return to Athens in triumph. He set sail, towing behind him a great sea parade of his war spoils. But after he entered the harbor of Athens, he remained aboard the flagship and would not go ashore until he saw his cousin and other friends, who invited him to land.

The people came in throngs, saluted him, followed him, and crowned him with garlands. They said that they could not have failed in Sicily or elsewhere if they had left the command of their forces to Alcibiades. They recalled that at the time he resumed responsibility they had almost been driven from the seas and were hardly able to defend their own suburbs. They were grateful that Alcibiades had not only restored them to their ancient dominion of the sea, but had also made them victorious on land. The people crowned him with golden crowns and gave him absolute power over land and sea forces. They decreed that his estates should be restored to him, and that he be absolved from the curses which they had pronounced against him.

In the height of his glory, Alcibiades conceived a brilliant exploit to dramatize for all Athenians both his piety toward the gods and his leadership against the Spartans. Traditionally the Athenians had celebrated the Eleusinian mysteries with a procession by land, escorting the image of the god Iaccus to Eleusis while performing sacrifices, dances, and other rites along the way. But since the Spartans had fortified Decelea, thus commanding the roads to Eleusis, the Athenians had been forced to conduct the procession by sea, omitting the proper ceremonies. Alcibiades reasoned that if he escorted the procession again by land, protecting it with his army, the Spartan king Agis would have no attractive alternative. If Agis did not oppose the procession, his prestige would suffer. If Agis did attack, Alcibiades would be engaged in a holy war in defense of the most sacred ceremonies, and all his fellow-citizens would witness his valor. Alcibiades stationed sentinels in the hills, and, at daybreak, he sent out his scouts. Surrounding the priests and novices with his soldiers, he led the procession in dignity and silence to Eleusis. The Spartans dared not attack. Having restored to the celebration its ancient splendor, Alcibiades led the procession back safely to Athens. There he was hailed not only as a general but also as a high priest, and urged by the common people to assume all powers.

But certainly, if a man was ever ruined by his own glory, it was Alcibiades. His continual success had produced such an image of his courage and ability that, if he failed in anything, the people thought he was being negligent, since nothing was considered beyond his power.

And so once again Alcibiades lost favor. The people never

stopped to consider that they provided little money for Alcibiades' wars against the Spartans, who were handsomely supplied by the king of Persia. Alcibiades repeatedly had to leave
his camp to raise money and provisions for his men. On one
such trip into Caria, he left his fleet to an experienced seaman
but ordered him not to engage in combat. His orders were
disregarded; the Athenian fleet sailed out and provoked the
enemy; and most of their men and ships were captured by the
Spartans.

When Alcibiades heard the news, he returned to Samos, but
his enemies had quickly gone to Athens to accuse him of neglecting his duty. The Athenians became resentful and chose
other generals.

Alcibiades immediately left the army, collected a body of
mercenary soldiers and declared his own war against the
Thracians. He tried to advise the new Athenian generals and
thus save the army, but his suggestions were rejected. When
Lysander, the Spartan, attacked the Athenians they were not
ready, and only eight galleys escaped. The Spartans captured
the two hundred other galleys and three thousand prisoners,
whom they put to death. Within a short time Lysander took
Athens itself, burned her ships and demolished her walls; and
the Spartans became the masters of both land and sea.

Alcibiades retired temporarily to Bithynia and once again
he prepared to interest the Persians in an alliance. The Athenians were completely crippled by the loss of their empire.
Then when Lysander also deprived them of their liberty by
setting up the Thirty Tyrants to rule over Athens, they began
to bewail their former errors. The most inexcusable of their
mistakes had been their second abuse of Alcibiades. They had
rejected him, not for any fault of his, but merely because they
were angry with his subordinates for the loss of a few ships.
The Athenians had behaved more shamefully than any soldier

ALCIBIADES

in depriving the city of its best and most valiant general. Yet they had still some faint hopes left as long as Alcibiades was alive.

Lysander eventually received secret orders from Sparta to have Alcibiades put to death. Whether this was because they feared his energy and boldness, or because King Agis wanted revenge, is not really known.

His assassins did not dare enter his house, so they surrounded it and set it on fire. As soon as Alcibiades discovered what was happening, he threw heaps of clothing and furniture on the fire to choke it. Wrapping himself in his cloak, and grasping his sword in his right hand, he dashed through the fire and escaped before his clothes were burned. The assassins saw him emerge, but still they kept their distance and killed him with darts and arrows. Timandra, his mistress, took up his dead body and wrapped it in her own robes. She buried, as decently and as honorably as circumstances allowed, the body of the dead Alcibiades—that Athenian whom the people loved, hated, and could not do without.

ALEXANDER

356–323 B.C.

*T*he most glorious exploits of men are not always the best indications of their virtues or vices. It is often in little things—expressions or jests, that we see the character and inclination of men. Portrait painters make great efforts to portray the lines and details of a face, particularly about the eyes, in order to reveal what a man really is. So, with Alexander, we must give more attention to the marks and indications of his character than to his great battles.

The night before the consummation of her marriage, Alexander's mother, Olympias, dreamed that a thunderbolt struck her belly, kindling a great fire, with flames leaping out in all directions. Philip, Alexander's father, later dreamed that he sealed up his wife's body with a seal bearing a design in the form of a lion. His court diviners told him the dream meant that the queen Olympias was pregnant, for a seal is never put upon anything that is empty, and that the child would be a boy who would one day be as strong and courageous as a lion.

It is said that Olympias took part in the ceremonies of Orpheus and orgies of Dionysius, and that she introduced tame serpents into the dances in order to give the ceremonies a stranger and more dramatic atmosphere. The serpents, creeping out of the ivy and coiling about the sacred spears and garlands of the women, made a spectacle which terrified the men who witnessed it. Philip once found Olympias asleep with a serpent lying beside her. Awed by the belief that the serpent might be the god Zeus in an earthly disguise, Philip consulted the oracle of Apollo at Delphi. The oracle commanded him to make a sacrifice to the god, and told him he would one day lose the eye with which he had peeped through the chink of the door to see the god Zeus, in the form of a serpent, in his wife's embrace.

When Alexander was yet quite young he entertained ambassadors from the king of Persia while his father was away. The ambassadors were impressed by Alexander and by the intelligent questions he asked about their country. He inquired about the distance between places, what kind of roads went into the upper provinces of Asia, about the character of the Persian king, and of the way he treated his enemies. He also asked what kinds of forces Persia could send to war. The ambassadors admired the young Alexander and considered his development and fine ambitions even more remarkable than the ability of his famous father.

Whenever, as a youth, Alexander heard that Philip had taken an important town, or won a victory, instead of rejoicing, he would say to his companions: "My father will have done everything already; nothing great will be left for you and me to do!" Intent upon action and glory rather than pleasure or riches, Alexander felt that every accomplishment of his father merely narrowed the possibilities for his own future. He did not want to inherit a kingdom which was already flourishing and settled. He hoped to be involved in troubles and wars, which would give him every opportunity to exercise his courage and increase his fame.

One day Alexander accompanied Philip and his attendants

ALEXANDER

to try the horse Bucephalus, which had been offered for thirteen talents of gold. Bucephalus was vicious and unmanage-
able, and he reared whenever any of the attendants attempted
to mount him. Philip rejected the horse as too wild and therefore useless. As they were leading him away, Alexander, who
stood by, remarked: "What an excellent horse they are losing
for the lack of skill and boldness to manage him!" Philip, over-
hearing, turned to his son and asked: "Do you reproach your
elders, as if you knew more and were better able to manage
him?" Alexander replied that he could indeed manage the
horse better than the others. "And if you fail," said Philip,
amused, "what will you forfeit for your rashness?" "The
whole price of the horse!" said Alexander.

The men began to laugh, but Philip and Alexander agreed
upon the wager. Alexander ran to the horse. Taking hold of
the bridle, he turned Bucephalus directly toward the sun. He
had noticed that Bucephalus was frightened by his own
shadow. Keeping the reins in his hand and stroking the great
horse gently when he became fiery, Alexander allowed Bucephalus to walk forward. Letting his mantle fall gently to the
ground, Alexander leaped nimbly to the horse's back. Without striking or spurring him, he gradually drew in the bridle.
When he found Bucephalus no longer rebellious but only impatient to run, Alexander let him out at full speed, urging him
on with his heel and his commanding voice. Philip and his
friends looked on in anxious silence. When the prince had
completed the course, he turned the horse and came back. All
the men burst into applause for his triumph; his father wept
for joy and kissed his son as he dismounted. Philip then said
to Alexander, "O my son, look for a kingdom equal to and
worthy of yourself, for Macedonia is too small for you!"

Alexander was fair-skinned and had a ruddy complexion.
His quick glance and a characteristic inclination of his head

toward his left shoulder were reflected in the sculpture of Lysippus, who alone was allowed to represent him. Though Alexander was eager and vigorous in other pursuits, he did not indulge himself in pleasures of the body, even in his youth. In his love of glory and in the pursuit of it, he showed a sense of fairness far beyond his years. Since he was a very fast runner, he was once asked whether he would run a race in the Olympic Games. Alexander answered: "I would if I had kings for competitors." He took no interest in famous athletes, and gave no encouragement to wrestling or boxing. However, he delighted in all sorts of hunting and cudgel-playing, and often gave prizes for tragedians and musicians, flute players and lyre players.

Philip realized that his son was easy to lead to duty by reason but could not be forced, and so he always tried to persuade Alexander rather than command him to do anything. He also realized that Alexander's education was too important to be entrusted entirely to ordinary masters in music, poetry, and common school subjects—his forming required, as Sophocles said, "the rudder's guidance and the bridle's restraint." So Philip sent for Aristotle, the most learned and celebrated philosopher of his time, and rewarded him in a way that was particularly appropriate. Only a short time before, Philip had demolished the city of Stagira, where Aristotle was born; he now returned to their homes all the citizens of Stagira who had been exiled and enslaved.

It seems that Aristotle instructed Alexander not only in ethics and politics, but also in those more abstruse and profound branches of learning which the philosophers reserved for oral communication to the selected few. Later, during his Persian campaigns, he heard that Aristotle had published some of these matters. Alexander wrote reprovingly to Aristotle: "Alexander to Aristotle. Greetings. You have not done well to publish your books of oral doctrine; for in what can we

ALEXANDER

now excel others if that knowledge has been laid open to all? For my part, I assure you, I would rather excel others in the knowledge of what is excellent, than in the extent of my power and dominion. Farewell."

Alexander owed to Aristotle his interest in medical practice and medical theory. When any of his friends were sick, Alexander often prescribed their diet and medicines. He was a great lover of all kinds of learning and reading and constantly kept Homer's *Iliad*—a copy corrected by Aristotle (called the casket copy)—with his dagger under his pillow, declaring that he valued it as the perfect, portable treasure of all military virtue and knowledge. But he valued many books and once, from the upper provinces of Asia, Alexander wrote home for a variety of books, including history, a great many of the plays of Euripides, Sophocles, and Aeschylus, and some odes.

For a while Alexander loved Aristotle no less, he said, than if he had been his father, saying that as he had received life from the one, so the other had taught him to live well. Afterward Alexander became suspicious of Aristotle and their friendship waned. But his violent thirst and passion for learning, once implanted, grew with him and never left him, as is seen by the honors he later bestowed on Anaxarchus and other philosophers.

When Alexander was sixteen, his father made him regent in Macedonia, entrusting to him the charge of the great seal. While Philip was on his expedition against Byzantium, the Medari rebelled, and Alexander acted vigorously. He defeated them, took their city by storm, drove out the barbarians, and installed a colony of several nations. He renamed the city Alexandropolis in his own honor. Later, at the battle of Chaeronea, which Philip fought against the Greeks, Alexander is said to have been the first man to break through the defenses of the dedicated men known as "the sacred band of Thebans."

This early bravery made Philip very fond of Alexander.

Nothing pleased him more than to hear the Macedonians call Alexander "king" and himself only "general." But later family disputes, caused chiefly by Philip's new marriages and love affairs, created a rift between Alexander and his father. Olympias, who was extremely jealous and stubborn, turned Alexander against his father. At Philip's wedding to an additional wife much too young for him, the bride's uncle, drunk with wine, proposed that the Macedonians ask the gods to grant to this new marriage a lawful successor to the kingdom. Alexander, outraged, threw his cup at the speaker, crying out: "You villain! What then, am I? A bastard?" Philip immediately took the side of his bride's uncle and would have stabbed his son with a spear. Luckily, either because he moved too quickly or because he had drunk too much wine, his foot slipped and he fell to the floor. Alexander reproached and insulted his father, saying, "There is the man who plans to pass from Europe into Asia; he cannot even pass from one table to another!" After this incident, Alexander moved his mother Olympias to Epirus and went himself to Illyria. Philip, reproved by a friend for causing so much discord in his own house, prevailed upon Alexander to return.

Their reconciliation was short. Soon the Persian governor of Caria offered his daughter in marriage to Arrhidaeus, a dull-witted, illegitimate son of Philip. Olympias and Alexander's friends persuaded Alexander that these negotiations meant that Philip intended Arrhidaeus, and not Alexander, to succeed as king. So Alexander sent the tragic actor, Thessalus, into Caria to persuade the governor to accept Alexander as his son-in-law, rather than Arrhidaeus. The governor was infinitely more pleased with this proposal. When Philip learned of it, he went to Alexander's apartment, taking with him one of Alexander's intimate friends, Philotas, the son of Parmenio. The King reproached Alexander for even contemplating be-

ALEXANDER

coming the son-in-law of a Carian, who was at best a slave of a barbarian king. Philip then insisted that the Corinthians return Thessalus to him in chains. He banished Ptolemy, Nearchus, and other friends of Alexander.

Shortly after this episode, Philip was killed. His assassin was a prominent young man who had been abused by Philip's new wife and who resented Philip's failure to punish her. It was generally thought that Olympias incited the assassin to murder, and even Alexander was censured. But Alexander ordered diligent search to be made for the men involved in the assassination and saw to it that they were punished.

Alexander was only twenty when he became king. At the time of his assumption of power, the kingdom was in great danger. The barbarian nations that bordered Macedonia were restless because they were not governed by their own princes. Though Philip had won victories over the Greeks, he had not had time to complete his subjugation of them and died leaving everything in disorder. Some Macedonians wanted Alexander to abandon the idea of subjugating the Greeks by force. They advised him to win the allegiance of the barbarians by treating them gently and indulgently when they first showed signs of revolt. Alexander rejected this counsel as weak, believing it was wiser to act decisively and with resolve. He believed that if he appeared to give ground to any tribe, he would invite all the others to trample on him.

Alexander acted on his convictions. He quickly went into the barbarian territory—as far as the Danube River—and defeated the barbarian king, Syrmus, thus putting an end to all possibility of further war in that region.

When he heard that the Thebans were in revolt and that the Athenians were allying with them, Alexander immediately marched through the pass of Thermopylae. "Demosthenes," he said, "called me a boy while I was in Illyria and a stripling when in Thessaly. I will show him before the walls of Athens that I am a man!"

When he came to Thebes, to show how willing he was to accept their repentance for past injuries, Alexander demanded only that they surrender to him the two Thebans who had begun the rebellion. He offered a general pardon to all those who would come over to him. But the Thebans responded by demanding that Alexander surrender his friends and lieutenants Philotas and Antipater. With a flourish of trumpets, the Thebans invited all who believed in the liberty of Greece to join Thebes. Alexander then applied himself to make the Thebans feel the harshness of war. Although the Thebans, outnumbered by Alexander's forces, defended themselves with a zeal and courage beyond their strength, the Macedonians surrounded them and slaughtered them. Thebes itself was taken, sacked, and razed to the ground.

In the midst of the fighting some Thracian soldiers broke into the house of the Theban matron Timoclea, who was renowned for her fine character. Their captain, after he had violently used her to satisfy his lust, asked if she had hidden any gold and silver. She readily answered that she had and told him to follow her into a garden, where she showed him a well. She said that when the city was taken, she had thrown everything of value into it. The greedy Thracian stooped to examine the well and Timoclea quickly pushed him into it and flung huge stones in on him until she had killed him. When the other Thracians discovered her, they carried her, bound, before Alexander. Her very presence and bearing showed that she was a woman of dignity and courage. Alexander, recognizing this, asked her name. She said, "I am the sister of Theagenes, who fought your father Philip for the liberty of Greece, and fell in the battle of Chaeronea." Alexander, admiring her boldness and her answer, commanded her to be set free with her children.

ALEXANDER

More than six thousand Thebans had been killed in battle; and the city itself suffered horribly and in many ways. Alexander hoped that such an example would terrify the rest of Greece into submission and at the same time please his allies, the Phocians and Plataeans. Alexander spared the priests, those who were bound to the Macedonians by ties of hospitality, the family of the poet Pindar, and those Thebans who were known to have opposed the public vote for war. All the others, numbering thirty thousand, were sold as slaves.

Alexander later repented of his severity to the Thebans. His remorse had such influence on him that he was never again so brutal to other men. He later blamed his murder of Clitus—which he committed while he was drunk—and the unwillingness of the Macedonians to persevere with him in his Indian campaign, to the wrath and vengeance of Dionysius, protector of Thebes. When any Theban fortunate enough to have survived asked him a favor, Alexander granted it.

As for the Athenians, Alexander forgave them, even though they expressed great concern at the misfortune of Thebes and gave all possible aid to those Thebans who had escaped. Perhaps the fury of Alexander, like that of the lion, was satisfied after the kill. Perhaps, after an example of such extreme cruelty, he wished to appear merciful. In any event he not only overlooked all the Athenians' past offenses, but he advised them to act wisely in their affairs because if he should fail, they would most likely become the arbiters of Greece.

Following the Theban war, the Greeks decided to join Alexander in the war against the Persians. They proclaimed Alexander their general, and soon many statesmen and philosophers came from all parts of the Mediterranean world to congratulate him. Diogenes the Stoic, however, who was then living at Corinth, never left his home. Alexander, intrigued by this indifference, sought out the philosopher and found him lying in the sun. When Diogenes saw so many people approach, he raised himself a little, and condescended to look at Alexander. The King addressed him courteously and asked whether there was any way the King might serve the philosopher. Diogenes replied: "Yes, you could remove yourself from between me and the sun." Alexander, surprised to find himself so lightly regarded, nevertheless saw something great in so careless an answer. While his followers were laughing at the bad humor of the philosopher, Alexander said, "If I were not Alexander, I would wish to be Diogenes."

He then went to consult the oracle of Apollo at Delphi about the prospects for the Persian war. He arrived on one of the days when it was deemed inauspicious for the oracle to reply to any questions. Alexander sent messengers to request the priestess to do her office. When she refused, pleading the law as her excuse, Alexander went up himself and began to pull her by force into the temple. Overcome with his boldness, she said, "My son, thou art invincible." Hearing this, Alexander released his grasp upon her and departed, saying he had received such an answer as he wished, and that there was no point in consulting the god any further.

Alexander recruited forty-three thousand foot soldiers and four thousand horse troops for the Persian campaign. He had only seventy talents for their pay, no more than thirty days' provisions, and was already two hundred talents in debt. Yet he would not let his army leave home until he had carefully determined and provided whatever his friends needed in order to follow him. To some he gave good farms, to one a village, and to another the revenue of a particular hamlet or harbor town. At last he had given away almost all his patrimony in Macedonia. When he was asked what he had retained for himself, Alexander replied, "My hopes." One of his officers responded, "Your soldiers will be your partners in those."

Satisfied with his preparations, Alexander crossed the Hellespont. At Troy he made a sacrificial offering to the goddess
Athena and honored the memory of the heroes buried there,
especially Achilles, whose grave he anointed with oil. Then,
with his friends, he followed the ancient custom and ran naked
around the tomb and crowned it with garlands. Alexander said
he envied Achilles, for Achilles had found a faithful friend
while he lived, and, after his death, a famous poet to sing his
praise. While looking at the rest of the antiquities of Troy, he
was asked whether he wanted to see the harp upon which
Paris had played. Alexander replied, "I do not think the harp
of Paris deserves attention. But it would give me great pleasure
to see the harp Achilles played when he sang the praises of
brave men."

While Alexander was inspecting the Trojan antiquities a
large Persian army was taking up its position on the opposite
bank of the river Granicus. Alexander was forced to fight at
the very gates of Asia in order to enter that part of the world.
Because of the depth of the river and the rough, uneven ascent
of the opposite banks, many of Alexander's officers were concerned. Some said it was the wrong time to fight because, according to tradition, the kings of Macedonia never marched
out to war in that month, called Daesius. Alexander overruled
all these objections and said that they would call the month a
second Artemisius, which was the name of the preceding
month. When Parmenio, his elder counselor, advised him not
to attempt anything that day because it was too late, Alexander replied, "I would disgrace the Hellespont were I to fear
the Granicus!"

Alexander immediately threw himself into the river with
thirteen horsemen. In spite of the swift current and the
showers of darts thrown by the enemy from the steep bank on
the opposite side, Alexander advanced. His action seemed
more desperate than prudent, but he persisted obstinately, and

at last, with great effort, made his way up the muddy, slippery banks of the river. Before he could reassemble his men, who were still crossing the river, Alexander was forced into a confused, hand-to-hand combat. The Persians pressed him, shouting loud warlike cries, charging horse against horse, attacking first with lances and, when these broke, fighting with swords. It was easy to distinguish Alexander from the others because of his buckler and helmet, which had a large plume of white feathers flying on each side. Many soldiers attacked him, and although his armor was pierced by a javelin in one of its joints, he was not wounded. At one point, two Persian commanders attacked him. He side-stepped one, and struck such a blow to the other that his spear splintered into pieces upon the breastplate of his enemy. In the meantime the first Persian commander, Spithridates, came up on one side, and, rising on his horse, struck a blow that cut off the plumed crest of Alexander's helmet and grazed his hair. As the Persian was about to repeat the stroke, Alexander's friend Clitus ran him through with a spear, while Alexander killed the other Persian with his sword.

Once the Macedonian phalanx had crossed the river to support the first horsemen, the enemy gave ground and fled, except for some Greek mercenaries. Alexander unreasonably refused their request that he spare them. He charged them himself first, and had his horse killed under him. His determination to kill these experienced, desperate men cost him more of his own soldiers' lives than he had lost in the actual battle. The Persians lost twenty thousand foot soldiers and five hundred horsemen; Alexander lost not more than thirty-four, nine of whom were foot soldiers. To honor their memory, Alexander commissioned Lysippus to erect a brass statue to each of them. So the Greeks might participate in the honor of his victory, he sent them a portion of the spoils; and to Athens he

ALEXANDER

sent three hundred bucklers. Upon all the rest he placed the inscription: "Alexander, son of Philip, and the Greeks, excepting only the Spartans, won these from the barbarians who inhabit Asia." Alexander then sent to his mother Olympias all of the plate, purple garments and other luxurious things that he took from the Persians.

This battle greatly improved Alexander's position. Sardis, the seat of the barbarian's sea power, and many other cities surrendered to him. He considered attacking Darius, the king of all the Persians, risking everything on the outcome of this one battle, but decided that he should first complete his domination of the entire Persian coast. At Pamphylia, where the waves usually come crashing in violently, rarely leaving so much as a narrow beach below the steep, broken cliffs, the waters quieted so that he sailed in easily. Menander in one of his comedies refers to the good fortune of Alexander:

> *Was Alexander ever favored more?*
> *Each man I wish for meets me at my door,*
> *And should I ask for passage through the sea,*
> *The sea I doubt not would retire for me. . . .*

At Gordium, said to be the seat of the ancient Midas, Alexander saw the famous chariot tied with cords made of the bark of the cornel tree. The legend was that whoever untied this Gordian knot would be emperor of the entire world. Some say Alexander cut it asunder with his sword; others that he loosened it by withdrawing the pin from the yoke and then drawing out the yoke itself.

In one way or another, Alexander seized every opportunity to invoke the aid of fate.

Learning of the death of Memnon, the most respected Persian officer in the maritime provinces, Alexander decided to march on into the upper provinces of Asia. Illness, however, detained him in Cilicia. His physicians considered his case desperate; but because they were afraid of the Macedonians if their cure should fail, none of them dared prescribe any remedies for Alexander.

Philip, the Arcanian, seeing how critical the illness was, and relying on his well-known friendship with Alexander, at last tried to cure him. He preferred to risk his own life and reputation rather than allow Alexander to die for lack of medical attention. On that very day Alexander had received and hidden under his pillow a letter from Parmenio warning him that the physician, Philip, had been bribed by Darius, the Persian king, to kill him. When Philip came in with the medicine, he extended the cup confidently to Alexander, encouraging him to take it. Alexander grasped the cup with cheerful assurance and drank down the potion, at the same moment handing Parmenio's letter to Philip.

What a spectacle! To see Alexander drink the medicine, Philip read the letter at the same moment, and each then turn and look at the other, but with different sentiments. Alexander showed his friendship and his confidence in his physician; Philip, overcome by the accusation, appealed to the gods to witness his innocence, threw himself down beside the sickbed, and implored Alexander not to be afraid but to follow his directions. The medicine at first worked so violently that Alexander lost the power of speech, became unconscious, and had scarcely any pulse left. But, with Philip's attention, his health and strength returned. He was soon able to appear in public to reassure the Macedonians, who had been constantly fearful and dejected until they saw him up and about again.

Meantime Darius had become extremely confident and had assembled an army of six hundred thousand. He erroneously attributed Alexander's long stay in Cilicia to cowardice. Darius

III

ALEXANDER

drew added confidence from the Persian soothsayers' interpretation of a dream in which he saw the Macedonian phalanx on fire, and Alexander waiting on him, wearing the costume which Darius himself used to wear, and then disappearing into the temple of Belus. The dream might well have been interpreted to prophesy the illustrious actions the Macedonians were about to perform and Alexander's mastery of Asia, as well as his death in the prime of his glory.

Darius ignored the good advice that he should fight in the open plains where his enormous army could maneuver. Instead, he decided to attack the Macedonians in the passes. He marched into Cilicia at the same time that Alexander advanced into Syria to meet him. In the night the two armies missed one another, and each turned back again. Alexander, delighted, hurried to engage Darius in the passes. Darius now realized his error in choosing to fight in country where the sea, mountains, and rivers necessarily divided his forces and rendered his horsemen almost useless at the same time that they covered and supported his enemy. Alexander was careful to improve upon the advantage fortune had given him by stretching his right wing out much farther than the left wing of the Persians. In this way he avoided being outflanked by their much larger army. Taking his place in the front ranks, Alexander put the barbarians to flight, although he sustained a thigh wound from an enemy spear.

Only the escape of Darius clouded this victory for Alexander. He had defeated more than one hundred and ten thousand Persians and had captured the chariot and bow of the great general Darius. His Macedonians, busily plundering the enormously wealthy camp of the barbarians, had reserved for Alexander the tent of Darius, which was full of splendid furniture, gold and silver. Alexander examined the bathing vessels, the water-pots, the pans, and the ointment boxes—all curiously wrought of gold—and smelled the exquisite fragrance which perfumed the whole place. He then entered a great, high pavilion, where the couches and tables and preparations for entertainment were magnificent. He turned to the men around him and said, "This, it seems, is royalty. Let us now cleanse ourselves from the toils of war in the bath of Darius." "Not so," replied one of his followers, "but in the bath of Alexander, for the property of the conquered is and should be called the conqueror's!"

Going in to supper, Alexander learned that the mother, wife and daughters of Darius mourned because they had seen his chariot and bow captured and assumed that he was dead. Alexander, more touched by their distress than by his own success, sent word to them that Darius was not dead and that they would continue to be provided with everything they had been used to receiving from Darius. Alexander gave them permission to bury any of the Persians they chose, using whatever clothing and furniture they saw fit. He made no reductions in their accommodations nor in the attentions and respect which had been formerly reserved for them; and he allowed even larger expenditures for their maintenance.

But the most noble and regal part of his treatment of Darius' family was that Alexander did not permit these virtuous prisoners to hear or experience anything unbecoming. It was as if they were lodged in a temple, with sacred and uninterrupted privacy, rather than in the camp of an enemy. Darius was considered the tallest and handsomest man of his time, his wife was believed to be the most beautiful princess, and the daughters not unworthy of their parents. But Alexander sought no intimacy with any of them; he considered it more noble to control himself than to conquer his enemies. He took no notice of the rest of the female captives, though they were remarkably beautiful, other than to say jokingly that the Persian

ALEXANDER

women were terrible eyesores. Displaying the equal beauty of
his own temperance and self-control, Alexander ordered them
removed from his presence. He severely reprimanded those
who wanted to bring him youths who were famed for their
beauty. He said that sleep and the act of generation reminded
him that he was mortal, implying that both weariness and sen-
sual pleasure reflect the frailty of man. Except for Barsine,
Memnon's widow, who was taken prisoner at Damascus, Alexander was intimate with no woman prior to his marriage.

Alexander did not indulge himself with food either. Every
day the lady Ada, whom he fondly called mother, and whom
he later made queen of Caria, sent him many different dishes,
and would have also furnished him with skilled cooks and pas-
trymakers. But Alexander refused all, saying that his tutor Leonidas supplied the best: a march before daybreak to whet his
appetite for the noon meal, and a light noon meal to whet his
appetite for the evening meal. When any rare fish or fruits
were sent him, he would give them to his friends, often keeping nothing for himself. But he always served a magnificent
table for his guests. He was very careful that everyone was
served equally and with proper attention. The cost of his
hospitality constantly increased, as his fortune did, until it
amounted to ten thousand drachmas a day. Alexander limited
the expenditure to that amount and would not allow anyone
else to spend more in entertaining him.

He was much less addicted to wine than had been generally
believed; and the truth is that when he had nothing else to do,
he preferred to talk rather than drink. Over every cup of wine
he held a long conversation, but when his responsibilities
called he did not delay as other generals did because of wine,
sleep, love, or entertainment. His life is proof of this, for
though it was short, he performed many great exploits.

When Alexander was not on the march, he sacrificed to the

gods first thing in the morning, then ate breakfast and spent
the rest of the day hunting, writing memoirs, giving decisions
on military questions, or reading. On the more leisurely
marches, he would exercise by shooting and darting the javelin as he went along, or by mounting and alighting from a
chariot at full speed. When he came in for the evening, he
would bathe and then dine. Although his conversation was always extremely pleasant, Alexander did indulge in soldierly
boasting. Those who flattered him took advantage of his vanity, and this made his closest friends uneasy because such
praise made them appear to think less of Alexander's accomplishments. After such an evening, he was likely to bathe again
and sleep, perhaps till noon, perhaps all day.

After the battle of Issus and the seizure of Damascus, the Macedonians became so accustomed to the Persian wealth and
women and their barbaric splendor of living that they were
ready to eagerly pursue the Persian way of life. But Alexander
felt they should secure the seacoast, and so he began the siege
of Tyre, which took seven months. Toward the end Aristan-
der the soothsayer predicted that Tyre would certainly be
taken that very month; but the soldiers laughed at him because
it was already the last day of the month. Alexander, anxious to
support the predictions, ordered that the day should not be
counted as the thirtieth, but as the twenty-third day of the
month. Then, calling for the trumpets to sound, Alexander,
with a small force, attacked the walls of Tyre more seriously
than he had previously intended. The rest of his men, who had
been left in camp, advanced to his support with such force
that the Tyrians gave up. The town was indeed taken that
very day.

During another excursion—against the Arabians—Alexander's tutor Lysimachus insisted on accompanying him, saying

ALEXANDER

that he was neither older nor less courageous than Phoenix, guardian of the legendary Achilles. When they reached the hills and dismounted to march on foot, Lysimachus lagged behind the main body of soldiers. Alexander stayed with Lysimachus to encourage and help the tired old man, risking his own life and enduring an extremely cold night in an exposed position to protect his teacher.

From the siege of Gaza, one of the largest cities of Syria, Alexander sent spoils to his mother and his friends. To his preceptor, Leonidas, he sent five hundred talents worth of frankincense and a hundred talents worth of myrrh, in grateful remembrance of the hopes Leonidas had held for Alexander as a youth. In the past, Leonidas, standing one day by Alexander when he was sacrificing, told him to be more careful of the quantities of incense he threw into the fire; he said he should not be so generous until he was master of the countries from which the spices came. So Alexander sent to Leonidas a note with the incense: "We have sent you an abundance of myrrh and frankincense, so that in the future you may not be stingy with the gods."

Among the treasures taken from Darius and brought before Alexander was a very valuable casket. Alexander asked those about him what they thought most worthy to be kept in it. After hearing their various suggestions, Alexander told them he would keep in it Homer's *Iliad*. Alexander relied on the wisdom of Homer during his expeditions. When he had conquered Egypt, he decided to build a great Greek city there and to give to it his own name. Homer then appeared to him in a dream saying:

> "*An island lies, where loud the billows roar,*
> *Pharos they call it, on the Egyptian shore.*"

Alexander immediately went to Pharos, which was above the mouth of the Nile. He found a long neck of land stretching like an isthmus between large lagoons a suitable site for his city. It had shallow waters on one side, and the sea on the other, thus providing a spacious harbor. Alexander declared that "Homer, besides his other excellences, was a very good architect!" He ordered the plan of the city of Alexandria to be drawn. Since the soil was black, and they had no chalk, they laid out their lines with flour, making a great semicircle with extensions at either end, so that the design resembled a Macedonian cloak. While the King was inspecting the design, a great flock of birds rose up from the river and devoured the flour used in marking out the lines. Alexander, although troubled by this omen, proceeded, after assurance from his diviners that this event signified that the city he was to build would be rich enough to care for all who would come from other nations.

While the construction of Alexandria proceeded, Alexander himself set out into the desert to visit the temple of Zeus. Alexander was warned about the lack of water, the violent winds, and the treacherous sands he would encounter on this long, difficult, and dangerous journey; but Alexander was not easily diverted from anything he set out to do. Fate, having supported him in his plans, made him even more resolute. His naturally bold disposition gave him a sort of passion for overcoming difficulties, as if it were not enough to be always victorious in battle, unless places, seasons, and nature herself submitted to him. Guided by ravens, which waited when the soldiers strayed or lagged behind, Alexander passed through the wilderness and presented himself at the temple. He asked whether any of his father's murderers had escaped punishment. The high priest, alluding to the legend that Alexander was the son of the god Zeus, told Alexander to speak with

ALEXANDER

more respect, since his was not a mortal father. Alexander, changing his expression, rephrased his question and also asked whether he was destined to conquer the world. The priest answered that Zeus had, indeed, granted to Alexander the distinguished fate to be the conqueror of the world. Others say that the priest, speaking out of courtesy in Greek, and intending to say, "O paidion" (O my son), instead, by a slip in pronunciation, said "O paidios" (O son of Zeus). Alexander was pleased, and let it be known that the oracle had called him the son of Zeus.

Alexander acted in a haughty manner with the barbarians, as if he truly believed his divine parentage, but with the Greeks he was reluctant to claim divinity. Once when he was wounded and bleeding, Alexander laughed, "This, my friends, is not the blood of a god, but real flowing, mortal blood." In another campaign, when it thundered terribly, Anaxarchus the philosopher asked Alexander if he, who was a son of Zeus, had the power to produce such a display. "No," answered Alexander, laughing, "I have no desire to be formidable in front of my friends. It was you, not I, who scorned my table for being served with fish instead of the heads of Persian governors!" Once when Alexander sent his closest friend, Hephaestion, a gift of small fish, Anaxarchus made fun of the gift and observed with irony that those like Alexander who sought magnificent goals by taking great risks rarely gained more pleasure than ordinary men. Alexander himself was not so vain as to think he was really a god; he simply used his claims to divinity to give people the impression that he was invincible.

When Alexander returned from Egypt to Phoenicia, he received a letter from Darius. The Persian offered, in exchange for Alexander's friendship and alliance, all the countries west of the Euphrates River, a thousand talents as ransom for cap-

tured Persians, and one of his daughters in marriage. Alexander
told his friends of this offer. Parmenio said that, if he were
Alexander, he would accept. "So would I," said Alexander, "if
I were Parmenio." Alexander replied that if Darius would
come and surrender to Alexander, he would be treated with all
possible kindness; if not, he would be hunted down.

Alexander soon regretted the severity of his demand for un-
conditional surrender. His royal prisoner, Statira, wife of Darius, died in childbirth, and because he was sorry he had not
given Darius a more gentle answer, Alexander gave her a
sumptuous funeral. One of the eunuchs escaped on horseback
to inform Darius of his wife's death. When Darius, in tears,
lamented that she had to endure captivity, and said that her
burial had probably been mean and obscure, the eunuch reported that Statira had been denied nothing. "I assure you," he
said, "she had not only all the ceremonies due her, but was
also honored by the tears of your enemies; for Alexander is as
gentle after victory as he is terrifying in the field."

The eunuch consoled Darius that he had been defeated by a
man whose virtues made him more than human—a man to be
loved and admired. When Darius heard this he turned toward
his friends and courtiers to utter this prayer: "Gods of my
family and of my kingdom, restore, I beseech you, the power
of Persia, that I may leave it as flourishing as I found it. But if,
indeed, the fatal time has come to put an end to the Persian
monarchy—if our ruin is a forfeit that must be paid to the
jealousy of the gods—grant then that no other man but Alexander may sit upon the throne of Cyrus!"

In the meantime Alexander proceeded with the conquest of
all of Asia west of the Euphrates. He then advanced toward
Darius, who was approaching Alexander with a million men.
As the two armies came within sight of each other, Darius reviewed his troops by torchlight. The plain between the moun-

ALEXANDER

tains shone with the lights and fires of the Persians, and the sound of their vast army was to the Greeks like the distant roaring of a vast ocean. Alexander's oldest commanders, particularly Parmenio, said it was too dangerous to fight such a huge army by daylight. They urged Alexander to attack Darius by night; but to this Alexander gave the celebrated answer: "I will not steal a victory." Some thought Alexander's answer juvenile, as if he was playing with danger. Others realized that he did not want to give Darius any excuse for a defeat or any pretext for trying his fortune again. Alexander knew that Darius still had great reserves of manpower and arms, and he reasoned that only a complete loss of courage and hope through undeniable defeat would induce Darius to give up the war.

After making this decision Alexander retired to his tent and slept soundly. Before daybreak Parmenio had to call him several times before he finally awakened Alexander. Parmenio asked how it was possible, before the most important battle of his life, that he could sleep as if he were already victorious. "And are we not so, indeed," replied Alexander, smiling, "since we are at last relieved of the trouble of wandering in pursuit of Darius, through a wide and wasted country, hoping in vain that he would fight us?"

Alexander rose and called for his famous horse Bucephalus, who was now growing old and whom Alexander never used except in actual battle. Mounting, he put on his helmet. He wore a Sicilian coat, girt close about him; over that a breast-piece of thickly quilted linen, which was part of the booty from the battle of Issus. The iron helmet made by Theophilus was so well wrought and polished that it gleamed like silver. To this was fitted a gorget of the same metal, set with precious stones. His light and well-tempered sword—the weapon Alexander used most in battle—had been given him by the king of the Citieans. His richest trapping was a belt, the work of the ancient Helicon, presented to him by the Rhodians as a mark of respect.

Alexander addressed his soldiers at length. They answered with loud shouts calling on him to lead them against the barbarians. He shifted his javelin into his left hand. With his right hand lifted up toward heaven, he entreated the gods: "If I be truly the son of Zeus, then aid and strengthen the Greeks." At the same time, a soothsayer rode by pointing to an eagle soaring directly above Alexander. It was soaring toward the enemy. This so excited the horsemen that, shouting encouragements and exhortations, they charged at full speed. The whole phalanx of foot soldiers followed *en masse*.

As before, so in this battle Alexander proved himself great and displayed the self-possession that comes from foresight and confidence. The left wing, commanded by Parmenio, was disordered and was forced to give ground. Parmenio sent messengers to tell Alexander that the Macedonian camp and baggage would all be lost unless a considerable reinforcement from the front were sent to the rear. Alexander's reply to Parmenio was, "You must surely have lost the use of your reason, and in your alarm, have forgotten that soldiers, if victorious, become masters of their enemies' camp and baggage, and, if defeated, fight gallantly and die with honor."

Before the front ranks could really come to blows, the Persians fell back. Alexander pursued Darius, whom he saw from a distance looking tall and handsome in a lofty chariot surrounded by royal guards. As the Persians drew close in order to repel the enemy, Alexander charged and terrified many, who fell back. But the bravest and most valiant attempted to hold their ground. Falling upon one another, they were slain in their king's presence, striving in the very pangs of death to control their horses.

ALEXANDER

Darius could no longer turn or maneuver his chariot. Its wheels were clogged and entangled with the dead bodies which almost covered the horses. They reared and plunged in front of the frightened charioteer. Seeing that all was lost, Darius abandoned his chariot and his weapons, and took flight upon a mare. Alexander, in pursuit, received a message from Parmenio asking for help against the Persians. Alexander, irritated at being so recalled from pursuing his victory, marched back toward the place of danger, only to find that the enemy had been totally overthrown.

Despite the escape of Darius, the battle seemed to put an end to the Persian empire. Alexander was proclaimed king of Asia; he returned thanks to the gods in magnificent sacrifices and rewarded his friends and followers with great sums of money, estates, and provinces. Eager to be honored by the Greeks, he wrote to them that he would have all tyrannies abolished so that they might live according to their own laws.

Alexander then set out for Persia. He was guided, as the priestess of Apollo had prophesied in his childhood, by a native of Lycia. The Babylonians surrendered to him and delighted him and his party with demonstrations of the peculiar qualities of naphtha, which issued from the earth like a spring at Ecbatana. They sprinkled the street leading to the King's lodgings with little drops of the naphtha, and then at dusk they applied torches at the opposite end. Instantly it caught fire from one end to another, so that the whole street was one continual flame.

At Susa, Alexander looted the palace of the Persian kings, who in better times had stored in their treasury water brought from the Nile and from the Danube as testimony to their power and the extent of their empire. Among other treasures of inestimable value, Alexander found forty thousand talents in coin and five thousand talents worth of Hermionian purple, which had been stored one hundred and ninety years yet still was fresh and colorful.

At Persepolis he found as much treasure as ten thousand pairs of mules and five thousand camels could carry. Here he happened to see a large statue of Xerxes, which had been accidentally thrown to the ground by the soldiers crowding into the palace. Gazing at it, he mused, "Now that you are prostrate on the ground, shall we neglectfully pass you because you once invaded Greece, or should we erect you again because of your great mind and virtue?" Here Alexander first sat on the royal throne of Persia, under the canopy of gold. An old man wept, deploring the misfortune of the Greeks whom death had deprived of the satisfaction of seeing Alexander on the throne of Darius.

Alexander stayed at Persepolis four months to rest his soldiers and pass the winter, diverting himself and his officers with entertainments, drinking, and other pastimes. He indulged his lieutenants so far as to allow their mistresses to sit and drink with them. Most celebrated of these women was Thais, an Athenian, mistress of Ptolemy, who later became king of Egypt. One night while all were drinking, Thais, exulting in being entertained in the stately palace of the Persian kings after all she had endured in following the Macedonian camp through Asia, addressed Alexander: "It would please me if, while you, great Alexander, look on, I with my own hand, may set fire to the court of that Xerxes who reduced the city of Athens to ashes. Then posterity will know that the women who followed Alexander took a revenge on Persians more severe than all the famed commanders have been able to do by land and sea." Alexander, affected by the enthusiasm of the company, rose, and with a chaplet of flowers on his head and a lighted torch in his hand, led the way. Shouting and

ALEXANDER

dancing, the King's party spread through the Persian palace
and was joined by the rest of the Macedonians, who hoped
that the firing of the palace meant that Alexander would return home. The King, however, quickly repented, and gave
orders that the fire be extinguished.

Alexander was by nature munificent, and he grew more so
as his fortune increased. He gave gifts freely and graciously
and with the manner which makes a gift most welcome. He
once saw a common soldier carrying on his back a part of the
King's treasure which had already exhausted a mule. Appreci-
ating the man's devotion in carrying the burden, Alexander
said to him, "Do not faint now, but finish the journey and
carry what you have there to your own tent for yourself!"

His mother Olympias wrote, telling him he should reward
and honor those about him in a more moderate way. "For
now," she said, "you make them all equal to kings; you give
them the power and opportunity to make many friends of
their own, and in the meantime you leave yourself destitute."
Only his dear friend Hephaestion was permitted to read Alexander's letters along with him, but their custom was that when
they had finished reading, the King would take off his ring and
with it set the seal of secrecy upon Hephaestion's lips. Alexander sent to his mother many presents, but never allowed her to
meddle with matters of state or war. When she complained
that he did not follow her advice, he bore her ill humor patiently. But when he read a long letter from Antipater, who
administered Macedonia in his absence, full of accusations
against her, he remarked that Antipater "does not know that
one tear of a mother effaces a thousand such letters as this."

Alexander's favorite commanders became luxurious and extravagant. One wore silver nails in his shoes; another employed several camels for the sole purpose of bringing him
body powder from Egypt to use when he wrestled. Many

used precious ointment rather than plain oil for their baths, and they carried about servants to massage them and wait upon them. Many had grown rich, and consequently proud. They were weary of marches and expeditions and wanted to indulge continuously in pleasure and idleness.

Alexander reproved them gently. He said he was amazed that they, who had fought so many battles, did not know by experience that those who work sleep more soundly than those who are worked for. He expressed his surprise that his followers, comparing the Persians' manner of living with their own, did not seem to realize that voluptuous living was abject and slavish, while a life filled with work and occasional pain was truly noble. "How," Alexander asked, "will a man who pretends to be a soldier keep his horse and his armor if his hands are too delicate to take care of his own body? Have you not yet learned that the greatest and most difficult of our victories lies in avoiding the vices and weaknesses of those whom we subdue?"

To strengthen his precepts by example, Alexander devoted even more time to hunting and warlike expeditions, seizing every opportunity to encounter hardship and danger. Once he met and mastered a huge lion. An ambassador, who happened to be present, said to him, "Alexander, you fought gallantly with the beast to determine which should be king!" Yet Alexander also showed tenderness and respect to his friends; on the smallest occasions he would write letters to help them. When he first sat in judgment upon capital cases, he would cover one ear with his hand while the accuser spoke, to keep that ear free from prejudice against the person accused. But so many accusations were brought before him—and so many proved true—that he eventually lost his tenderness and began to believe even those who made false accusations.

Finally some men censured and spoke ill of Alexander him-

ALEXANDER

self. At first, he bore this patiently, saying that it became a king well to do good to others and be evil spoken of. But later, when anybody spoke ill of him, Alexander became inflexible and severe, valuing his glory and reputation above all else.

Again Alexander set out to search for Darius, expecting they would have to fight another battle. But he soon heard that Darius was held captive by Bessus. After eleven days of marching more than four hundred miles, his soldiers were without water and ready to quit the search. Some Macedonians passing by offered to Alexander a helmet filled with water. Without drinking from it, he returned it with thanks, saying, "If I alone should drink, the rest will be disheartened." Hearing this, the soldiers all cried out to him to lead them forward and began spurring on their horses. While they had such a king, they said, they would feel neither weariness nor thirst, but would look upon themselves as little less than immortal.

Yet not more than sixty horsemen were able to keep up with Alexander and arrive at the camp of the enemy. When at last they found Darius, he was lying in a chariot, wounded from darts and at the point of death. Darius asked for water, which the Macedonians gave him. When he had drunk a little, he said to those who had given him water, "This is the last measure of my misfortune, that I may not return your kindness. But Alexander will thank you for your humanity to me, as the gods will reward him for his kindness to my mother, my wife and my children. Tell him I give him my hand as I now give it to you." With these words, Darius died.

When Alexander came up to them, he was filled with sorrow, and taking off his own cloak, he covered the body of Darius. He ordered the body to be carried in state to Darius' mother for burial, and received Darius' brother into the circle of his intimate friends. When Bessus was taken, Alexander or-

dered two trees bound down to meet, and one of Bessus' legs
fastened to each, so that when the trees were set free, returning to their natural positions with great force, each carried
half of the body of Bessus with it.

Alexander marched into Hyrcania with the best of his army,
leaving most of the Macedonians who were weary of war in
their quarters. It was in Hyrcania that he first put on the Persian costume. Perhaps he did this with the idea of making the
work of civilizing the Hyrcanians easier, since nothing appeals
more to men than conformity with their own fashions and
customs. Or it may have been as a first trial to see whether the
Macedonians might be led gradually to forget the more democratic relationship of Macedonians to their king and adopt instead toward Alexander the deference which the Persians accorded their kings as divine rulers. Alexander adopted neither
the trousers nor the sleeved vest, nor the tiara for the head,
but a middle course between the Persian and the Macedonian,
not so flaunting as the one, yet more pompous and magnificent
than the other.

In other ways, too, Alexander gradually accommodated his
way of life to that of the natives, while trying to bring them to
adopt Macedonian customs. Alexander believed that it was
wise to rely upon the good will which might arise from inter-
mixture and association as a means of maintaining peace rather
than to rely upon force. He put thirty thousand Persian
youths under masters to learn the Greek language, and to be
trained to fight with Macedonian discipline. He then married
the Persian princess Roxana, whom he truly loved. Her
youthfulness and beauty immediately charmed Alexander
when he first saw her taking part in a dance. Yet this marriage
contributed also to his larger purposes, because Roxana's people were pleased to see him take a Persian wife and they were

ALEXANDER

sympathetic to his honorable approach to Roxana, the first woman he had ever loved passionately.

He noticed that, among his favorites, Hephaestion most approved all that he did and imitated him in his change of habits; while Craterus, his faithful lion-hunting companion, continued his strict observance of Macedonian customs. So Alexander used Hephaestion in all dealings with the Persians, while Craterus became his advocate with the Greeks or Macedonians. In general Alexander showed more affection for the former and more respect for the latter, saying that Hephaestion was Alexander's friend while Craterus was friend of the king.

Next to Alexander, Philotas, the son of Parmenio, was the most munificent of the Macedonians. He was valiant and had great endurance in war, but Philotas fell short of true greatness. He carried arrogance and luxury to a degree not becoming in a private citizen; by his spurious majesty he inspired envy and ill will. His father Parmenio sometimes told him, "My son, to be not quite so great would be better." Philotas' enemies eventually persuaded Alexander that Philotas was implicated in a plot against Alexander's life. Philotas was tortured to death while being interrogated by Hephaestion and the principal officers in the presence of Alexander, who was concealed behind some tapestries. Parmenio, who had already lost his other two sons in battle, was executed on Alexander's order.

These actions made Alexander an object of terror to many of his friends, since Parmenio had done brave service under Philip and was the only one among Alexander's older friends and counselors who had encouraged him to go into Asia. The deplorable end of his friend Clitus was perhaps even more inhuman than that of Philotas. However, considered in its circumstances and weighing the cause, it may be thought of as an unfortunate accident which occurred when the King's anger

LIVES FROM PLUTARCH

and excessive drinking encouraged the insolence of Clitus.

Alexander had received a present of Grecian fruit from the seacoast. It was so fresh and beautiful that he called Clitus to see it and share it with him. Clitus stayed for supper with the King, and the company, when they had drunk a good deal, began to sing songs ridiculing some Macedonians who had been recently worsted by the barbarians. Though Alexander and the younger men were amused, some of the older men reprimanded both the author and the singers. Clitus, who had drunk too much and was by temperament rough and willful, was so annoyed that he could contain himself no longer. He said it was not right to make sport of Macedonians in front of barbarian enemies—that although some Macedonians had been overcome, they were much better than those who laughed at them.

Alexander remarked that Clitus was pleading his own cause when he gave cowardice the name of misfortune. Clitus started, "This cowardice, as you are pleased to term it, saved the life of the 'son of the gods' from Spithridates' sword! It is by the spilling of Macedonian blood that you are now raised to such a height as to disown your father Philip and call yourself the son of Zeus!"

"Base fellow," cried Alexander, now thoroughly exasperated, "do you expect to utter these things everywhere, and stir up the Macedonians to sedition and not be punished for it?"

"We are sufficiently punished already," Clitus answered, "if we must envy those of us who did not live to see their countrymen beaten by the rods of Median slaves and forced to make entreaties through Persians in order to speak to their own king."

While this exchange continued, the older men did what they could to restore harmony. But Clitus would not quit, demanding that Alexander speak out if he had more to say. "Else

ALEXANDER

why do you invite freeborn men, accustomed to speak their minds openly, to dine with you? You would do better to live and talk with barbarians and slaves, who would not scruple to bow their knee to your Persian girdle and white tunic!"

These words so provoked Alexander that he grabbed an apple lying on the table and threw it at Clitus. He would have taken up his sword if Aristophanes had not hidden it. Breaking from those restraining him, Alexander called out aloud to his Macedonian guards, a certain sign that he was greatly agitated. He commanded a trumpeter to sound and struck the trumpeter with his fist for not instantly obeying him. Clitus still refused to yield and was, with difficulty, forced from the room by his friends. But he came in again at another door, singing, disrespectfully, the verses out of Euripides' *Andromache:*

> *"Are these your customs? Is it thus that Greece*
> *rewards her combatants? Shall one man claim*
> *The trophies won by thousands?"*

Alexander snatched a spear from one of his soldiers and ran it through Clitus' body. As Clitus fell, groaning, to his death, the King's anger vanished. Seeing his friends standing about him in profound silence, Alexander withdrew the spear from the dead body. He would have thrust it into his own throat if the guards had not held his hands and forced him away. All that night and the next day he wept bitterly. Finally, spent with lamenting, he lay speechless, emitting only deep sighs and ignoring worried friends who forced their way into the room.

Callisthenes, kinsman and pupil of Aristotle, tried to soothe Alexander by reasoning gently with him. Anaxarchus, who was contemptuous of his fellow philosophers, entered the room, demanding, "Is this the Alexander whom the whole world looks to, lying here weeping like a slave? Do you fear

the censure and reproach of men, to whom you ought to be
yourself the law and full measure of equity? Use the right
your conquests have given you as the supreme lord and governor of all and do not be the victim of a vain and idle opinion!
Do you not know that Zeus is represented to have Justice
and Law beside him to signify that all the actions of a conqueror are lawful and just?"

With such speeches Anaxarchus allayed the King's grief but
corrupted Alexander's character and made him more bold and
lawless than he had been before. At the same time Anaxarchus
insinuated himself into the King's favor at the expense of Callisthenes, whom he envied and resented. Callisthenes was austere and indifferent, and admired for his serious and orderly
life and his eloquence as a speaker. Once when Anaxarchus
argued that the climate of Greece was colder than that of Persia, Callisthenes silenced him by saying, "You must admit this
country is colder than Greece. There you had but one threadbare cloak to keep out the coldest winter, while here you wear
three rich mantles, one over another!"

Callisthenes frequently refused public entertainments.
When he did attend, he seemed to disapprove of what he saw.
At dinner with the King, when the cup came to him, he was
asked to make a speech in praise of the Macedonians. After he
had spoken everyone rose to applaud his eloquence and reward him with garlands. Alexander, however, quoted Euripides:

> *"I wonder not that you have spoke so well,*
> *'Tis easy on good subjects to excel."*

"Therefore," said Alexander, "to show the force of your eloquence, dispraise my Macedonians and tell them their faults,
so that by hearing their errors they may be better in the future." Callisthenes obliged, retracting all he had said, criticiz-

ing the Macedonians freely. He went even so far as to berate
Alexander's father, Philip, applying to him the verse:

In civil strife e'en villains rise to fame.

Alexander observed that instead of his eloquence, Callisthenes
had made only his ill will appear in what he had spoken.

Though he ruined himself by his lack of discretion, Callisthenes saved the Greeks and Alexander from great dishonor.
After Alexander had drunk some wine at a particular banquet,
he extended the cup to one of his friends. When the friend had
drunk, he worshiped and then kissed Alexander. All present
did the same, one after another, until Callisthenes' turn came.
He took the cup and drank and then came and offered to kiss
Alexander. One of the party objected, saying to Alexander,
who had not noticed, "Sire, by no means let him kiss you, for
he alone of us all has refused to worship you." Alexander declined the kiss. Callisthenes appeared unconcerned, and said
aloud only, "Then I go away with one kiss the less."

Hephaestion and others of Alexander's friends resented Callisthenes' failure to pay the King the same veneration they did.
But by positively refusing to pay adoration to Alexander and
by speaking out openly, Callisthenes set an example for the
best Macedonians. The practice of worshiping Alexander
was finally given up. Callisthenes was later suspected of conspiring against Alexander's life; he died after being kept in
chains seven months awaiting trial before the full council,
when his friend and kinsman Aristotle could be present. In
accusing Callisthenes, Alexander had plainly turned against his
old mentor Aristotle.

Alexander, by this time determined to invade India, realized
his soldiers were so laden with booty that marching would be
difficult. So at break of day—when the baggage wagons were

loaded—he set fire first to his own wagon and those of his friends. Then he commanded that the rest of the baggage belonging to the army should be burned. Most of the soldiers, with loud war-whoops, saved what was absolutely necessary, and burned all the rest. In the Indian campaign Alexander overcame difficulty and opposition by his own resolution and virtue: he thought nothing was impossible for the brave, and nothing secure for the cowardly. When told that the commander of an impregnable position was the greatest coward alive, Alexander observed, "Then what you are telling me is that the place may be easily taken, since what commands it is weak." When he saw his soldiers advance excessively slowly to attack a town surrounded by a deep river, Alexander stood upon the bank and said, "What a miserable man am I, that I have not learned to swim!" It was only after considerable persuasion that Alexander did not attempt to cross the river on his shield. After the assault was successful, ambassadors seeking peace were surprised to find him still in armor and without attendants. When at last someone brought him a cushion, he made the oldest of the ambassadors sit upon it and demanded of him only that the old man rule his own people, sending to Alexander one hundred of his best men as hostages. In surprised relief the old man laughed and replied, "I shall be able to govern better if I send you one hundred of my worst men."

King Taxiles, whose dominions in India were thought to be as large as Egypt, asked Alexander, "Why do we make war upon one another, if you have no intention of robbing us of our water or food, which are the only things that wise men must fight for? If I have more riches and possessions than you, I am ready to let you share with me, but if fortune has given you more, I have no objection to sharing your wealth." Alexander was pleased and embraced Taxiles, saying, "Do you think your kind words and courtesy will let you off without a

ALEXANDER

contest? No, I shall compete with you in courtesies and will win!" They exchanged gifts of great value, and Alexander won the affection of many of the Indians.

The best Indian soldiers soon became paid soldiers of several Indian cities, however, defending the cities and causing Alexander a great deal of trouble. After a final capitulation and surrender, Alexander attacked these mercenaries as they were marching away and killed them. This one breach of his word remains as a mark upon his achievements in war, in which he had otherwise acted throughout with the justice and honor of a just king. Alexander was also inconvenienced by the Indian philosophers, who opposed those Indian princes who allied themselves with Alexander. When he captured several of the philosophers, he had them hanged.

Alexander gave in his own letters an account of his war with Porus. The armies were separated by the river Hydaspes, and on the opposite bank Porus kept his elephants with their heads toward their enemies, in battle order, ready to attack. Every day Alexander had a great deal of noise made in his camp, so that the Indians would become accustomed to it and would not think it unusual. Then, one dark, stormy night, Alexander made his way into the river with a part of his foot soldiers and the best of his horsemen. They reached a small island where they encountered a violent rainstorm, with lightning and tremendous winds. Although some of his men were burned and dying from the lightning, he left the island and continued across the swollen river. This is the occasion on which Alexander is supposed to have said: "O Athenians, will you believe what dangers I incur to merit your praise?"

The men left their boats and made their way through the high water onto the beach. With Alexander and his horsemen about twenty furlongs ahead, the Macedonians were charged by a thousand horsemen and sixty chariots. Yet they took all the chariots and killed four hundred of the Indian horsemen on the spot. Porus, guessing that Alexander had himself crossed the river, attacked with the greater part of his army. Alexander realized the number of his enemy and the effect the attack of the elephants would have on his own men; so he divided his forces. He attacked the left wing himself, while one of his commanders attacked the right wing. Both wings of the Indian army were broken and retreated in confusion upon the elephants that were in the center. They rallied there and continued to fight for eight hours before Alexander's forces prevailed.

Porus himself was said to be over seven feet tall; and when he sat upon his elephant, which was one of the largest, he appeared, in proportion to the elephant, as the usual horseman on his horse. During the battle this elephant showed extraordinary wisdom and concern for the King, his rider. As long as Porus was strong enough to fight, the elephant courageously defended, repelling all who attacked him. When Porus was overpowered by the darts thrown at him, the elephant knelt down and began to pull out the darts from the King's body with his long trunk.

When Porus was captured, Alexander asked him how he expected to be treated, "As a king," replied Porus. When asked to be more specific, Porus said he had nothing more to request, "for everything is understood in the word king." Accordingly, Alexander not only allowed Porus to govern his own kingdom as a satrap under himself, but added to it several other territories of independent tribes.

The battle with Porus took the edge off the Macedonians' courage, and discouraged them from advancing further into India. They had heard that the Ganges River was thirty furlongs wide and one hundred fathoms deep; that the enemy awaited them there with eighty thousand horsemen, two hun-

ALEXANDER

dred thousand foot soldiers, eight thousand armed chariots, and six thousand fighting elephants. At first Alexander was so hurt and enraged at the reluctance of his men to continue that he secluded himself in his tent, declaring if they did not pass the Ganges, he would owe them no thanks for anything. He said that to retreat now would amount to a confession that he had been vanquished. But the logical arguments of his friends and the misery of his soldiers made him decide to return. Before he left he distributed various deceptive reminders, which exaggerated his glory for posterity, including weapons and armor larger than those actually used. He erected altars to the gods, which the Persian kings continued to honor when they passed the Ganges.

Alexander was now anxious to see the Indian Ocean. He ordered towboats and rafts to be built; and on these he went down the rivers, at his leisure, only occasionally subduing cities on either side of the rivers. During this voyage he captured ten of the Indian philosophers, called Gymnosophists, who were reputed to be the quickest and most succinct in their answers to philosophical questions. Alexander put them on trial, letting them know that those whose answers were not pertinent would be put to death. He designated the eldest of the philosophers to be the judge of them all.

Of the first Alexander demanded, "Which are most numerous, the living or the dead?" He answered, "The living, because those who are dead do not exist."

Of the second he inquired, "Does the earth or the sea produce the largest animals?" He answered, "The earth, for the sea is but a part of it."

Of the third, Alexander inquired, "Which is the most cunning of all animals?" The answer: "That animal which man has not yet discovered."

Alexander bade the fourth tell him what argument the philosopher had used with Sabbas to persuade him to revolt. The philosopher replied, "No other than that he should either live or die nobly."

Of the fifth, Alexander asked, "Which is the older, night or day?" The answer, "Day, by one day at least," appeared not to satisfy the King, so the philosopher added the observation that strange questions require strange answers.

Alexander inquired of the next, "What should a man do to be very much loved?" The sixth replied, "Be powerful, without being too much feared."

The seventh was asked, "How might man become a god?" He replied, "By doing that which is impossible for man to do."

The eighth question was, "Which is the strongest, life or death?" To which the eighth philosopher answered, "Life is stronger than death, because it endures so many miseries."

The King's last question was, "How long is it good for a man to live?" "Until death appears more desirable than life," replied the philosopher.

Then, turning to the philosopher he had made judge, Alexander commanded him to give sentence. "All that I can determine," said he, "is that each has answered worse than the other." "Then you shall die first," replied Alexander, "for giving such a sentence." "Not so, O King," replied the Gymnosophist, "unless you said falsely that he should die first who made the worst answer." The King gave them presents and dismissed them.

After going down the rivers for seven months, Alexander came to the Indian Ocean. He went ashore upon an island and sacrificed to the gods. Then he prayed that no other man might exceed the glory of his expedition.

Sending part of his men by sea, Alexander began the trip

ALEXANDER

home to the Mediterranean by land. Because of a shortage
of provisions his army was reduced to one quarter of the hundred and twenty thousand foot soldiers and fifteen thousand
horsemen he had brought out of India. Then in Gedrosia he
found great plenty and refreshed his army. He continued
marching through Carmania, feasting all the way and reveling
night and day upon a platform drawn by eight horses.

When he met his men who had come by sea, he decided to
sail out of the Euphrates with a great fleet to go all the way
around Arabia and Africa, and thus, by Heracles' pillars, back
into the Mediterranean. But news of revolt among the conquered nations and unrest in Macedonia itself forced him to
give up his great adventure.

Alexander sent his fleet back to subdue the maritime provinces
and he himself returned into Persia. Finding that a Macedonian had opened and rifled the sepulchre of Cyrus, he had him
put to death. Reflecting upon the uncertainty of the affairs of
man, Alexander had the original inscription on the tomb recut
to read, in Greek characters, "O man, whomsoever thou art,
and from whencesoever thou comest, for I know thou wilt
come, I am Cyrus, the founder of the Persian empire. Do not
grudge me this little earth which covers my body."

At Susa, Alexander married Statira, a daughter of Darius,
and celebrated also the nuptials of his friends, giving the noblest Persian ladies to his best men. At this magnificent festival
there were nine thousand guests, who each received from Alexander a golden cup for the libations. Alexander found that
the thirty thousand Persian boys whom he had left behind to
be taught and disciplined were wonderfully improved: they
were strong and handsome and performed their exercises with
marvelous dexterity. The Macedonians were at first jealous of
his pride in the Persian youths and Persian satraps, but eventu-

ally they were reconciled with their king. Alexander dismissed those who were no longer able to serve, and gave them magnificent rewards when they came home. At all public shows and in the theaters, these veterans were to sit on the best and foremost seats and were to be crowned with chaplets of flowers. He also ordered that the children of those who had lost their lives in his service should continue to receive their fathers' pay.

In Ecbatana Alexander began to divert himself again with spectacles and public entertainments, performed by three thousand actors and artists who had recently arrived from Greece. Then Hephaestion became ill with a fever, and while his physician attended the theater, the young soldier ignored his diet, drank wine and ate a whole fowl for dinner. Shortly afterward he died.

Alexander was completely undone by the loss of Hephaestion. He ordered the manes and tails of all his horses and mules to be cut as a gesture of mourning, and forbade any music to be played in the camp. In his wild grief he crucified the poor physician, and then he fell upon the Cossaeans and put the whole nation to the sword. This was called a sacrifice to Hephaestion's ghost. Alexander planned a monumental tomb for Hephaestion which would cost ten thousand talents.

While on his way to Babylon, Alexander met Nearchus, who brought him warnings from soothsayers not to go there. Alexander ignored the warnings, but when he approached the walls of Babylon, he was shaken by incidents which were interpreted as bad omens by the diviners and priests who crowded about his court. He was sorry that he had not listened to Nearchus; he remained most of the time outside of Babylon, moving his pavilion from place to place and sailing up and down the Euphrates. As Alexander became more and more influenced by superstition, his mind grew so disturbed that, if anything unusual happened, he thought it was a prophecy of

ALEXANDER

trouble. Soon after his arrival at Babylon, a tame ass attacked the largest and handsomest of Alexander's lions and killed it with a kick. Then one day, when Alexander was preparing to dress after exercising and oiling his body, he discovered an escaped convict wearing his robes, with the crown on his head, seated on the throne. At first the man would not answer any questions. Finally rousing himself as though from a trance, the man claimed that he had been directed by the god Serapis. The soothsayers condemned him to death.

But Alexander had lost his spirit and his confidence in the idea that the gods favored him. So miserable a thing is disbelief and contempt of divine power on the one hand, yet so miserable also is superstition, which fills the mind with slavish fears and follies. So it was with Alexander. He became suspicious of his friends, particularly of Antipater and of his sons, Iolaus, who served as chief cup-bearer to Alexander, and Cassander, who had only recently arrived from Macedonia. The first time Cassander saw some of the Persians worship Alexander, he could not help laughing aloud. Alexander was so incensed that he seized Cassander by the hair with both hands and dashed his head against the wall. When other Macedonians came to accuse Antipater of misrule at home, Cassander defended his father. Alexander interrupted him: "Do you think men who have no just complaint would travel so far to complain?" Cassander argued: "The fact that they travel so far from the evidence is a strong indication that their complaint is not just." Alexander smiled and said, "Those are some of Aristotle's sophisms which can be used on either side of an argument. You and your father will both be punished severely if you are guilty of the least injustice!" Long after Alexander's death, when Cassander ruled Macedonia and all of Greece, he came upon a statue of Alexander. Cassander trembled and grew weak at the sight, recalling the terror of Alexander's severity.

Some ancient writers thought a drama as noble as the life of

Alexander should have a dramatic ending; they invented tales that he was seized by pain in his back as if he had been struck by a lance, or that he was poisoned and died, as if he had drunk the "cup of Heracles." It is true that some answers he received from the oracle about Hephaestion turned Alexander's thoughts from fear and from sorrow over the death of his friend; he began sacrificing to the gods and drinking wine. One night he gave a splendid banquet for Nearchus. Afterward, when he was preparing to sleep, his friend Medius invited him to continue the revelry. All that night and the next day he drank. Alexander's own journals tell the rest. On the eighteenth of June, finding himself feverish, he lay in his bathing room. The next day, when he had bathed, he returned to his bedroom and spent the day playing dice with Medius. That evening he bathed again, offered sacrifices to the gods, and ate his supper. On the twentieth, after the usual sacrifices and bathing, Alexander remained in his bathing room and listened while Nearchus told the story of his voyage and repeated the observations he had made about the ocean. The twenty-first he spent in the same manner, except that his fever increased and he had a very bad night. The next day he had a severe attack; he ordered his bed moved beside the great bath. There he talked with his generals about filling vacancies in the army with experienced men whose bravery had been tested. On the twenty-fourth Alexander was much worse. He was carried out to assist in the sacrifices. He gave orders that his generals should remain with him, while other officers kept watch outside. On the twenty-fifth he was moved to his palace on the other side of the river. Although he slept a little, his fever did not fall. When his generals came into his bedroom, Alexander was speechless. He continued so the following day. His Macedonian soldiers, believing him to be dead, came to the gates with great clamor, demanding to see their king and threatening the friends who guarded him until they were ad-

ALEXANDER

mitted. Each soldier laid down his weapons and passed silently and respectfully by his king's bed. On the twenty-seventh two friends were sent to the temple of Serapis to inquire whether Alexander should be brought there but were told they should not move him. On the twenty-eighth, in the evening, Alexander died. (This account is almost word for word as it is written in his journal.)

After Alexander's death his generals disputed among themselves for many days to determine which among them should succeed to his vast power. One of them exercised the chief authority by manipulating Arrhidaeus, Alexander's weak half-brother, who was now ruined by the drugs Olympias had given him. The Macedonians, however, paid great honor to Roxana, who was pregnant. But Roxana was jealous of Statira, and sent for her by a forged letter, as if Alexander were still alive. When she had lured Statira into her power, Roxana, with the help of one of the generals, killed both Statira and her sister, threw their bodies into a well, and filled it with earth.

At the time of his death there was no suspicion that Alexander had been poisoned, but six years later Olympias put many to death and scattered the remains of Iolaus, claiming he had administered poison to her son. Some who insisted that Alexander was poisoned produced a witness who, they said, heard King Antigonus speak of it. They claimed that Aristotle himself persuaded Antipater to poison Alexander and provided the poison—a water of a deadly quality, cold as ice, distilled from a rock, gathered like a thin dew and kept in an ass's hoof, so cold and penetrating that no other vessel would hold it. This tale, however, is generally rejected. The best evidence that Alexander had not been poisoned was the fact that his body stayed clear and fresh, without any sign of corruption, although it lay neglected for many days in his hot and sultry quarters.

CORIOLANUS

5TH CENTURY B.C.

$\mathcal{M}$arcius leaped from the trenches with a few comrades and killed the first Volscians who charged from the besieged city of Corioli. Having slowed the Volscian attack, Marcius called to his fellow Romans to attack again. The young aristocrat had great qualities for a soldier; not only was he strong but he also had a voice and bearing that inspired terror in the enemy. Part of the Roman army which had remained at the siege of Corioli rallied to Marcius' side, and the Volscians retreated. Marcius, not content with this, pressed hard and drove them to the very gates of their city. There the other Romans fell back, beaten off by the shower of darts poured down upon them from the walls of the city.

Marcius, however, stood his ground and urged his followers to slip in among the Volscians who were retreating into the armed city. He cried, "Fortune has opened Corioli, not so much to shelter the vanquished as to receive the conquerors!" Followed by a few Romans willing to venture with him, he thrust himself through the gate. At first, no one dared resist him. Then a wild fight began, but Marcius, by strength, swiftness, and daring spirit, overpowered every adversary. He succeeded in driving most of the enemy to seek refuge in the interior of the town; they threw down their arms in surrender.

The Roman commander, Larius, then brought the rest of the Roman soldiers easily and safely into the city.

Once inside the walls, the soldiers began looting Corioli. Marcius indignantly told them it was dishonorable to act so selfishly while the other half of the Roman army was still fighting Volscians outside the walls. Few paid him any attention, but some followed him down the road by which the Consul Cominius had departed with the Roman column.

When Marcius came upon the forces of Cominius, the enemy had advanced within view. The Romans were getting ready for battle, and some according to Roman custom, were making an oral will before three or four witnesses to name their heirs. When Marcius appeared, covered with blood and sweat and leading such a small band the men were alarmed; but when he told them how Corioli had fallen, they regained their courage and cried out to be led to battle. First, however, Marcius decided that he and his followers should be in battle position opposite the best Volscian warriors. The Consul embraced and saluted him, and granted his request, greatly admiring his gallantry.

When the fighting began, Marcius ran out before his comrades and successfully broke the Volscian ranks. The fighting became intense around him, and many fell dead. The Romans bore so hard upon the enemy and attacked them with such violence that the Volscians abandoned their ground and quit the field. The rest of the Volscian army was defeated—many were killed, and many were taken captive.

The day after the battle, the army assembled at the Consul's tent. Cominius rose. After thanking the gods for their success, he turned to Marcius and said, "I witnessed part of your brave leadership in our recent battle. More stories of your valor have been told by Larius. As a just reward for one so brave, you must choose, before all of the others, a tenth of the treasure,

CORIOLANUS

horses and captives that have fallen into our hands. In addition I give to you, as a special present, this mighty horse with trappings and ornaments in honor of your deeds."

The entire army applauded. Marcius stepped forward. He gratefully accepted the horse, but added: "I am pleased by the praises of my general. I cannot, however, accept spoils, which I look upon as mercenary rewards rather than as a mark of honor. I have, instead, one special favor to ask. There is a certain friend of mine among the Volscians, a man of great integrity and virtue, who is now our prisoner. Let me redeem him from being sold as a common slave."

There was silence; then the men cheered. Marcius' refusal of spoils, followed by such a humane request, had left the army temporarily stunned. This act gained him as many admirers as had the bravery he had shown in battle. Those who envied his special honors had to admit that anyone who could so nobly refuse reward was, more than all others, worthy of it. It is a higher accomplishment to use money well than to use arms well; but not to need money is more noble than to use it.

When the applause had stopped, Cominius said, "It is futile, fellow-soldiers, to force our gifts on one who is unwilling to accept them; let us therefore give him the kind of gift that he cannot reject. Let us vote that he shall hereafter be called 'Coriolanus' in honor of his courage and leadership in the victory at Corioli."

Marcius had been preparing himself for this day since his early childhood. The one thing the Romans held in highest esteem was military achievement, and they even spoke of "virtue" by using a word which meant "manly courage." Marcius believed that the mastery of weapons would be of little use unless he himself was well prepared for service. So he exercised and conditioned his body to every sort of activity and punishment. He developed both the lightness of a sprinter and an extraordinary power in hand-to-hand combat, hard to overcome.

When Marcius was a youth the Roman dictator saw him bravely fight to save the life of a Roman soldier fallen in battle. The dictator crowned him for his act with a garland of oak branches, which was the way the Romans honored anyone who had saved the life of a citizen. This early fame may well have satisfied a less determined young man, but for Coriolanus it only served as a spur to pursue even greater honor. He looked upon the garland not as a reward for an act already performed, but as a pledge of what he would do in the future. He went from one heroic feat to another, accumulating trophies, while his commanders vied with each other to see who would pay him the greatest honor.

While glory was the goal of most men's brave deeds, Coriolanus' goal was his mother's joy. Her delight in hearing him praised and seeing him crowned made him feel as if he were the most honored and happy person in the world. Born Caius Marcius, of the patrician house of the Marcii, which produced many distinguished Romans, Marcius was brought up by his widowed mother, Volumnia. Though the early loss of a father may have disadvantages, Marcius' life shows it need not prevent a youth from becoming both good and great in the world. Marcius believed that he owed his mother all of the respect he would have given his father, had he lived. He could never be satisfied that he had given her, in his tenderness, all the respect she was due. He took a wife at her request, but even after he had children, he continued to keep his family in his mother's household.

Coriolanus' reputation for honesty and courage gave him considerable authority in Rome at a time when the people began to disagree with the Senate, which favored the wealthier

CORIOLANUS

citizens. The poor complained of inhuman treatment by the moneylenders and consented to fight against the Sabines after being promised by their rich creditors that they would be more gently treated in the future, a promise that had the backing of the Senate. After they had fought courageously and won, the Senate professed to remember nothing of the agreement. The Senators showed no concern at the fact that veterans, because of their debts, were being dragged away like slaves, their few goods seized as before. When the Consuls directed all who were of age to appear for military duty, no one answered the summons. Some members of the government said the laws should be relaxed in favor of the poor, but Coriolanus disagreed and suggested that money was not the main question. It was his thought that the failure of the people to appear as ordered was the first insolent step toward an open revolt against the laws. He encouraged the government to check the *plebs* at the earliest moment.

The poorer people were disgusted. Realizing that their condition was not likely to be improved, they left the city of Rome and seized the hill called Holy Mount. There they sat by the river Anio, committing no violence, but saying that they had been forced out of the City by the cruelty of the rich. They said they could find anywhere in Italy air, water, and a place to be buried, and that the only privilege they were giving up was that of being wounded or killed in a war for the defense of their creditors.

The Senate, highly disturbed, sent out its most moderate and popular men to talk to them. The chief spokesman concluded negotiations with this celebrated fable:

"Once," he said, "all the other members of a man mutinied against the stomach, which they accused of being the only idle, uncontributing part in the whole body while the rest were put to hardships and the expense of much labor to supply and minister to its appetites. The stomach, however, merely ridiculed the silliness of the members, who appeared not to be aware that the stomach certainly does receive the general nourishment, but only to return it again, and redistribute it amongst the rest. Such is the case," he said, "ye citizens, between you and the Senate. The counsels and plans that are there duly digested, convey and secure to all of you proper benefit and support."

The people returned to the City; the Senate agreed to establish for them five protectors, called Tribunes, who were to be elected annually by the *plebs*. Thus satisfied, the common people appeared for military duty and enthusiastically followed their commanders to attack the Volscians. Coriolanus, disgusted by the fact that the plebeians had prevailed, appealed to the patricians to prove that they were superior not only in power and riches, but by their zeal and bravery in war. It was in this campaign that Coriolanus had distinguished himself so nobly and had won his name at Corioli.

However, no sooner had the Volscian war ended than domestic troubles in Rome began again. While the people had been off fighting, the land had not been farmed, and there was no corn to be bought. Even if there had been corn, there was no money; and the poor began to talk as if the rich had purposely contrived the famine.

Meanwhile a group from Velitrae arrived in Rome, saying that a disease had reduced their city to barely a tenth of its population, and that the survivors wished to place themselves under Roman rule and protection.

The Senate hoped to alleviate the famine in Rome by sending the more quarrelsome people as colonists to Velitrae. The Consuls selected some citizens to move to Velitrae and gave notice to others to march again against the Volscians. The Senators hoped that the rich and poor, mingling in the same army and fighting for the same cause, would be reconciled.

CORIOLANUS

Orators for the *plebs* spoke out against both maneuvers. It was not fair, they cried, to send their citizens into a colony where the air was filled with disease and the ground was covered with dead bodies. They also argued against sending the remainder of the citizens off to fight a needless war. The people refused to do either. The Senate was at a loss to know what to say or do.

Coriolanus had always had confidence in himself and knew he had the admiration of the finest men of Rome. He openly took the lead in supporting both ventures. With his support, the proposal to colonize Velitrae was approved.

The colonists were chosen by lot and were sent by force to Velitrae. Then Coriolanus led as many men as he could persuade to join him against the Antiates, and in this campaign they captured much corn. They returned to Rome with great wealth including cattle and prisoners—none of which Coriolanus kept for himself. Those who had refused to go looked at their more fortunate fellow-citizens with envy, but for Coriolanus they felt only hostility and dislike. They surmised that his growing power would eventually be used against them.

Not long after his return, Coriolanus became a candidate for the consulship. As was the custom in those days, Coriolanus, presenting himself for election, appeared before the people in only a toga, with no tunic under it. His battle scars and gashes, which were very much in evidence, reminded the people clearly of his seventeen years of military duty. The people began to feel that it would be wrong to reject a man of such high birth who had so distinguished himself in their service. They told each other he should become Consul. But on the day of the election Coriolanus appeared in the Forum with a pompous train of Senators attending him. People who had felt kindly toward him now felt indignant and envious. They feared that, if they elected a man of such an aristocratic temper, the *plebs* certainly would lose the little freedom they had left.

Coriolanus was defeated. He could not bear this rejection; and as he had always indulged his temper—regarding contentiousness as a sort of nobleness—he retired full of fury and obvious bitterness against the people. He had never learned how essential it is for anyone who undertakes public office to be able to adjust to ill-treatment. Coriolanus, in his straightforward and direct way, thinking that to overcome all opposition is the true part of bravery, never once suspected that in this attitude he was revealing the weakness of his nature.

In the midst of all this, a large quantity of corn reached Rome, part of it as a gift from Syracuse. The people flocked to the senate house, expecting that what the Senate had received as a gift would be distributed to the people in the same manner. Some of the Senators agreed, but Coriolanus criticized them as flatterers of the rabble and traitors to the nobility. Coriolanus argued that since the Senate had granted the plebeians the Tribunes as their representatives, the common people were now a threat to the state. Everything they desired was given them; no restraint was placed on their will; they refused to obey the Consuls. Ignoring the law, they gave the title of judge to the leaders of their private factions.

Coriolanus said, "When things are in such a state that we must sit here and decree bounties for them, what is left for us but to pay them for their disobedience and take care of them so they may ruin us all? They certainly can't look upon these gifts as a reward for public service, which they have too often deserted, or for slandering the Senate and renouncing their country. They can only believe that we give out of fear, so from this point on, they will set no limit to their disobedience. Concession is mere madness. If we have any wisdom and will power, we won't rest until we have recovered the power of the Tribunes which the people have extorted from us."

CORIOLANUS

The young men who were most proud of their noble birth had always been devoted to Coriolanus. He had been their captain, their instructor in the arts of war, and their model of excellence. But their unquestioning faith in him was no help, for it was their indignation at his ill-treatment that had aggravated his resentment against the *plebs*. Now in this speech in the Senate he inspired these young men, and indeed almost all the patricians, who spoke of him as the only citizen who was above both force and flattery.

The assembly met in wild confusion. It appeared that Coriolanus would prevail. The Tribunes ran out into the crowd and incited the people to such fury that they were ready to break in upon the Senate. To prevent this, the Tribunes then demanded that Coriolanus come before them to defend himself. Coriolanus contemptuously ignored the officers who brought him the summons; and so the Tribunes came themselves, threatening to force him to appear. As the patricians came to his rescue, night fell and the contest was ended.

By daybreak the City was in turmoil. The people, highly agitated, came from all parts of the City and gathered in the Forum. With the approval of the Senate, the Consuls, who were very alarmed, pacified the angry crowd. The Tribunes, however, demanded that Coriolanus answer to several charges: Could he deny that he had encouraged the Senate to overthrow the government and annul the privileges of the people? When called to account for it, did he not disobey their summons? Had he not done all he could to begin a civil war?

Coriolanus arrived at the Forum as if to make his apology. The people quieted down to hear him, and the Tribunes listened while planning to humiliate him. But when he began to speak, his expression and the tone of his voice conveyed an offensive kind of freedom that seemed contemptuous. Instead of the submissive language the people expected, his words seemed to accuse rather than to apologize. Pride, and also will-fulness—which Plato called the consort of solitude—made Coriolanus insufferable.

The crowd became angry. The Tribunes conferred; and the boldest of them proceeded solemnly to announce that Coriolanus was condemned by the Tribunes of the people to die. He ordered guards to take Coriolanus to the Tarpeian rock and, without delay, to throw him headlong from the precipice.

Many, even of the plebeian party, felt the sentence was horrible and extravagant. The patricians hurried to the rescue and surrounded Coriolanus. They spoke to the crowd, beseeching them not to allow the execution. They said to the Tribunes: "What do you think you are doing, dragging one of the worthiest men of Rome, without trial, to a barbarous and illegal execution?" The Tribunes' allies saw that it would be impossible to carry out the sentence without killing many of the nobility. They persuaded the Tribunes to be more moderate. "Very well," said the Tribune who had pronounced sentence, "you shall have no grounds for complaint against the people. The people grant your request, and your man shall be tried. We order you, Coriolanus, to appear on the third market day and defend yourself, and to try to prove your innocence to the Roman citizens, who will then judge your case by vote."

In the weeks before the day of the trial, the Senate was in a state of suspense, divided between their concern for Coriolanus and their fear of the plebeians. Some declared that, if the Senate once allowed the people to assume the authority to pronounce sentence upon any of the patricians, the Senate would completely destroy itself and betray the government. The oldest Senators, and those best liked by the people, urged that it was not contempt of the Senate which made the people assume such powers, but, rather, the impression of the people

CORIOLANUS

that the Senate was contemptuous of them. They argued that if the people were once allowed such a mark of respect, the mere possession of it would dispel their anger.

Coriolanus asked the Tribunes what were the charges against him. They replied that he was to be impeached for attempting to usurp power and to establish arbitrary government. Coriolanus stepped forth, saying, "Let me go then to clear myself of that charge before them; I freely offer myself to any sort of trial, and I accept whatever punishment I am given; only make certain that the charges that you have mentioned are the charges upon which I am tried, and do not play false with the Senate."

When the people convened on the day of the trial, the Tribunes contrived to substitute a new method of voting calculated to work against Coriolanus. Instead of prosecuting him on the charges agreed upon, which could never be proved, they tried him on other charges, including the distribution he made of the booty taken from the Antiates. They claimed that he should have brought it into the public treasury instead of dividing it among those who had followed him. By way of excuse, Coriolanus began to praise the courage of those who had fought with him. These words further irritated the masses, who cried out against him. A majority of tribes voted against him. The sentence of his condemnation was pronounced; the penalty was perpetual banishment.

The people went away with greater joy than they had ever displayed over any military victory. Among the distraught patricians, Coriolanus alone appeared unmoved, but inwardly he was seething with indignation and resentment. When he returned home, he comforted his mother and his wife, who were in tears, and proceeded at once to the City gates, where all of the nobility attended him.

Coriolanus spent the next few days alone, distracted by the

various alternatives which his rage and indignation suggested
to him. Without considering any honorable or useful course
of action, he concentrated on a plan for revenge upon the
Romans. He decided at last to incite Rome's neighbors to war
against her, and he selected the Volscians as a likely prospect.
He knew that Tullus, a mighty man among the Volscians,
hated him above all other Romans, but that Tullus also sought
revenge against Rome. He decided to gamble on the chance
that Tullus' desire to defeat Rome was stronger than his bitterness against Coriolanus.

Dressing in disguise, Coriolanus went to the home of Tullus
and, without speaking to anyone, sat down by the fireplace.
Tullus was at supper, but he was curious about the mysterious
visitor with his head covered, so he went in to see him immediately. Coriolanus told Tullus simply that he had been stripped
of Roman citizenship by the envy and cowardice of the Roman
people. Thus driven out as an exile, he had come to Tullus, not
for safety or protection, but to seek vengeance. He said, "It
would be to your advantage to use my talents, for I know all
the secrets of the enemy. If you decline my help, kill me."

Tullus welcomed Coriolanus. Together they urged the
Volscian chiefs to ignore the two-year truce the cities had
sworn, and to attack Rome while it was distracted by the
growing differences between its Senators and plebeians. After
Rome itself provided the means for a dispute by mistreating
the Volscians who were attending its games and spectacles, the
Volscian chiefs sent ambassadors demanding that Rome give
up the Volscian territory and cities it had seized in the recent
war. The Romans were indignant. They replied that the
Volscians were the first to take up arms, but that the Romans
would be the last to lay them down!

Tullus and Coriolanus were immediately commissioned as
Volscian generals; without waiting to assemble regular troops,

CORIOLANUS

Coriolanus marched with volunteers into Roman territory. His object was to make the Roman patricians even more unpopular with the plebeians. He took special care not to touch the farms and lands of the patricians, while he destroyed the property of other men. In Rome the old quarrels broke out afresh, and the Senators reproached the people for their recent injustice to Coriolanus. The plebeians answered by accusing the Senators of conspiring with Coriolanus while they sat themselves like unconcerned spectators, knowing that their properties were protected.

When the entire Volscian army was finally mobilized, Coriolanus marched against the Romans with half the force, while Tullus remained to defend the Volscian cities and to supply the army in the field.

Coriolanus first took Circaeum and then destroyed the country of the Latins. Here he expected to meet the Roman army, but the Roman *plebs* had shown little inclination for military service. Furthermore, the Consuls were unwilling to demand it when the term of their offices was about to expire. Coriolanus marched on to take a number of other Roman colonies. When the Volscians at home heard of his success, they quickly joined Coriolanus and acknowledged him as their sole commander. His fame spread throughout all Italy. Everyone was amazed at the sudden change in the fortunes of two nations, caused by the loss to one, and the gain by the other, of a single man, Coriolanus.

At this time Rome was in complete disorder; the people, unwilling to fight, spent all their time arguing and reproaching each other. But when news came that the enemy had attacked Lavinium—the city where all the sacred images were kept and from which the Roman nation had sprung, the first city Aeneas had built in Italy—there was a complete reversal of the positions of the plebeians and patricians. The people now called for a decree repealing the sentence against Coriolanus and recalling him to Rome.

When the Senate assembled to consider the decree, the patricians rejected the proposal. They were angry with Coriolanus. He now threatened Rome as a declared enemy of his whole country, though he knew well enough that the best men of Rome had always supported him and suffered with him the injustice of the people.

When Coriolanus heard of the Senate's action, he was more exasperated than ever. He abandoned the siege of Lavinium and marched furiously toward Rome, camping within five miles of the City. Rome was in terror: the women ran up and down the streets, and the old men prayed tearfully in every temple. Without courage or wisdom to provide for their own safety, the patricians and plebeians agreed that it was time to forget the offenses of Coriolanus and appease him.

Ambassadors chosen from his family and friends were led to Coriolanus through the enemy camp. They found him sitting in state with the Volscian chiefs, looking proud and arrogant. Gently they offered him the right to return to his country, so that the war would stop. Coriolanus answered with anger and resentment. He demanded that the Romans return to the Volscians the cities and lands they had seized; he also demanded for the Volscians rights at Rome equal to those of the Latins. Coriolanus then dismissed the Roman emissaries, giving them thirty days to consider his terms.

He then withdrew his forces from the approaches to Rome and attacked the allies of Rome for thirty days, ravaging their lands and capturing seven great cities. Meanwhile the Romans dared not venture out to relieve their allies and showed no more capacity for action than if they had lost the power of motion. When Coriolanus appeared again near Rome with his whole army, the Romans sent ambassadors to say that Romans would make no concessions to threats, but if Coriolanus would withdraw the Volscian army, Rome would grant the Volscians any favor Coriolanus thought they should have. Coriolanus rejected their answer, advising the Romans to return within three days with approval of his original demand. Otherwise, he said, they would no longer be free to pass through his camp upon idle errands.

A third time the Roman Senate attempted to negotiate more dignified terms with Coriolanus. They sent to him the whole order of Roman priests, in their sacred vestments and in full procession. Coriolanus remained unmoved, and told them sharply to make up their minds whether they would surrender or fight. He said that the original terms were the only terms of peace.

In Rome the people seemed incapable of making plans for their own safety. They sat within the City, watching their walls, placing their hopes chiefly in the accidents of fate, while the women went to the temples to pray. One of the most honored aristocratic women praying to Jupiter was Valeria. By instinct, and with divine guidance, she realized what must be done; she rose from her prayers and, taking the others with her, went directly to the house of Volumnia, mother of Coriolanus.

They found Volumnia sitting with her daughter-in-law; her little grandchildren were on her lap. Valeria, surrounded by her female companions, spoke in the name of them all: "We come as mere women to women, not by direction of the Senate, or an order from the Consuls, or the appointment of any other magistrate; but the god himself, I believe, has been moved to compassion by our prayers and has prompted us to visit you in a body to make a request on which our own and the common safety depends. If you consent, your fame will be greater than that of the Sabine daughters, who won their fathers and husbands from deadly hatred and established peace and friendship. Arise and come with us to Coriolanus and join in our pleas."

Volumnia answered: "My countrywomen, I share with you our common miseries, and I bear the additional personal sorrow of losing the reputation of Coriolanus. But the greatest of all misfortunes is that the affairs of Rome have sunk to a point where they are dependent upon us. But let us serve; lead us to him so that we may be able, if nothing more, at least to spend our last breath pleading to him for our country."

It was pathetic to see the women walking through the camp of the Volscians, who watched them in respectful silence. As Coriolanus became aware that his mother led the party of women, he abandoned his stately position upon a raised platform and came down hastily to meet her. Overcome by his feelings, he greeted his mother first, embracing her, and then with tears and caresses he embraced his wife and children. Volumnia spoke in the presence of the Volscian chiefs:

"We are the most unfortunate of all women. The sight which should be sweetest is the most dreadful: your mother to behold her son, and your wife, her husband, threatening the walls of Rome. Prayer, which usually is a comfort, adds most to our confusion because we cannot ask at the same time for Rome's victory and your safety. As for myself, I will not wait for war to determine for me whether I must lose you or my native soil. I would rather aid both than destroy either one. If I cannot persuade you to prefer peace to war, then be assured that you will not be able to reach your country unless you first trample upon the corpse of her who gave you life. I will not live to see a child of mine led in triumph by his own countrymen or triumphing over them. Remember also that the fortunes of war are uncertain. Yet this much is certain, that by conquering Rome you will gain only the infamy of having

CORIOLANUS

undone your country. But if the Volscians are defeated under your command, the world will say you brought misery on those who placed confidence in you. You need not betray the Volscians to save your country. They have a superior army and will therefore be thought to grant freely the two greatest of blessings: for peace and friendship, both will thank you. Otherwise, you alone must expect to bear the blame from both nations."

While his mother spoke, Coriolanus listened, without a word. When he stood silent, Volumnia continued: "Oh, my son, why are you silent? Is it the mark of a great man to remember wrongs done to him and not to remember and honor the good things that a child receives from his parents? You are relentless in punishing the ungrateful; yet you are the most ungrateful of all! You have punished your country already; but you have not paid your debt to me."

With this she threw herself down at his feet. Coriolanus cried out, "Oh, Mother, what have you done to me?" Raising her up from the ground, he added, "You have saved Rome, but I am destroyed, and by you alone!"

The next morning, Coriolanus broke up his camp and led the Volscians homeward. They followed him obediently, more out of admiration for his virtue than out of respect for his authority. The Romans began to crown themselves with garlands and to prepare for sacrifices to the gods, showing highest honors to the women, who had brought safety to Rome.

The Volscians were about to forgive Coriolanus when he was killed in Antium by extremists among the followers of Tullus, who now feared him. The Volscians buried him with the honors of a noble hero and famous general.

In Rome, the Senate passed a decree offering to the women whatever favor or honor they asked, and granted their simple

LIVES FROM PLUTARCH

request that a temple be erected to Female Fortune. Romans say that, as the statue of Fortune was hoisted and set into place, it uttered the words "Blessed of the gods, O women, is your gift."

MARCUS CATO

234–149 B.C.

$\mathcal{M}$arcus Cato, the stern and stoical advocate of the simple and noble Roman virtues and tradition, was born in Tusculum and grew up on his father's farm among the Sabines. Little is known of his plebeian ancestors, but he praised his own father as a worthy man and a brave soldier. He said that his great-grandfather had won military prizes and once was even reimbursed for five horses killed under him in battle.

Early in his career Cato was called an upstart; he confessed that this was true insofar as there were no public officials among his ancestors, but he asserted that he recognized ancient foundations for honor in the work and virtue of his ancestors. His name was originally Priscus, but the Romans gave him the name Cato because of his abilities (Cato means "skilful" or "experienced").

He had a ruddy complexion and gray eyes; he was both strong and healthy. He developed good physical habits by working with his hands, living temperately, and serving diligently in the army.

When he was young he practiced public speaking in small towns. He considered it essential to have a trained voice in order to lead an active public life. He became a capable lawyer and never refused counsel for those who needed it. He also became a fine orator, and was known for the conciseness and brevity of his speeches.

His strong character and sound wisdom gradually became well known and he soon had a strong position in public affairs. He often refused pay for his counsel and legal aid, and he seemed unimpressed by the honor he achieved through oratory and the law. It was on the battlefield that Cato sought honor. At seventeen he fought in the ranks against Hannibal; while still a youth, Cato's chest and face bore scars from Rome's enemies.

In battle he was both steadfast and bold. He stared defiantly at his enemies and shouted at them with a harsh, threatening voice, believing that such action often terrified the enemy more than the sword itself. When marching, he carried his own arms and was followed by only one servant, who carried food. He helped his servant, with whom he was never short-tempered, in preparing food whenever his military duties allowed. He was never angry or hasty with this servant. And he drank only water along with the rest of the soldiers.

Cato admired his neighbor, Manius Curio, a great general who was three times carried into Rome in triumph. Curio lived extremely simply in a small, plain house. Once when the Samnites came to this farm to bribe Curio they found him boiling turnips for supper. They made their proposal, to which Curio answered that he who was content with such a supper had no need for gold. Curio believed that it was more honorable to conquer those who possessed the gold than to have it himself. Marcus Cato tried to follow Curio's example; he worked harder, spent little money and lived simply.

As a youth Cato served under Quintus Fabius Maximus, "the Great Delayer," who wore out Hannibal's army by retreating and avoiding battle. In this campaign, the young Cato was lodged with a Pythagorean philosopher and learned from

MARCUS CATO

him some conservative Greek ideas—that pleasure leads to evil, that the body is a liability to the soul, that thought must discipline the body and purify the soul. Cato became a strong advocate of the ideals of frugality and temperance. Cato followed Quintus Fabius Maximus as an example.

Valerius Flaccus, a man who was a good judge of men's potential, became interested in Cato's good character. He admired Cato's hard work and sacrifices, his plain living, his ability to endure hardships, his moderation and fair dealing, and so he wanted to help Cato advance. He also appreciated Cato's voluntary counsel and pleading for those who needed help but could not afford it. Valerius thought that such a fine character, like a plant, needed the right atmosphere in which to flourish; he urged him to begin a public career at Rome. He sponsored Cato as a candidate first for Tribune, then for quaestor, and finally for Censor. He served with him as Consul.

Cato opposed Scipio the Great for being overly generous in distributing wealth among the soldiers. He contended that Scipio was corrupting the character of the soldiers by giving them the money to indulge themselves in unnecessary pleasures and luxuries. When Cato returned from inspecting Scipio's army, he spoke against Scipio in the Senate, asking that he be called back to account for his wasting money and time. Scipio answered the Senate's order by saying he had a plan for victory and he needed to prepare; so they let him go forward.

Cato was called the Roman Demosthenes because of his eloquence, but he gained far greater honor for his virtuous living. It was rare at that time for a public leader to cultivate the old habits of physical labor, poor clothes and simple living, and few orators preferred a cold breakfast and a light supper. However, Cato did all of this and chose to do without luxuries rather than to have them. As Rome became powerful, the influence of foreign customs and luxuries began to turn many

LIVES FROM PLUTARCH

Romans away from hard work and strict living. While Rome became the greatest power on earth, it lost its purity at home. Life in the City grew more complicated but in the midst of this confusion, Cato persevered in his discipline of restraint; he stood for character and stability.

No matter how cheap an article might be, his rule was that nothing was a bargain that was not needed. He refused to pay a high price for any one slave; he sought plain, sturdy slaves who could work hard. He bought lands only for sowing and feeding, not for visual pleasure. He was called greedy and miserly by some men, and his sharp criticisms of other people were resented. He used to say that he had only two ways of gaining—agriculture and thrifty saving. His books on farming tell in detail how to plow, to care for crops and animals, even how to make cakes and to preserve fruit.

Cato's economy in personal expense saved money for himself and for the Republic: he never wore expensive clothing, and when as Consul he led the war in Spain, he left his horse there rather than charge the state the expense of returning him to Rome. He spared his workmen and his soldiers. In public justice he was inflexibly severe and strict, but at the same time he was precise and exacting in following the law and the constitution. The Roman government never seemed more severe and yet more mild than under his administration.

He spoke courteously, yet forcibly; he was pleasant, yet impressive; humorous, yet austere; terse and philosophical, although at times violent. He was compared to Socrates, who outwardly seemed to be a simple, blunt, talkative fellow, but actually was serious and deep and extremely wise.

A man's character is expressed by his words; Cato's remarks are famous. Trying to stop the plebeians from shouting for free food and circuses, he said, "It is hard, O citizens, to make speeches to the belly, which has no ears." He said it is hard to

MARCUS CATO

preserve a city where a fish sells for more than an ox. Cato accused the Roman people of being like sheep, for they did not obey as individuals, but only as a flock would they follow their leaders. Speaking of the Romans, he said, "Men usually command women; but we command all men, and the women command us." He claimed that, just as demand in the Roman market set the price for purple dyes and other luxury items, so the tastes of the Romans set the pattern for habits of life to be followed by other people. Thus the Romans' responsibility to set good examples was most important.

He told the Romans that if they had grown great by their virtue and temperance, they should not change for the worse; but if it was intemperance and vice that had given them power, they should change for the better, since in those particulars they had grown indeed quite great enough.

He criticized the citizens for electing the same men to office again and again: "For it seems that you either do not judge government office to be worth much, or you think there are few worthy of holding it."

Pointing to one man who sold a seashore estate left to him by his father, Cato asked if the man were stronger than the sea, for what the sea washed away slowly and with great effort, this man drank away quite quickly.

Cato claimed that his enemies envied him because he started work before daylight and served the public before tending to his own personal business. He said he would rather be deprived of the reward for doing well than not to suffer the punishment for doing ill. He was able to pardon all offenders but himself.

He used to assert that wise men profited more by fools than fools from wise men; because wise men avoided the faults of fools, but fools did not imitate the good example of wise men. Once when Cato was being reviled by a dishonest man, he

LIVES FROM PLUTARCH

charged him: "A contest between us would be unequal; for you can hear and speak bad words easily, because you are used to them; but it is both unpleasant to me to speak them, and unusual to hear them."

He said that the soul of a lover lived in the body of another. In his whole life the three things he regretted most were: trusting a secret to a woman, that he once went by water when he could have gone by land, and that he had remained one whole day without really accomplishing anything.

Once when he saw an old man committing a crime, he said, "Friend, old age has blemishes enough itself. Do not add to it the deformity of vice." He cherished old age as a significant and rewarding time of life, and until his death at eighty-five he remained active and vigorous.

The Romans sent three ambassadors to Bithynia: one had gout, another had undergone a brain operation, and Cato considered the third to be a fool. Cato laughingly said, "The Romans have sent an embassy lacking feet, head, and heart." (The Romans considered the heart to be the source of judgment and practical sense as well as emotion and courage.)

As Consul he led an army to fight in Spain. When they were surrounded by a large band of barbarians, Cato called on a neighboring tribe for help. They demanded 200 talents as payment for their help, which the other Romans thought was intolerable. But Cato said that if he won he would pay his allies from the spoils of those they defeated, but if they were defeated there would be nobody left either to demand the reward or to pay for it.

With the help of these tribesmen, Cato won the battle and the war. He averaged more than a victory each day during this campaign. When he left Spain to return to Rome, he divided the spoils among all his soldiers—a pound of silver to each man—saying it was better that everyone return home with silver than just a few men with gold. He took nothing for himself except for his actual expenses in Spain. He said, "I don't find fault with those who seek to profit by these spoils, but I myself would rather compete in valor with the best than in wealth with the richest or with the most covetous in love of money."

On the way home from Spain, he defeated a group of tribesmen who had been harboring 600 Roman deserters; he had all the deserters beheaded. Scipio criticized him for the mass execution of these deserters, and then got himself appointed as Cato's successor in Spain. The Senate voted, however, to uphold all that Cato had previously established. Very little was accomplished under Scipio, so that Scipio eventually lost credit himself instead of reducing Cato's prestige. Cato contended that prestige should be based on achievements rather than on nobility of birth. He said that a plebeian should not hesitate to compete against a patrician, nor should a patrician rest on his rank.

After Cato was honored for his victories in Spain, he went to assist his former lieutenant in Greece. There he became a Tribune in the army fighting Antiochus the Great. Thus, by continuing to serve, he proved his commitment to virtue and discipline. He was not like those who strive not so much for virtue's sake as for vainglory; for many men who have attained honors quit public affairs and pass the rest of their lives in pleasure and idleness. Cato, on the contrary, seemed as if he had just entered public life: he still offered his legal and military services to his friends and to the public.

Although he could speak and read Greek efficiently, he spoke to the men of Athens through an interpreter in order to emphasize his character as a pure, simple Roman. He said that the Athenians admired the quickness, brevity, and force of his speech, for the interpreter took a long time to translate what he had stated in a few Latin words. Cato believed that the words of the Greeks came only from their lips, while those of the Romans came from their hearts.

In the war with the Greeks, Antiochus fortified the famous narrow pass at Thermopylae. Cato remembered how the Persians had found a way around the pass to trap Leonidas and his brave Spartans. During the night he climbed around the mountain on a dangerous path and captured an enemy soldier; from him he learned that there were only 600 Greeks in the pass. Early in the morning the Romans attacked; shouting and making a great clamor, they descended from the mountains on all sides. They drove the 600 back against Antiochus' main army, throwing the entire Greek force into confusion. Antiochus was struck in the mouth by a stone, which broke his teeth, and in his pain he failed to provide effective leadership. His army was crushed by the combined efforts of Cato and Manius the Consul, who gave all the credit to Cato.

Full of pride, Cato wrote that many said that Cato owed not so much to the public as the public did to Cato. He himself returned to Rome with the news of victory, thus increasing his conceit and self-satisfaction. He then concentrated on finding, accusing, and convicting dishonest officials; he even accused Scipio. He himself tried to be honest, but he was accused at least fifty times of violating his public office. When he was again accused in his old age, he objected that it was hard for him, who had lived with an earlier generation, to plead now before their sons.

Ten years after he had served as Consul, he was elected Censor, a high office charged with investigating the life, morals, and manners of all Romans. There were two Censors, one a patrician and one a commoner, whose duties were to watch, correct, and punish immorality or the violation of Roman customs. The Romans believed that marriage, the rearing of children, feasting and drinking were all matters of public concern and subject to inquiry and examination. The Censors also had the power to expel a Senator from the Senate and to take away horses, thus demoting men from equestrian rank.

Cato's opponents in the election for Censor made many promises and indicated they would provide a soft, easy administration. They said Cato was uncompromising and severe, Cato, in response, promised to punish evil-doers. Cato contended that the City needed thorough discipline, and he suggested the people choose not a gentle physician, but the roughest one to correct the evils of the time. The people rejected the smooth promisers and chose the severe countenance of Cato.

As Censor he threw out of the Senate certain corrupt and immoral Senators. In the case of Manilius, a Senator who was a candidate for Consul, Cato expelled him from the Senate because he had kissed his wife in the sight of his daughter and in open day. Cato said that his own wife never came into his arms except when frightened by great thunder.

Cato interfered with the luxuries and the reveling of the idle rich. He greatly increased the tax on all extremely expensive dresses, carriages, jewelry, and furniture. What Cato hoped for was that the burden of higher taxes on luxury items would encourage thrift and moderation. Actually both those who had to pay the tax on their luxuries and those who sacrificed the luxuries to avoid the tax came to hate Cato for his severity.

Some people had inserted pipes secretly into the public aqueducts to steal water from the City. Cato had all of these secret pipes discovered and cut off. He checked buildings that extended over onto public property and had their walls torn down. He bargained closely in behalf of Rome, beating down the contract prices of public construction to the lowest and reducing the tax collectors' commissions.

By thus recalling Rome to its tradition of pure, simple, honest virtue, he angered those who had abused the Republic, but he was praised by the people. Indeed the people set up a statue of Cato in the temple of health, praising him for his good discipline and wise and temperate laws, which reclaimed the Roman commonwealth from the vice into which it was sinking. Cato was proud of this statue, although before it was raised he had bragged that while others took pride in the work of sculptors and painters, the citizens carried his praise in their hearts. When asked why he had no statue, he had said, "I would much rather be asked why I have no statue than why I have one."

Cato had indicated he did not want any citizen to be praised unless it were advantageous to the Republic, but he still enjoyed his own praise and repeated it. He said that those who did wrong or were criticized used to say they shouldn't be blamed, for they were not Catos. He also frequently repeated that those who awkwardly imitated his deeds were called left-handed Catos.

Cato definitely had enormous authority among the Romans. The Senate often turned to him for counsel as if he alone were its leader. Sometimes when he was not present they would postpone discussing the most important questions.

He was a good father, an excellent husband, and an extraordinarily good businessman, whose thrift and investments were sound. He married a wife more noble than rich, believing that the rich and the noble were equally proud, but that a noble lady would not act unbecoming in any way and that she would be more obedient to her husband. Cato thought it was more important to be a good husband than to be a good Senator. He admired Socrates for having lived a temperate life with a wife who was a scold and children who were half-witted.

MARCUS CATO

Cato paid a great deal of attention to his son. He himself taught him to read, although he had a good tutor, because Cato did not want his son punished by a servant, nor did he want his son to be beholden to a servant for so great a blessing as knowledge. Therefore he also taught him grammar, law and gymnastics. He taught him how to endure heat and cold, to swim over the most rapid rivers, to ride, and to fight in armor. He wrote histories so that his son might know the traditions of Rome and the achievements of his forefathers without leaving home.

The books Cato produced for the education of his son are early examples of good Latin prose. His histories, which reviewed the origin of Roman institutions and traditions, he wrote in Latin so that the youth would avoid the influence of Greek learning. He also wrote on oratory, law, and military science, and he published many of his speeches. His book on agriculture is a classic that influenced the course of farming in Italy. In it he indicates that profitable cattle raising is the best use of the land, moderately profitable cattle raising the next best use, unprofitable cattle raising third, and plowing the land only fourth.

He tried to set a good example for his son by clean speech, clean living, temperance, and self-discipline. The son was guided toward virtue and wisdom by his father's discipline: he was ready, obedient and docile. He was not as sturdy physically as Cato the Elder, so his father did not insist on as austere a life, but he fought bravely in battle. Serving under Paulus Aemilius against Perseus, his sword was struck from his hand because the sweat on his hand and arm made him lose his grip. He so resented losing his sword that he rallied a group of Romans, drove the enemy back from the spot where his sword had fallen, and recovered it from under the bodies of those he had killed.

LIVES FROM PLUTARCH

Cato the Elder also trained his slaves to his own way of life. He did not tolerate gossip or laziness, and if anyone asked a slave about Cato's activities, he answered merely that he did not know. He encouraged his slaves to sleep a lot, because he wanted them to be constantly either working or sleeping. He was very severe in his discipline and whipped those who cooked, cleaned, or served carelessly. Those who had committed a crime calling for death were punished if they were found guilty by their fellow-servants. When a slave became old and unprofitable, Cato believed in selling him.

He invested his money in such a way as to bring him the best return. He owned ponds, hot baths, grounds containing fuller's earth, mines, and woods. When he invested in ships and merchandise on the basis of a 2 per cent share in fifty ships, he sent his own freedman along on the voyage to protect his interests. He also spread the risk in his investments by having many partners. Cato claimed that it was noble, and even godlike, to increase an estate he had received; he told his son that it would be behaving like a weak widow to decrease it.

When two philosophers, Diogenes and Carneades, came as deputies from Athens to beg relief from a penalty levied by Rome, the young Romans became interested in their philosophy and spent hours listening to them. Many were pleased to see the young men interested in philosophy and Greek literature, but Cato objected to the flow of words. He wanted the youths to pursue the glory of arms and of virtue rather than eloquence; so he had a law passed to banish all philosophers from Rome. He criticized the Senate for delaying these deputies by not giving a decision: "Let them go back to their own schools and declaim to the Greek children, and leave the Roman youth to be obedient to Roman laws, customs and governors." He actually despised philosophy and scoffed at Greek

MARCUS CATO

studies, predicting that the Romans would be destroyed when they became infected with Greek literature. He also was suspicious of physicians and claimed to know how to heal himself by diet, sleep, and rest. Because of this presumption he lost both his first wife and his first son in illness, although his own strong physique insured a long life for Cato.

When Cato was old, he was asked advice by a friend about a suitable marriage for his daughter; Cato recommended himself for the young girl. His own son and daughter-in-law asked if they had offended him to cause him to bring a stepmother into the household over them. "Far from it, my son," he replied, "I simply want to leave the commonwealth more sons like yourself." And he did.

Cato continued in public service even in old age, but he enjoyed using his leisure in writing and in supervising his farms. He stayed active as a lawyer before the courts, even past the age of eighty, and he was still a strong leader of the Senate at eighty-five, when he died.

Cato was a great host, inviting friends of all ages to his farm for delicious dinners and interesting conversation. He thought that meals were the best place for making friends, so, at his table interesting experiences were discussed and good citizens were praised. He disdained gossip, and he cherished friendship among honest and trustworthy men as one of life's great blessings.

As one of his last acts of state, he was sent to Carthage to investigate the cause of a dispute between Carthage and Numidia, both of which had been defeated by Rome. When he discovered that Carthage was not, as the Romans had thought, in poor condition but was rather well armed, not to mention proud and ambitious, he quickly returned to Rome. Instead of helping Carthage to make peace with its neighbors, he began to check this rapid new growth of Rome's old enemy. He reported to the Senate that the former defeats by the Romans had not so much decreased the strength of Carthage as it had made them less foolish and more determined to become great. He showed the Senate some giant figs from Carthage and reminded his hearers that they were raised just three days sail from Rome.

It seemed dangerous to Cato that a city always great, and now grown wise by reason of its calamities, should still be waiting for the follies and excesses of the powerful but overconfident Roman people to ruin Rome. He thought that the best course of action was to remove all outside dangers, since Rome was threatened by rottenness within.

Cato now ended every speech with the sentence, *"Carthago delenda est"*—"Carthage ought to be destroyed." Thus he pushed the Romans toward a third war for the final destruction of Carthage. Soon after the war began, he died, predicting that the young Scipio would be the man to crush Carthage.

Cato Salonius, his son by his second wife, became a praetor. His grandson Marcus was Consul, and his great-grandson by this line was the eminent Roman philosopher and Senator who became a friend to Cicero and an obstacle to Julius Caesar.

* * *

Cato was a hard, disciplined, tough Roman who believed in the plain, honest life and who tried to set a good example for others. He believed in hard work, constructive planning, and sacrifice. He admired bravery and believed that Romans must fight strongly and courageously to preserve the Roman way of life. He respected custom, law, and order. He liked plain living; simplicity was his guide.

Cato waged war all his life against vice, dishonesty, immo-

MARCUS CATO

rality, and waste. He feared the corruption of luxury, drunkenness, soft living, and love of riches. He was suspicious of foreign ways of life, particularly the softness of Greek culture. He opposed everything Greek and Oriental as an invasion of the 100 per cent Roman way of living.

Cato's influence helped to make Rome a strong Republic. He was respected even by those who resisted his reforms. It was clear that he loved Rome.

THE GRACCHI

TIBERIUS GRACCHUS
162–133 B.C.

CAIUS GRACCHUS
153–121 B.C.

*T*he Gracchi, Tiberius and Caius, were sons of an elder Tiberius Gracchus, who had served as Censor, had been Consul two years, and had twice celebrated a Roman triumph for his military victories, but who was more famous for his virtues than for his honors. Their mother was the noble and lovely Cornelia, daughter of Scipio, the brave Roman who had defeated Hannibal. These two outstanding people, Tiberius and Cornelia, had twelve children.

There was a story that Tiberius once found two snakes in his bedchamber. When he consulted the soothsayers about it, he was told that he should neither kill both nor let them both escape; but that, if the male snake were killed, he would soon die, and if the female snake were killed, Cornelia would soon die. Tiberius, already an old man, loved and admired Cornelia so much that he killed the male serpent and let the female escape. And, indeed he soon died, leaving his young but wise wife with the responsibility of their twelve children. Cornelia proved to be a discreet matron, an affectionate mother, and a thoroughly constant and noble-spirited widow. King Ptolemy offered her a crown, but she refused him and chose to remain a widow, devoting herself to her children. Unfortunately she lost all her children before they reached maturity, except one daughter, who eventually married Scipio the Younger, and the two sons Tiberius and Caius. Cornelia diligently prepared both sons for great careers of public service.

Tiberius and Caius were alike in their courage and temperance, in their liberality, eloquence, and intelligence. Because of their integrity and their lack of greed for money they were never accused of being unjust or corrupt. But in their actions and in their administrative methods in public affairs they were quite different one from another. Tiberius seemed to be gentle and composed, whereas Caius seemed intensely earnest and violent. In speaking, Tiberius was quiet and orderly, standing in one spot, whereas Caius rushed about as he spoke, gesturing wildly, and once in the heat of his argument, pulled his gown off his shoulders. Tiberius spoke gently and persuasively, arousing sympathy, whereas Caius' oratory was impetuous and passionate, making every point count. In choice of words Tiberius was pure and carefully correct, while Caius used a richer and more colorful vocabulary.

In his way of living, Tiberius was frugal and plain; Caius, although temperate and even austere compared to other leaders, differed from his brother by his fondness for new fashions and rarities. For example, he was criticized for having bought some silver dolphins valued at 1250 drachmas per pound.

Whereas Tiberius had a mild temperament, Caius was so passionate that when speaking he often became so carried away that his voice lost its tone and he shrieked abusively. To correct this, Caius had a discreet servant stand behind him with a pitch pipe. When Caius heard a soft tone on the pitch pipe, he would check his vehemence and force himself to speak more calmly.

Both brothers were remarkable for their courage in war, justice in the government, care and hard work in office, and self-control in their private lives. If they had not died so young, they might well have made great generals and conquerors. Tiberius was older by nine years, and so he held pub-

THE GRACCHI

lic office before Caius was old enough to serve. Perhaps a principal cause of the failure of their enterprises and reforms was the interval between their careers and the fact that they could not combine their efforts. The power they would have exercised, had they both flourished together, might have overcome all obstacles and resistance.

Tiberius was admitted to the College of Augurs at a very young age because of his obvious ability. Appius Claudius, the great Consul and Censor and the head of the Senate, arranged for his daughter's marriage to Tiberius. When he returned home one day, Appius told his wife that he had contracted their daughter in marriage. In surprise, she asked, "But why so suddenly? Why should you hurry—unless it is Tiberius Gracchus who will be her husband?"

Tiberius served in Africa under the young Scipio, his sister's husband. He was closely associated with the great commander in action and learned to appreciate his noble spirit. He followed Scipio's example, and soon was the most courageous and obedient of all the young men in the army. He was very popular and much admired among the soldiers; he was the first to mount the enemy's wall at Carthage, a remarkable feat that spurred other Romans to fight well.

After Scipio's triumph, Tiberius served as paymaster for the Roman army that was defeated by the Numantines. Even in the great misfortune of defeat Tiberius showed courage and good judgment; he maintained his respect and honor towards the losing general at a time when others criticized him. When the commander, obviously surrounded and defeated, asked for a truce, the Numantines refused to deal with anyone except Tiberius Gracchus. Not only did the Numantines respect the young officer, but they also remembered his father, who had subjugated many Spaniards but had granted peace to the Numantines.

Tiberius worked out acceptable peace terms to save 20,000

Roman soldiers, but the Numantines kept all the spoils, including Tiberius' account books and his records as quaestor. After the army was on its way back to Rome, Tiberius returned to the Numantines to plead for his records, lest he not be able to give an account of the money entrusted to him by the Republic.

The Numantines were delighted at this opportunity to extend hospitality to him and invited him into their city. As he stood hesitating, they took him by his hands and begged him not to look upon them as enemies but to accept them as friends. Tiberius decided to consent, anxious to have his books returned, and careful to avoid showing any distrust of their hospitality. After a friendly dinner, they returned his records to him and offered him whatever else he wanted; he refused everything except the records and some incense to use in an offering of thanksgiving.

When the army returned to Rome all who had any connection with it were severely criticized. But the families of the soldiers rallied to the defense of Gracchus, since it was he who had saved their lives. The Consul therefore was blamed and humiliated, while the other officers were spared for the sake of Gracchus.

When he was elected Tribune of the people, Tiberius became concerned with the abuse of rights to the public lands and with the need of the common soldiers and the poor to own their own land. Of the land that Rome's armies won by conquest, part was sold publicly and part was defined as common. This common land was supposed to be assigned to poor citizens who could pay little rent. When rich men offered higher rents they drove the poor men out. To remedy this inequity a law was passed to limit each man to only 500 acres of such land. At first this law protected the poor, but later the rich learned to register the land in the names of others, so that once more they took the land away from the poor.

Deprived of their farms, the poor despaired and became careless in educating their children. They soon even became unfit to serve as soldiers. In a short time the proud free farmer of Italy was replaced by work gangs of foreign-born slaves.

Cornelia chided her sons that the Romans still called her the daughter of Scipio, rather than the mother of the Gracchi. Perhaps it was she who inspired Tiberius to fight for the poor. His brother Caius said it was the sight of deserted farms and of slaves working the fields instead of free Romans that inspired Tiberius to recover the public lands for the poorer citizens.

In drawing up his land law, Tiberius consulted Senators well known for their judgment and authority. The law was unprecedented inasmuch as it appeared to be so moderate and gentle, especially considering the oppression and greed against which it was aimed. Those who should have been punished for violating the former laws and therefore should have lost title to the lands they had unjustly gained were to be paid a reasonable price for relinquishing their claims in favor of those legally qualified to own the land. In this gentle way Tiberius wanted both to forget and forgive all the former transgressions and to prevent such abuses in the future.

But the greedy landowners bitterly opposed Tiberius' law, declaring that he was trying to overthrow the government and confuse the issue. Tiberius, however, won wide support for the law among the people. "The savage beasts in Italy," he said, "have their particular dens, they have their place of repose and refuge; but the men who bear arms and expose their lives for the safety of their country enjoy nothing in it but the air and light, and because they have no houses they have to wander from place to place with their wives and children." He asked how the army commanders could urge the soldiers to fight for their homes and altars, when they actually had neither homes nor altars of their own. Tiberius argued that they fought, instead, only to maintain the luxury and wealth

of other men. He said that they were called the masters of the
world, but had not one foot of ground they could call their
own.

His opponents were unable to answer or oppose these arguments. They therefore went to the Tribune, Octavius, and
persuaded him to stop the passage of the law. For the protection of the people any one Tribune by opposing a law could
veto it. Octavius distorted this power to stop the protection of
the peoples' rights.

Tiberius, blocked by these proceedings, put aside this leni-
ent bill and introduced a new one which was more severe. It
provided that those illegally holding land had to surrender it
immediately. Octavius and Tiberius debated the issues every
day. Tiberius observed that Octavius was one of the men who
would lose lands if the law were passed, so Tiberius offered to
pay Octavius personally from his own small resources for the
lands he would lose.

Although he fought passionately and determinedly for his
land laws, Tiberius never lowered himself to personal re-
proaches or derogatory remarks against Octavius, nor did Octavius against him. As in all other situations, a noble nature and
a temperate education controlled and overrode political contentions.

Tiberius got an edict passed that all magistrates should stop
working and that the treasury should be closed until the land
law was either approved or rejected by popular vote. The
landowners went into mourning. They hired men to murder
Tiberius, who armed himself in self-defense. On the day when
the people were supposed to vote, the landowners seized the
voting urns by force and carried them away. When Tiberius
began assembling the people to oppose this violent interfer-
ence, Manlius and Fulvius, two highly respected citizens, took
Tiberius by the hand and, with tears in their eyes, begged him

to stop. Because he respected these two fine men, Tiberius asked them what they would advise him to do. They admitted they did not know, but they pleaded with him to leave it to the Senate to decide. Tiberius agreed, but this time the land-owners blocked his action in the Senate.

Tiberius finally appealed publicly to Octavius for coopera-tion, but he was again refused. He then declared that since they each had equal authority, their differences on this impor-tant question might lead to civil war. He proposed that one of them be deposed from office. He asked Octavius to have the verdict brought against him, Tiberius, first, saying he would willingly give up his authority if the citizens desired it. Octa-vius refused, and Tiberius told him that, if he would not change his mind, he would put the question to the assembly for Octavius to be forced to give up his authority. He then adjourned the assembly.

The next day he gave Octavius another chance to change his mind, and when he did not, Tiberius asked the assembly to vote as to whether Octavius should be deposed or not. In such cases the Romans voted by tribes, each citizen being a member of one of the thirty-five traditional Roman tribes. After seven-teen of the thirty-five tribes had voted against Octavius, Tibe-rius stopped the voting and begged Octavius to cooperate for the land law rather than be disgraced by being thrown out of office. Octavius seemed to weaken, but when he saw the landowners encouraging him, he boldly told Tiberius to use any measures he pleased. The vote continued, Octavius was voted out of office by the people, and Tiberius forced him to leave the rostra. Instead of employing public officials, Tiberius ordered one of his own servants to remove Octavius. The ig-nominious manner in which he was dragged out heightened the drama of the event. The people immediately assaulted Oc-tavius, but his rich friends surrounded him and got him out of

LIVES FROM PLUTARCH

the crowd. A servant of Octavius, while protecting his master from the multitude, had his eyes struck out. Tiberius was extremely distressed by this violence, and he rushed to stop the rioters.

The land law of Tiberius was next voted on and ratified by the assembly, and three commissioners were appointed to make a survey of the lands to see that they were equally divided. Tiberius, his brother Caius, and his father-in-law Claudius Appius were named as commissioners. Tiberius got one of his clients named to succeed Octavius as Tribune. This offended many, and the landowners became more open in their insults and opposition to Tiberius. The Senate refused him the usual support and expenses for enforcing the new law. Once, when he asked for a tent to be used on location as they divided the lands, the allowance was refused. But the people became more loyal and more intensely emotional about Tiberius. When one of his friends died suddenly, it was said that he had been poisoned by the landowners.

At about this time, King Attalus of Pergamum died, having made the Roman people his heirs. Tiberius suggested that all of the King's money be divided among the poor citizens who were eligible for the distribution of public lands, so that they might have the means to begin cultivating their ground. He also declared that the disposal of the cities in the territories of Attalus did not concern the Senate, but the people. This made the Senators even more hostile towards him. Deposing Octavius had offended even some of the common people for whom he did it, because they hated to see a Tribune, who had been elected to represent them, deposed from office.

When Tiberius began to understand that his suggestions had offended many of his followers as well as the Senators, he made a speech to explain why Octavius had been deposed. A Tribune, he said, is supposed to represent the people, and as

THE GRACCHI

such he should be defended. A Tribune of the people is sacred indeed and ought to be inviolable. On the other hand, if a Tribune degenerates to a point where he oppresses the people and takes away their power and their right to vote, he has deprived himself of his honors and immunity through the neglect of the duty for which he gained the honors and immunity. "Is there anything in all Rome that we hold as sacred and honered as the vestal virgins, to whose care alone the preservation of the eternal fire is committed? Yet if one of these transgresses, she must be buried alive. In the same way a Tribune loses his inviolability when he attacks the foundations of that authority from whence he derived his own. He who attacks the power of the people is no longer a Tribune at all, regardless of what he might be called. Can a Tribune have power to imprison a Consul, and yet the people not have power to degrade him if he abuses the power they gave him as their representative?"

When his term expired Tiberius boldly stood for reelection as Tribune, fearing for his safety if he were to go out of office. To secure good will and votes, he sponsored new laws, which reduced the amount of time soldiers had to spend in the armies, which granted liberty of appeal from judges to the people's assembly, and which created new judges from among the equestrian ranks equal to the judges from the senatorial rank. In this way he reduced the power of the Senate and enhanced the prestige and influence of the businessmen.

Tiberius went among the people in the marketplace before the day of voting and spoke humbly and tearfully. He told the people that the landowners might break into his house and kill him. His supporters pitched tents around his house to guard him. On election day, Tiberius was frightened by superstitious omens, but in spite of them he went to the Capitol. The people welcomed him with loud applause and gathered around him, but in the meantime the election was delayed by fights between the opposing parties. One of the Senators forced his way through the crowd to warn Tiberius that his opponents in the Senate planned to kill him that day. Those close to him armed themselves, but those at a distance were confused by what was going on. Trying to signal that his life was in danger, Tiberius pointed to his head.

The enemies of Tiberius ran to the Senate, pretending that Tiberius was seeking a crown, and indicating that this was the meaning of his touching his head. Nasica, a Senator who had many acres of public land, demanded that the Consul punish Gracchus as a tyrant. The Consul refused to act against Tiberius without a fair trial; Nasica arose and shouted, "Since the Consul regards not the safety of the Republic, let everyone who will defend the laws follow me."

Nasica and others picked up pieces of stools and chairs which had been broken by the milling of the crowd. They joined their attendants, who had come to the Senate armed with clubs and staves, and together they hastened towards Tiberius.

Tiberius himself tried to flee, and many around him were killed. One pursuer caught him by his gown, which he threw off, continuing to flee in his underclothes. As he stumbled in the crowd, a fellow Tribune hit him over the head with the foot of a stool; many blows followed, and he was killed.

Since the deposing of the last Roman king, this was the first conflict between the Senate and the people that ended in blood. Prior to this, such quarrels had been resolved on a friendly basis, with concessions on both sides, the Senate yielding for fear of the *plebs* and the people out of respect for the Senate.

Tiberius was killed out of hatred and malice against him personally, rather than for the reasons which were publicly

THE GRACCHI

stated. The Senate would not allow Caius the privilege of a decent burial for his brother, and his corpse was thrown into the river. However, to appease the people, the Senate proceeded with the division of the public lands and permitted the people to choose another commissioner in place of Tiberius. In spite of these concessions, the people still showed their anger over the murder of Tiberius.

After his brother's death, Caius Gracchus stayed out of public affairs and lived quietly at home. Whether he did this out of fear of his enemies or because he wished the people to hate them is uncertain, but many people were misled into thinking that Caius was unambitious, or that he did not feel a strong loyalty to his brother's ideas. But perhaps the real reason for this "retirement" was his youth; he was not yet thirty.

Caius studied oratory to prepare himself for a public career. He did not care for a life of moneymaking, eating, and drinking, and he certainly did not intend to pass his days in obscurity. After a time he appeared to plead the cause of a friend, and his speech made the other orators of his time seem childish. His eloquence and passion so filled the common people with joy and hope that the Senators became determined to prevent him from being elected Tribune.

Caius then went to Sardinia as quaestor under Orestes, a mission he liked because he had been well prepared for war. It is said that the ghost of Tiberius appeared to him in a dream, saying, "Why do you tarry, Caius? There is no escape; one life and one death has been given to us both, to spend the one and to meet the other in the service of the people." Although Caius was later criticized for being a demagogue, it was certain from the beginning that it was necessity that brought him into public affairs rather than any ambition of his own.

While Caius was in Sardinia he proved to be courageous, just to the men under his command, obedient to his commanding officers, self-controlled, frugal and industrious. During the bitter cold of that winter, the general demanded that several Sardinian towns supply warm clothes for the soldiers. The unwilling citizens appealed to Rome, and the Senate ordered the general to find some other way to clothe the army. The soldiers were in distress from the cold, so Caius went from town to town getting the people to voluntarily contribute clothing for the army. Then an African king, out of respect for Gracchus, sent corn to the Roman troops in Sardinia. The Senate was offended by these honors to Caius, so they sent new men as replacements for the soldiers for whom Caius had secured these benefits.

Caius returned to Rome to face various accusations. When he had completed his eloquent and successful defense, it seemed to everyone that it was he who had been injured rather than the state or those who accused him. He cleared himself of all suspicion and ran for Tribune with vast popular support but with strong opposition from the Senate. At the time of the election so many citizens came from the rural areas to the City to vote for Caius that they could not find lodgings. The Field was not large enough to hold all that came to vote, and many climbed on nearby roofs to voice their support of him. Opposition by the nobility, however, was so effective that Caius ranked only fourth in the race, but his ability made him the strongest of all the Tribunes. He constantly reminded the people of the injustices to his brother, and of how Tiberius and his close followers were put to death without a trial, contrary to Roman law. He recalled that, according to Roman custom, whenever one was accused of a capital crime and failed to appear in his own defense, a trumpeter was to be sent to his home to summon him to appear in court. Before this was done the judges could not vote. In this way he emphasized how cautious the early Romans were in cases involving life and death.

Having incited the people, he proposed two laws. The first was that whoever had been voted out of office by the people should become ineligible to hold any office afterwards. The second law provided that if any magistrate condemned a Roman to be banished without legal trial, the people could take action to prevent the banishment. The purpose of these laws was revenge on Tiberius' tormentors. Caius voluntarily withdrew the first law at the request of his mother Cornelia, who sought no vengeance. Cornelia was a strong influence on Caius as Tribune and Caius frequently referred to her noble character in publicly attacking his adversaries. Eventually the people erected a brass statue of her, inscribed with the legend: "Cornelia, the mother of the Gracchi."

Caius introduced other laws to divide the public lands among the poor citizens, to provide clothing for the soldiers, to exempt boys under seventeen from military service, to extend the franchise to all Italians, to reduce the price of corn to the poor, and to regulate the courts of justice. As he argued for these laws, he turned towards the people, whereas all other speakers had addressed their remarks to the Senate. This change of direction marked a revolution in state affairs—the conversion of the Republic from an aristocracy to a democracy.

When he was given the power to select the new judges, Caius wielded such authority that even the Senate followed his advice in difficult problems. He was wise and fair in the counsel he gave. He proposed that new colonies be founded to provide homes for the poor; he built public roads and granaries. Caius was very efficient in supervising all of these public works, and showed a remarkable ability to be responsible for details. In dealing with the variety of public officials—contractors, scholars, soldiers, Senators, and workmen—he was courteous and friendly but always dignified and thorough. He treated all these various men with an easy familiarity, yet in a businesslike way. This gentleness won admiration for him even among those who opposed his policies.

The roads he built made travel through Italy more comfortable and convenient than ever before. They were marvels of engineering and good construction; they were built to last. He had instructed that the roads were to be made as beautiful and pleasant as possible. They were run exactly in a straight line, partly paved with hewn stone and partly laid with solid masses of gravel. Valleys and gullies were either bridged or filled with solidly packed foundations of rubble and dirt, so that the roadway would be uniform, level and attractive. He also had the roads divided into miles, with pillars of stone signifying the distance from one place to another. To help travelers mount their horses without the help of a groom he placed other stones beside the roads.

The people of Rome and of all Italy appreciated all his other achievements, but especially the roads; they liked to travel through the beautiful Italian countryside in comfort and safety. The *plebs* were particularly devoted and loyal to Caius. Some believed that he wished to become Consul, or even to break precedent by becoming Consul and Tribune simultaneously. This belief was based upon a mysterious passage in a speech Caius made to the people: "I have only one request; if it is granted, I will consider it the greatest obligation in the world; if it is denied I will not complain." Yet Caius never stood as a candidate for Consul, although he supported others for the office.

Caius was elected Tribune the second time on the voluntary motion of the people; he had not sought office. He then pro-

posed colonies for Tarentum and Capua and he also proposed
that the Latins should enjoy equal privileges with the citizens
of Rome.

The Senators and big landowners, seeing that Caius was
gaining power by favoring the people, decided to fight fire
with fire. They employed Livius Drusus, a fellow Tribune
with Caius, to introduce laws favorable to the masses in such a
way as to outdo Gracchus. When Caius proposed two colonies, Livius proposed twelve. When Caius divided the public
land among poor citizens and charged a small rent to be paid
annually into the public treasury, Livius revoked even the
small charge. Caius proposed equal rights for the Latins;
Livius made it unlawful for a Roman captain to whip a Latin
soldier. In each case, the Senate opposed Caius' reform but
supported the reform proposed by Livius. The Senators made
it plain that they opposed Gracchus personally instead of his
public measures and principles. They were determined to ruin
him.

While Caius was away in Africa supervising a new colony
which was being founded on the site of the ruined city of Carthage, Livius gained popularity with the people. He was careful to take no personal advantage for himself and he encouraged the people to be loyal to the Senate. But Livius opposed a
close friend of Caius, a man named Fulvius, who was very
temperamental and notoriously hated by the Senators. Livius
attacked Fulvius for fomenting differences among the citizens
and inciting the Italians to rebel. When Scipio Africanus died,
his body bore the marks of recent violence and suspicion was
directed towards Fulvius, because he was Scipio's enemy and
had that very day publicly criticized him. Because Fulvius was
his friend, Caius was implicated in the criticisms of Fulvius. It
is possible that his association with the unpopular Fulvius may
well have contributed to his own downfall.

At this time Caius was concerned about the state of affairs at Rome and especially about the candidacy of a strong enemy for the consulship. He quickly finished his business at Carthage in order to protect his interests in Rome. When he returned, he presented new laws for the people. On the day the assembly was to vote, the Consul ordered all who were not born Romans to leave the City. Caius opposed this, but was unsuccessful.

On the day of election a gladiator show was to be held in the marketplace; certain magistrates had built grandstands and sold tickets. Caius demanded that the grandstands be taken down so that the poor people could watch the show without paying. When he was not obeyed, he had workmen tear them down by force.

In the next election for Tribune he was defeated; he claimed the election judges cheated and made false returns. The conflict between Caius Gracchus and the Senate, between poor man and landowner, between Latin and Roman, became much more bitter.

The new Consul revoked some of the laws sponsored by Caius and tried to irritate Gracchus so that he would lose his temper and provoke violence that might lead to his death. At first Caius and his supporters bore this opposition peacefully, but at last he could stand no more and so he brought armed men to the marketplace. One of the Consul's attendants pushed his way through them, saying, "Factious citizens, make way for honest men." As he pointed his arm at them in contempt and scorn, someone picked up a stylus and killed him. Caius regretted the murder and reprimanded his followers for becoming violent. The Consul insisted on revenge but was thwarted by a sudden downpour of rain, which stopped the fighting. The next day the Senate gave the Consul extraordinary power "to protect the Republic and to suppress all tyrants." The Consul ordered the Senators and the Equestri-

THE GRACCHI

ans to arm themselves and to bring armed attendants to the next assembly.

On learning this Caius went to the marketplace and stood staring up at his father's statue for a long time, and he shed tears. Impressed by this, his followers guarded his house all through the night; early the next morning they went armed and shouting to the Capitol, ready to fight. Caius went separately and unarmed except for a small dagger under his robe, although his wife had warned him against the danger:

"Caius, I do not say good-bye to you to let you address the people, either as a Tribune or a lawmaker, nor as if you were going to some honorable war—if you were to die under such circumstances, my mourning would be respected and honored. But you go now to expose yourself to the murderers of Tiberius. You are rightly unarmed, because you choose to suffer the worst injuries rather than to harm anyone yourself. But even your death now will not serve the public. Faction prevails; power and arms are now the only measures of justice."

Caius slowly withdrew from her embrace and silently departed with his friends. When he left she fell prostrate on the ground, lying speechless in her despair.

A young boy was sent to the Consul to propose peace, which many Senators wanted, but the Consul insisted on fighting. He took the boy captive and led experienced soldiers, including archers, against Caius' followers.

Caius was never once seen acting violently against anyone. Abhorring the outrages that were a part of the day's violence, he withdrew to Diana's temple. The Consul then proclaimed that he would pardon all those who would desert Gracchus; many accepted this pardon. When Caius learned how many of the people had left him, he prayed to the goddess that the Roman people, as a punishment for their ingratitude and treachery, might always remain in slavery.

As Caius attempted to escape from Rome his enemies pursued closely, nearly capturing him at the wooden bridge over the river. Two trusted friends guarded the bridge while Caius fled with one servant. As he ran people encouraged him and wished him success, as spectators cheer athletes in a race, but nobody helped him, nor would anyone lend him a horse, even though he repeatedly asked for one. Finally in a little sacred grove, Caius' obedient servant drew his sword and ended his master's dedicated but turbulent life as well as his own.

A reward had been offered for the head of Gracchus—its weight in gold. One of the leaders of the Senatorial party brought the Gracchan head in and claimed seventeen pounds of gold. (He had replaced Caius' brains with lead.)

His body was thrown into the river, his house was burned, and his wife was refused his inheritance and the right to a period of mourning. The Consul, as if he gloried and triumphed in the slaughter of the three thousand citizens killed in this upheaval, erected a temple of Concord. During the night someone wrote across the temple "Folly and Discord Concord's temple built."

Most of the people were humbled and frightened at the time of Caius' death, but before long they demonstrated their respect for the memory of the Gracchi. They set up statues of both brothers and consecrated the places where they were killed; there the Romans annually offered the first fruits of the harvest and daily made their devotions, as at the temples of the gods.

Cornelia, having lost her husband, father, and two sons tragically, bore her grief nobly. It was startling to hear her give a full account of their deeds and misfortunes in a calm, objective way; her generous nature and sound education gave her a stoical strength. Although misfortune may often defeat the efforts of virtue, it cannot prevent us from enduring tragedy with serenity and fortitude.

CICERO
106–43 B.C.

*A*s a young student, Cicero was so inquisitive and talented that his school was often visited by men who had heard of the youth's quick thinking and ability to learn. He was eager for every kind of knowledge. Although he was a capable and fluent poet as a boy, he never became a great classical poet. Instead he devoted his literary efforts to the eloquence of forceful oratory and to the precision and clarity of prose.

Although he was not of senatorial rank by birth, he was elected to the Senate because of his eloquence, his diligent political efforts, and his loyalty to the orthodox Roman tradition. Cicero studied with a well-loved scholar in Rome and acquired a knowledge of the law from his close association with eminent statesmen in the Senate. Then he served for a short time in the Marsian war under Sulla. The trend of Roman government—toward civil war and eventual dictatorship—alarmed Cicero. Cautiously he withdrew from public life until Sulla gained control and established order. It was during this period that Cicero studied with the Greek philosophers living in Rome.

At this time one of Sulla's freed slaves bought, with Sulla's approval, the property of a political enemy who had been put to death. He was challenged by the heir, a young farmer, Roscius, who claimed the estate was worth many times what had been paid for it. Sulla, angry that his authority was questioned, charged Roscius with the murder of his father. Because they all were afraid of Sulla's cruelty, none of the advocates dared defend Roscius, so the young man went to Cicero. His friends encouraged him to take the case, saying that he was not likely to have a more favorable and honorable introduction to public life. Cicero undertook the defense and conducted it successfully; he became famous for it, but incurred Sulla's wrath.

Sulla's vengeance was well known, so Cicero fled to Greece, giving his poor health as an excuse. Indeed he was thin and weak, and his voice, though strong, was harsh and uncontrolled. While he studied at the New Academy in Athens he further developed his interest in Greek philosophy. He said that if he failed in public affairs at Rome, he would return to the academy, to pass his life quietly studying philosophy. In Greece he strengthened his body by exercise and learned to control his voice.

When Sulla died, Cicero's friends urged him to return to Rome. But Cicero, who was cautious and thorough, continued diligently to practice and study with the most celebrated speakers of the time. He traveled from Greece to Asia, and then to Rhodes. There the scholar Apollonius, who was helping Cicero perfect his skill at oratory, requested one day that Cicero speak in Greek, thinking thus to point up his faults. Other hearers were astonished by Cicero's fluency, but Apollonius showed no excitement and just sat quietly after Cicero had finished. Cicero was disconcerted by his silence. Finally Apollonius said to him, "You have my praise and admiration, Cicero, and Greece has my pity and commiseration, since those arts and that eloquence which are the only glories that remain to her will now be transferred by you to Rome."

When Cicero was again ready for political affairs, an oracle discouraged him. When he asked at Delphi how he could attain

CICERO

the most glory, the priestess replied, "By making your own genius, and not the opinion of the people, the guide of your life." Therefore, when he first returned to Rome, he passed his time quietly. But when his own wish for fame and the encouragement of his relatives made him begin to practice law seriously, he became immediately successful and outshone all the advocates of the bar.

He had learned well his lessons in oratory, but because he had once been defective in his delivery, he continued to try to improve himself. He even sought the help of famous actors, including Aesop the tragedian. He had learned to manage his voice effectively and ridiculed loud speakers, saying that they shouted because they could not speak, in the same way that lame men get on horseback because they cannot walk. His quick sarcasm and witty remarks strengthened his pleading.

At the time of a great corn shortage, Cicero was appointed quaestor for Sicily. His stern discipline offended many natives, because he demanded sacrifice in order to send quantities of corn to Rome. But eventually his diligence, care, justice, and clemency made him honored among the Sicilians. At the same time, Cicero successfully defended a group of Roman youths who were charged with neglect of discipline and misconduct in the army.

When he returned from Sicily, he was quite proud of his achievements as quaestor. On meeting a friend who was an eminent citizen, he asked him what the Romans thought of his actions, expecting that all of Rome was talking about his record. His friend asked, "Where is it you have been, Cicero?" He was humiliated that the report of his Sicilian record had sunk into the city of Rome as into a vast ocean, without any visible effect on his reputation.

As a politician he diligently memorized the names of as many citizens as possible. He remarked that mechanics and artisans who work with lifeless instruments know the name,

place, and use of every one, yet statesmen, who carry out their
work through men, are often negligent in their knowledge of
individuals. He not only learned their names, but he also
learned where each citizen lived, what lands each possessed,
and who his friends were.

Representing the cities of Sicily, Cicero brilliantly prosecuted for corruption in office a rich Roman Senator, Verres,
who had served as governor of Sicily. The praetors, sitting as
judges, favored Verres. They delayed the trial so that there
would not be enough time for the oral arguments of the prose-
cutor. Cicero came forward saying there was no need of
speeches; he quickly examined his witnesses in the time remaining, thus leaving the judges no choice but to pass sentence on
the accused. It was said that in this case Cicero won not by
speaking, but by holding his tongue. Verres was convicted
and Cicero won a tremendous victory over senatorial corruption.

Cicero then married Terentia, whose dowry enabled him
to live well but temperately. They lived in a house near the
Palatine Hill so that visitors did not have to make a long journey to see him. Many who knew of his reputation came to
him for advice and counsel, and even Pompey paid court to
Cicero. Indeed it was Cicero's support and speeches in his favor that helped to establish Pompey's authority.

Cicero served with distinction as praetor, and became
known for his efficiency and justice. The first time he stood
as a candidate for Consul, he was the only candidate descended from a father of the equestrian rather than the senatorial order. His main opponent was the unscrupulous Catiline, a
daring, restless young man who was accused of killing his own
brother. Catiline had assembled the discontented and unem-
ployed veterans of Sulla's old army in the hope of overthrow-
ing the very government which he sought to direct.

CICERO

The conspirators had incited Etruria, as well as a large part
of Gaul, to revolt. Rome itself was most dangerously inclined
to change because of the unequal distribution of wealth and
property. Many patrician Roman citizens had foolishly thrown
away their money on lavish entertainments and sumptuous
buildings, and so the riches of the City had fallen into the hands
of the less noble.

After a very bitter campaign, Catiline was defeated; Cicero
was elected to the consulship along with Antonius, a man who
was not fit to lead but was a valuable ally. As Consul, Cicero
had to contend with the developing conspiracy of the defeated
Catiline (who now turned to open revolt), with the incom-
petence of his colleague Antonius, and with unreasonable laws
introduced by the Tribunes. The worst of these laws proposed
to set up a commission of ten persons with great power. It was
proposed that they could sell the public lands recently conquered by Pompey and others, judge and banish whomever
they pleased, plant new colonies, draw on the public treasury,
draft whatever soldiers they thought necessary, and pay them.
Antonius supported the measure, hoping to be one of the commissioners.

Cicero then managed to obtain for Antonius the province
of Macedonia, although he himself declined patronage. This
pleased Antonius so that he was ready to follow Cicero's lead
thereafter. Cicero then spoke out against the law to establish
the ten commissioners, confounding those who proposed it.
The Senate not only threw out the law but also rejected its
proponents to such an extent that they proposed that no such
autocratic measures should again be suggested. Cicero made
the entire Senate feel that eloquence lends great charm to
what is good and that justice can be invincible when it is
clearly expressed.

Cicero believed that any man who wanted to effectively

govern a commonwealth must always prefer the honest action
to the popular one when the two are in conflict, and in speaking, he must propose right and useful measures with such clarity that the issues cannot be confused by opponents.

Idle veterans from Sulla's old army, dreaming of plunder
and a share of Italy's riches, inspired Catiline to act. He organized an outlaw army in Etruria. In Rome, Catiline continued to gather support for himself, and by arranging wild parties he won to his banner a group of reckless young men who
were in debt and eager for change. In the midst of preparing
to overthrow the government, he stood as a candidate for Consul the second year. Catiline planned to have Cicero murdered
on election day. When Cicero accused him in the Senate of
conspiracy against the Republic, Catiline brazenly replied,
"What harm is there if of two bodies—the one lean and con-
sumptive with a head, the other great and strong without one
—I put a head to that body which lacks one?" This distorted
comparison of the Senate and the people made clear Catiline's
intent to divide the people and overthrow the Republic. Cicero
began wearing armor under his toga, and once he purposely
allowed his tunic to slip from his shoulders, revealing the
armor. When those around him discovered his danger, they
were disturbed; and so thereafter the noblest young men in the
City accompanied Cicero as an armed guard.

The day appointed for the *coup* drew near. At midnight,
some of Rome's most powerful citizens knocked at the gate of
Cicero's house, commanding the porter to awaken him. They
had intercepted letters from Catiline which indicated the wide-
spread support for the conspiracy. At dawn Cicero summoned
the Senate and delivered each of the intercepted letters to the
man to whom it was addressed, demanding that they be read
publicly. The aroused Senate passed a decree temporarily
giving Cicero absolute power to save the state in its danger.

Following an attempt early one morning by Catiline's men

CICERO

to murder Cicero at his own gate, Cicero summoned the Senate to the temple of Jupiter. When Catiline arrived, none of the Senators would sit by him, and all left the bench where he had seated himself. Cicero denounced him and commanded him to leave the City, saying that since one governed the Republic with words and law, and the other attempted to control by force of arms, there must be a wall between them.

Catiline and three hundred men left the City, carrying ensigns, rods and axes as though they represented the Republic. They joined the veteran's army in Etruria; Antonius led the Roman legions against them.

Lentulus, Catiline's partner, assembled those conspirators who remained in Rome and established communications with Catiline. Cicero watched carefully as this group of reckless men plotted against Rome.

By thorough detective work Cicero unraveled the entire plot; he revealed the conspiracy to the Senate in a series of brilliant orations. When all agreed upon the guilt of the conspirators, a terrific debate arose over suitable punishment. Cicero was reluctant to demand death—the only punishment fit for such crimes—not only because of his clement nature but because he did not want to exercise his authority insolently. He would have liked to avoid treating too harshly men of noble birth who had powerful friendships in the City. Yet he knew the double danger of any milder punishment: he himself would be in danger of reprisal if they lived, and the multitude would think him guilty of cowardice.

Cicero was encouraged to be severe by his wife Terentia, who, according to Cicero, would rather impose herself into his public affairs than to tell him of her domestic matters. She brought him signs and omens from the vestal virgins, who had been sacrificing in the Consul's home, and commanded him to act for the good of his country.

One Senator proposed the death penalty. The young Julius

Caesar, however, suggested that the conspirators' estates should be confiscated and they be confined to whichever Italian cities Cicero should designate. Actually Cicero suspected that Caesar was involved with Catiline, but Caesar was so popular with the people that if Caesar were accused with the conspirators, they were more likely to be saved with him than he to be punished with them.

Caesar's plea for mercy to the conspirators brought a sympathetic response. Cicero spoke on both sides of the argument, but his friends thought Caesar's sentence best for Cicero, in that he would be blamed less by the people if the conspirators were not killed. As the Senate was about to grant mercy, Cato pleaded violently for justice and full punishment. He attacked Caesar bitterly, casting suspicion on him, and demanded the death sentence on the basis of the evidence Cicero had given. Swayed by Cato, the Senate decreed death for the conspirators.

Cicero then personally supervised the execution of the condemned, going with an armed guard to capture each leader individually and escorting him to his execution. At first, the people, frightened, just watched in silence—especially the young men—as if, in fear and trembling, they were undergoing an initiation rite of some ancient, sacred mystery of aristocratic power. When all of the condemned had been executed, Cicero saw some of their followers in the marketplace, standing in groups. It was obvious that they thought their leaders were still alive and were waiting for darkness to rescue them. To put an end to such hopes, but carefully avoiding, out of deference to Roman custom, reference to the dead as dead, Cicero called loudly out to them, "They did live!"

By evening the citizens broke their silence and applauded him as he passed from the marketplace to his own house. The women burned torches from the rooftops to honor Cicero

CICERO

and a splendid train of the most important citizens followed him home. They said that though the Roman people were indebted to their military commanders for wealth and power, it was to Cicero alone that every one owed his safety, for delivering Rome from the Catilinian conspiracy.

The execution of the leaders broke the conspiracy; so many abandoned Catiline that his army was easily defeated by Antonius. Catiline himself was killed in this battle.

Although Cicero became very powerful, some remained opposed to him, including Caesar, the newly elected praetor, and some of the Tribunes who took office a few days before Cicero's term expired. To prevent his addressing the people, they threw benches before the rostra and told Cicero that he might only make the oath of withdrawal from office before stepping down. Accepting these conditions, Cicero recited his oath in a new form, proclaiming that he had saved his country and preserved the empire. The people heard him and confirmed the truth of it by their applause. Caesar and the Tribunes, all the more exasperated, proposed recalling Pompey with his army to put an end to what they termed Cicero's usurpation. Fortunately for Cicero and the whole commonwealth, Cato was one of the Tribunes at that time, and had not only power equal to the others, but also greater wisdom and force. In an oration to the people, Cato highly praised Cicero's conduct as Consul and called him the Father of Rome, thus preserving his popularity with the *plebs*.

Although Cicero's authority remained great, he continued to offend many people by always praising himself and reminding the people that he had broken Catiline and Lentulus and saved the Republic. He was intemperately fond of his own glory, but at the same time he felt no envy for others. He freely praised both the ancients and his contemporaries. The combination of his intelligence and mastery of expression produced comments which have survived for centuries. He called Aristotle a river of flowing gold, and said of Plato's dialogues that if Jupiter were to speak, it would be in such language. He called Theophrastus his special luxury, and when asked which of the orations of Demosthenes he liked best, he replied, "The longest!"

Yet, Cicero wanted to be praised; and to make his orations more startling, he would often compromise his own dignity, by being sarcastic toward his antagonists. On one occasion a rich Senator, publicly reproached by Cicero, called to him, asking, "Did not you yourself, two days ago in this same place, commend me?" "Yes," said Cicero, "I exercised my eloquence in declaiming upon a bad subject!" When one of the oldest Senators objected to a proposed law and said it would never pass while he lived, Cicero replied, "Then let us postpone it. He does not ask us to wait long!" To a young man who was suspected of having given poisoned cake to his father and who now threatened to make speeches against Cicero, he replied, "Better those than your cakes!" In a lawsuit Cicero questioned a witness who, though ignorant, professed to be a lawyer. When the man answered, "I know nothing about that matter," Cicero retorted, "You think, perhaps, we ask you about a point of law!" In another court, after hearing the opposing lawyer say his client had asked him to use industry, eloquence and fidelity in representing him, Cicero rose and demanded of his opponent, "How have you had the heart not to grant a single one of your client's requests?"

His conceit and his sarcasm earned him many enemies, but his downfall came about through the vengeance of a reprobate. Clodius, a handsome and wealthy young nobleman, fell in love with Pompeia, Julius Caesar's wife. He sneaked into Caesar's house during a ritual of the women, disguised as a music girl; when he was discovered, he was prosecuted for profaning

CICERO

the religious rites. As a result of this episode Caesar divorced his wife, saying that Caesar's wife must be above suspicion.

Clodius, who had helped Cicero to obtain information about Catiline, claimed in his defense that he was not in Rome on the specified day, but that he was away in the country. Cicero testified that Clodius was indeed in Rome on that day, that he had come to Cicero's house, and he cited their conversation. It was said that Cicero testified not only out of his duty but also because he wanted to preserve peace with his wife Terentia, who despised Clodius. Cicero's testimony and that of others clearly showed Clodius' guilt, but the bribes and pressures of Clodius' supporters persuaded the judges to acquit him by a vote of thirty to twenty-five.

After the verdict, Clodius told Cicero that the judges had not trusted his testimony. "Yes," said Cicero, "twenty-five of them trusted me and condemned you; the other thirty did not trust you, for they did not acquit you until they got your money."

Later Clodius was elected Tribune and devoted himself to ruining Cicero. The principal charge he brought against Cicero was technically valid—that he had put Lentulus and Cethegus to death without a fair trial. To escape this charge, Cicero became one of Caesar's lieutenants in Gaul. Clodius then seemed to be friendly and pretended to drop his charges; Cicero became so secure that he resigned his commission to Caesar. Receipt of the resignation exasperated Caesar, who demanded complete loyalty and hated anyone to quit him. He joined Clodius in pressing the accusation of execution without a fair trial.

The people were divided over the accusation, but the failure of Pompey and other former friends to support him in this crisis discouraged Cicero. He finally decided to go to Sicily until the uproar died down. As soon as it was known that he

had fled, Clodius proposed a decree of exile and issued an order denying Cicero "fire and water," thus prohibiting anyone
within five hundred miles of Rome to provide hospitality and
shelter for him. Many people, respecting Cicero, ignored the
edict and offered help, but the praetor of Sicily discouraged
his coming there.

Cicero therefore went to Greece, where he was received
with respect, and where cities even competed to honor him.
In the past, Cicero had often wished that his friends would call
him, not orator, but philosopher, because he thought knowledge was most important and had used rhetoric only to become a public figure. But a desire for glory has great power to
wash the patterns of philosophy from men's souls and to im-
print instead the passions of the common people in the minds
of those who govern them. In spite of Greek hospitality, Cicero remained disheartened, like an unfortunate lover; his looks
and his thoughts kept returning to Italy.

Clodius meanwhile burned Cicero's villas and announced
daily that his property was for sale, but none came to buy.
Clodius, encouraged by the easy support of the people, criticized even Pompey for the treaties he had made in the countries he had conquered. Pompey began to regret his own
cowardice in deserting Cicero and devoted himself to bringing
Cicero back. The Senate soon resolved that no public measure
could be ratified or passed until Cicero returned. The people
then began to turn to Cicero's side, and a Tribune of the people
summoned Clodius to trial for acts of violence. Pompey, with
popular support, drove Clodius out of the Forum and summoned the people to vote on Cicero's return. When Cicero
returned, just sixteen months after his banishment, he had an
overwhelmingly popular homecoming.

Cicero himself took revenge by going with his followers to
the Capitol and defacing the tables which contained the records of Clodius' acts as Tribune. Cicero claimed all his acts

CICERO

were illegal since Clodius was a patrician and therefore could not legally serve as a Tribune. Cato was displeased at this, not because he favored Clodius, but rather because he contended that it was irregular and violent for the Senate to vote the illegality of so many decrees, including those of Cato's own government in Cyprus and at Byzantium. This caused Cato's and Cicero's friendship to be more reserved.

Cicero served as Augur, and then was sent to Cilicia to end a revolt against its king. He was able to diplomatically effect a reconciliation without war, and thus he strengthened the loyalty of Cilicia to Rome. He accepted none of the presents offered him by the King and other leaders, but rather he saved money for the government by receiving his visitors simply at his own home. Cicero employed few servants; early each morning he would receive guests personally at his gate. While serving in Cilicia he discovered a large embezzlement from the public money and thus relieved the cities of this financial drain. He was gentle but firm in discipline, and his administration was highly praised.

Cicero returned from Cilicia to Rome just before the conflict between Caesar and Pompey flamed into civil war. The Senate planned to honor Cicero with a triumphal parade for his accomplishments in Cilicia, but Cicero replied that he would rather reconcile his differences with Julius Caesar and follow Caesar's triumphal chariot than to be accorded his own triumph. He privately advised both Caesar and Pompey and tried to reason against their conflict. As Caesar approached Rome with his powerful army and Pompey and many honest citizens left the City, Cicero wrote in a letter: "To which side shall I turn? Pompey has the fair and honorable plea for war; and Caesar, on the other hand, has managed his affairs better and is more able to protect himself and his friends. So that I know from whom I should fly, not whom I should fly to."

A friend of Caesar wrote to Cicero that Caesar thought it

best for Cicero to come out openly for Caesar's cause, but that if he considered himself too old for this, he should retire to Greece and stay out of the way. Cicero, annoyed that Caesar had not approached him directly, angrily replied that he would not do anything unbecoming his past life.

Finally he sailed to join Pompey, although he was half-hearted in his support of Pompey because he thought that Caesar would triumph. Cicero was ill and unable to fight in the battle of Pharsalia. After Pompey's defeat Cato gathered many of Pompey's men and maintained a great fleet of ships. He offered the command to Cicero on the basis of his consular dignity, but Cicero declined and refused to take any further part in the war.

He returned to Italy to meet Caesar at Brundusium, not altogether without hope, but with some fear of publicly testing the temper of an enemy and conqueror. There was no need to worry. As soon as Caesar saw him, he came down to meet him, saluted him, and, leading him away from all the others, spoke to him privately.

Caesar continued to treat Cicero with honor and respect, in spite of the times Cicero had opposed him. When Cicero presented an oration in praise of Cato, Caesar answered, calling his own speech anti-Cato but praising Cicero's own life and eloquence. When Ligurius was prosecuted for bearing arms against Caesar and Cicero undertook his defense, Caesar said mockingly, "Why not once more hear a speech from Cicero? There is no question that Ligurius is a wicked man and an enemy." But as Cicero spoke Caesar was impressed by the language and pathos of his defense. Caesar's expression changed often as he listened, and it was obvious that he was deeply moved—he actually trembled in commotion as Cicero discussed the Pharsalian battle. Overpowered by Cicero's eloquence, he acquitted Ligurius. Such is the power of clear, eloquent, forceful speech, to sway even the most powerful of men.

As the Republic gave way to the dictatorship of Caesar, Cicero withdrew from public life and instructed young men in philosophy. He translated Greek philosophical works and, for the first time, translated a number of Greek logical and physical terms into the natural Roman idiom.

He occasionally did, however, publicly praise and patronize Caesar, such as the time when the fallen statues of Pompey were restored by Caesar. Cicero came forth from his private life to say that by this act of humanity Caesar had indeed set up Pompey's statues, but he had made sure that his own would be erected.

Cicero planned to write a history of Greece and of Rome, but circumstances prevented it. He divorced Terentia charging that she had neglected him during the war and had been unkind after his return. Terentia denied the charges, and Cicero's real motives were soon revealed when, after the divorce, he married a rich young girl. When his daughter Tullia died, Cicero divorced his new wife because she seemed to be pleased by Tullia's death; and so ultimately Cicero found little happiness in his late years.

After Caesar was murdered, Antony convened the Senate and made a short address recommending peace and harmony; Cicero, following him, persuaded the Senate to follow the example of Athens and decree an amnesty for Caesar's murderers, giving Brutus and Cassius each governorships in the provinces. But when the people saw the dead body of Caesar being carried through the marketplace, his bloody clothing ripped from sword thrusts, they became enraged and began to search for the murderers with torches in their hands, hoping to burn their houses.

It seemed that Antony would now be sole ruler of Rome.

Cicero had had no part in the murder of Caesar; he had been the closest confidant of Brutus, and so in fear of Antony, he left for Athens. When he heard that Antony was cooperating with the Senate, Cicero felt he had been a coward and returned to Rome. Antony summoned Cicero to the Senate, but he claimed he was ill and remained at home. Cicero and Antony maintained a guarded politeness toward each other until the young Octavian, soon to be called Caesar, arrived on the scene. He came to claim his inheritance from Caesar and to dispute the money which Antony had kept from Caesar's estate. Caesar, who had no children, had designated in his will that Octavian, his nephew, was to be the heir of his estate. Octavian's relatives asked Cicero to use his eloquence and political influence with the Senate and the people to help Octavian against Antony. They offered Cicero, in return, the support of the wealth and military following Octavian had inherited from Caesar.

Long before this Cicero had dreamed that he witnessed Jupiter pointing out one young man who would end all Rome's civil wars. When he first met Octavian, he instantly recognized him as the youth of his dream; but his principal reasons for helping Octavian were his hatred of Antony and his inability to resist an opportunity for fame. Octavian treated Cicero with respect, calling him Father, which sickened Brutus, who said that Cicero, in courting Octavian, was not trying to free his country, but was rather seeking an indulgent master for himself.

Nevertheless, this alliance with Octavian enabled Cicero to rise to such power that he could do whatever he pleased. He completely overpowered Antony, driving him out of the City and sending the two Consuls with an army to defeat him. At the same time, he persuaded the Senate to treat Octavian as if he were praetor. The two men, old and young, were immensely successful together and even stood for election as Consuls. Cicero campaigned vigorously for Octavian and won the support of the Senators as well as others for him; he and Octavian were elected Consuls.

Once established as Consul, the young man bade Cicero farewell. Reconciling himself with Antony and Lepidus, Octavian formed the Triumvirate, from which he would emerge as "Augustus." Cicero now realized that he had ruined himself and betrayed the liberty of Rome.

Dividing the government like a piece of property, the Triumvirate decided to choose two hundred persons to be put to death. Antony wanted Cicero to head the list, but Octavian protested for two days and then yielded. The three made concessions to each other by adding to the list the strongest supporter of each: Cicero, Antony's uncle, and the brother of Lepidus. The Triumvirs had allowed their anger to deprive them of all humanity; their callous agreement seemed to demonstrate that no beast is more savage than man is when he holds absolute power to indulge his rage.

Hearing the news, Cicero and his brother, Quintus, started for Cicero's villa near the sea. They planned to take a ship from there to find protection with Brutus in Macedonia, but because they were short of supplies, Quintus returned to his home for provisions, leaving Cicero to go ahead. Quintus was betrayed by his servants and was slain. Cicero, reaching his villa, found a ship and went immediately on board. With a good wind, he sailed along the coast, but when the pilots were ready to turn toward Macedonia, Cicero changed his mind and went ashore. He traveled a short distance toward Rome, but then turned again to the sea. There he spent a frightened night, unsure of what he should do. At times he resolved to return secretly to Octavian's house in Rome, and there kill himself upon the altar of Octavian's household gods in order to bring divine vengeance upon Octavian, but the fear of torture prevented him. At last he allowed his servants to take him to another of his villas, where he lay down upon his bed to rest. His servants were unwilling to stand idly awaiting their master's murderers; so they alternately persuaded and forced Cicero to allow himself to be carried again in his litter toward the seaside. There his assassins caught up with him. When he saw a Tribune of Rome, a centurion, and the party of soldiers, Cicero told his servants to set the litter down. Putting his left hand to his chin, a habitual pose, he sat calmly, looking steadfastly at his murderers. As the centurion advanced, sword drawn, Cicero stretched his neck out of the litter to receive the blow.

His head and his hands, the hands with which he had written the "Philippics," his great orations denouncing Antony, were carried to Antony in Rome. Antony ordered that they be fastened above the rostra, a sight which horrified the Roman people.

A long time later, Augustus found his grandson with a book by Cicero in his hand. The boy, in fear, tried to hide the book, but Augustus lovingly turned the pages of the book and said, "My child, this was a learned man and a lover of his country."

CAESAR

100–44 B.C.

Caius Julius Caesar traced his ancestry through Aeneas to Venus, thus claiming a connection with the beginnings of Rome and laying a basis for his claim to immortality. In spite of financial hardships, his mother insisted that he be properly educated. He was tutored by a Gaul, who may have inspired the boy's dream of the man's Gallic Wars. Caesar showed promise in oratory but enthusiastically left his studies to become a military aide with the Roman army in Asia.

At the age of sixteen he married to please his father; after his father's death, he divorced his young wife to marry Cornelia, daughter of Cinna, who was trying to revive Marius' revolution. Marius, married to Caesar's aunt, was the fiery popular leader against the aristocratic legions of Sulla. The year Caesar was born, Marius had retired from the consulate in frustration and defeat. He left Rome to travel in Asia, and returned twelve years later to be crushed in an unsuccessful attempt to prevent a dictatorship by Sulla.

*I*n 83 B.C., when Sulla finally became master of Rome, he ordered Caesar to divorce Cornelia. Caesar refused, and Sulla confiscated her dowry. Caesar said nothing, but offered himself to the people as a candidate for the priesthood, although he was very young for the office. Sulla managed his defeat, but still was unable to make Caesar divorce Cornelia.

Not satisfied, Sulla discussed with his principal supporters whether Caesar should be put to death. When some of them said it was not worthwhile to plot the death of a boy, Sulla replied, "You know little if you do not see that there is more than one Marius in that boy!"

LIVES FROM PLUTARCH

When Caesar learned of Sulla's remark he decided to keep out of the way by going to the country of the Sabines. He moved frequently from house to house to avoid detection, but one night, as he was moving, he was seized by Sulla's soldiers, who were looking for followers of Marius. Caesar bribed their captain, paying him two talents, and was released.

The young fugitive immediately left Italy to avoid Sulla. While at sea, he was captured by pirates, who demanded twenty talents for ransom. He laughed at them for not understanding the value of their prisoner and offered to secure fifty talents ransom. His followers were sent to raise the money for the ransom, leaving him alone with the pirates. He treated his bloodthirsty captors like servants, ordering them to be quiet while he slept, to listen to his poetry, and to play at sports with him. He threatened them with hanging and crucifixion, and for thirty-eight days he amused himself by joining in their exercises and ridiculing them. They laughed with him because they thought his free talking and abuse were due to a kind of simplicity and boyish playfulness. When his ransom arrived and he was released, Caesar immediately procured Roman ships from the nearby port of Miletus and returned to pursue the pirates. Surprising them while they were still in the port where they had held him prisoner, he captured most of them and retrieved his ransom. He put the pirates in prison at Pergamus and then applied to the Roman praetor who governed Asia, asking how they should be punished according to Roman law. The praetor, with his eye on the pirates' prize money, said he would think, at his leisure, about what to do with the prisoners. Leaving the praetor, Caesar returned to Pergamus. He reminded the pirates of the punishment he had often threatened when they little dreamed that he was serious. Caesar then had them crucified. He next went to Rhodes to study oratory and philosophy with the famed Apollonius. Al-

CAESAR

though Caesar had the ability to become a great statesman and orator, he, unlike Cicero, studied speech only to the extent he felt necessary to secure a second rank in that art. He did not care to be a great orator, but wanted rather to be first among men of political and military power.

He returned to Rome and began to win supporters by his friendliness, enthusiasm and energy, as well as his real ability. He was generous and hospitable, thus appealing primarily to the plebeians. He aroused the old loyalties to Marius by his funeral oration to his aunt Julia, who was Marius' widow. He set up the statues of Marius, which had been forbidden ever since Sulla had declared the followers of Marius to be the enemies of the Republic. When some opposed the revival of homage to Marius, the people supported Caesar. When his own wife Cornelia died, Caesar also made an oration at her funeral, which won the people's sympathy for his great kindness and tenderness.

After serving well in the army in Spain, Caesar married Pompeia, the daughter of Pompey. Later he married his own daughter, Julia, to Pompey. Thus he early sealed an alliance with Rome's greatest soldier.

There were two major factions in Rome at this time: Sulla's powerful group and the broken remnant of Marius' revolutionary party, which Caesar began to revive into his own strong party. Again he had the statues of Marius carried secretly at night and placed in the Capitol. When the people saw them the next morning they were amazed at the boldness of the man who had set them up again. It was not difficult to guess who had done it, and soon a great crowd gathered to see the statues. Some criticized Caesar as openly defying the established government by reviving honors which had been buried by the Senate, but others thought that Caesar was testing the people, to see if they would quietly accept him and the changes he would make in the government. The old followers of Marius took courage and suddenly came shouting into the Capitol. Many wept for joy as they rallied to Caesar as the one man who was a successor worthy of Marius.

When the Senate met, one of Rome's most eminent citizens criticized Caesar. He closed his speech by saying that by his actions Caesar was not only undermining the government but also preparing to destroy the Republic. Caesar's apology satisfied the Senate; but his admirers advised him to go forward with his plans, since the people's favor would allow him to overcome all and become the first man in the commonwealth.

Little by little Caesar developed and increased his political influence. His power among the *plebs* continued to grow, and indeed, he was so profuse in distributing gifts that before he gained any public office he was already in debt 1300 talents. As aedile he entertained the people not with a few gladiators but by three hundred and twenty public combats.

He made all previous demagogues seem nothing, as he used all the public funds he could control, all his own money, and all he could borrow for his magnificent shows, processions, and public feasts.

At first Caesar's enemies thought little of the growth of his political influence, assuming it would fail when his money was gone. Many thought that, by spending so much to be popular, he exchanged a solid good for what would prove to be a short and uncertain reward. But actually Caesar was purchasing popular support for a relatively cheap price. When his power later became established so that he could openly alter the Roman constitution, his enemies realized too late that no matter how insignificant a beginning may seem, with continued effort it can become a strong threat. They were to learn that merely despising a danger at first may make it in the end irresistible.

CAESAR

Cicero was among the first to see Caesar's scheming nature through his disguise of good humor and courtesy. Although he detected Caesar's ambition for absolute power, Cicero said, "When I see his hair so carefully arranged, and observe him adjusting it with one finger, I cannot imagine that such a man could conceive of subverting the Roman state."

When Cicero exposed Catiline's conspiracy to overthrow the Republic and the conspirators were convicted in the Senate, Caesar spoke against the severity of the death sentence. He argued that it was unjust and without precedent to take the lives of persons of such high birth and distinction without a fair trial, unless there were an absolute necessity for it. He urged that the conspirators be confined in certain Italian towns to be designated by Cicero. He recommended that only when Catiline's army was defeated should the Senate determine what should be done about the conspirators.

Caesar's plea seemed so humane and was presented with such eloquence that those who spoke after him adopted it. Even Cicero seemed to agree with him, although he spoke on both sides of the argument. Others who had previously argued for execution now acceded to Caesar, until old Cato spoke. In his speech Cato hinted that Caesar himself might be suspected. Cato pressed the charges against the conspirators so strongly that they were condemned to death.

Some time later Caesar returned to the Senate to clear himself of suspicion. Because this Senate session lasted longer than usual, the people surrounded the Senate and demanded both Caesar's safety and that the Senate excuse him.

When Caesar was about to begin his term as praetor, Cato was afraid that the poor citizens, who placed all their hopes in Caesar, might start an uprising. Knowing that Caesar would be even more formidable once he was in office, Cato persuaded the Senate to give to the poor a monthly allowance of corn. This expedient cost the Republic 7,500,000 drachmas that year, but Caesar's power was weakened by the Senate's generosity. The immediate cause of alarm was removed by feeding the poor, and indeed, they caused no disturbance during Caesar's praetorship.

The high priest (Pontifex Maximus), whose greatly prestigious office was a lifetime one, had died. Usually an older man of great wisdom, piety, and dignity was chosen as high priest, but though very young and not very experienced in religious matters, Caesar stood for office against two older men. One of his opponents, afraid of the loss of prestige if Caesar defeated him, offered Caesar a large sum of money to withdraw. The young candidate retorted that he was ready to borrow a larger sum in order to carry on the contest. On election day, he embraced his weeping mother as he left for the Forum. "My mother," he said, "today you will see me either Pontifex Maximus or an exile." He won.

Because Caesar was praetor, his wife Pompeia celebrated the sacred rites of the goddess Bona in her home. During these ceremonies Caesar's house was off limits for all men. The noblest ladies of Rome were assembled there for the rituals, but one night Clodius, a rich but wild patrician who secretly loved Pompeia, sneaked into the house disguised as a maid. He was discovered, amid shrieking and excitement, while Caesar's mother covered the sacred relics and terminated the rituals. The women drove him out and reported the incident to their husbands. Clodius was tried for impiety. Caesar divorced Pompeia, but for political reasons he would not accuse Clodius, thus allowing him to go free. He said he did not know whether any wrong had been done, but "Caesar's wife must be above suspicion."

Caesar now made an alliance with Crassus, the richest man in Rome, who helped him pay part of his debts. Caesar then

CAESAR

assumed his authority as governor of Spain and set about to subdue his province, where the wild Spanish tribes had never been brought under control. In a miserable mountain village his officers were making fun of the natives, mockingly wondering if they competed among themselves for hollow honor in so poor a place. Caesar said seriously, "For my part, I had rather be the first man among these fellows than the second man in Rome." While subduing these wild tribes in Spain, he read the history of Alexander the Great and wept bitterly, crying, "Have I not reason to weep, when Alexander at my age had conquered so many nations, and I have all this time done nothing that is memorable?"

He raised new armies, conquered all of Spain for Rome, and established good relations among the various Spanish tribes. Debts were the source of immense problems among the Spaniards, so Caesar ordered that each debtor surrender two-thirds of his income to his creditors until his debts were paid, but that the debtor should be free in his use of the other third.

He returned from Spain in glory, having expanded Rome's power and having enriched himself and his soldiers. Having already received from his armies the title of Imperator, he determined to be elected Consul. Because of his achievements and victories in Spain he was due a triumph, but custom required that he wait outside Rome until the Senate decreed the triumph. At the same time, the law required that one who stood for the consulship must appear personally in Rome before the election. Caesar arrived outside Rome just in time for the election and requested of the Senate that since he was obliged to be absent before the triumph, his friends be allowed to seek the consulship for him. Cato and others opposed this and then delayed the decision. Caesar therefore passed up the triumph in order to enter the City immediately and to push his campaign for Consul.

He persuaded both Pompey and Crassus, thus far bitter enemies of each other, to unite with him in a triumvirate. Thus seeming to do something good for Rome, he gained the power to win as Consul and to work towards the downfall of the Republic. Indeed it may be that it was not the later quarrel between Pompey and Caesar which was the origin of the civil wars so much as their union, their conspiring together first against the patricians, which led later to quarreling between themselves. Cato foretold the consequences of this alliance, but at that time he was criticized as being sullen and interfering. In the end, however, he gained the reputation of a wise but unsuccessful counselor.

When Caesar became Consul, he introduced bills more characteristic of the most audacious Tribune than of a Consul. He proposed divisions of lands among the common people and the opening of new colonies for the poor. The Senate opposed him, but the *plebs* were pleased. He loudly proclaimed that the Senators' insulting and harsh conduct left no other course open to him than to support the cause and interests of the *plebs*. He hurried out of the Senate and brought Pompey and Crassus to stand beside him in front of a mass of the plebeians. Together they defied the Senate and gained the applause of the crowd. Caesar asked the people whether they agreed with the bills he had introduced; they cheered. He then asked them to help him against those who had threatened to oppose him with their swords. Pompey also made a speech about fighting against the patricians, which the Senators also resented; but the people loved Caesar.

Caesar changed his daughter Julia's plans for marriage to another man and betrothed her to Pompey. He himself married Calpurnia, daughter of Piso, and then later got Piso elected Consul. Pompey, after he was married to Julia, filled the Forum with his soldiers and supported Caesar's laws. He

CAESAR

also arranged for Caesar to become governor of all Gaul at the end of his consulship.

Old Cato protested Caesar's assuming so much authority and arranging for power and position through marriage contracts. Caesar had him seized and led off towards prison. He had thought Cato would argue and appeal to the Tribunes, but Cato meekly followed without protest. Not only were the nobility outraged by Cato's arrest, but the *plebs* also, in respect for Cato's virtue, followed in dejected silence. Caesar, sensitive to the people's attitude, secretly requested one of the Tribunes to rescue Cato.

As the Triumvirate took greater control of Rome's business, many Senators frequently missed the meetings. One among them, Considius, a very old man, once told Caesar that the Senators were not meeting because they were afraid of his soldiers. Caesar's impudent answer was, "Why don't you then, out of the same fear, keep at home?" Considius replied that age was his guard against fear and that the small remains of his life were not worth much caution.

Bibulus, Caesar's colleague who was supposed to have equal power with him, saw that he had little authority compared to Caesar. But because he was afraid of Caesar, he stayed at home and left the government to Caesar. Many of his acts as Consul were disgraceful and aimed only at supporting his future ambitions. He even assisted that same Clodius who had earlier disgraced his wife; and while Consul he supported the campaign of Clodius to disgrace Cicero and to drive him out of Italy.

After his year as Consul, Caesar made a fresh start by leading his armies to Gaul. In the Gallic Wars he established his reputation as a soldier and a general, who was greater than any other generals of his time or of the past. One he outdid on the basis of the difficulty of the country in which he fought, another in the extent of territory conquered, some in number and strength of enemies defeated; one because of the wildness and treachery of the tribes whose goodwill he finally gained, another in his humanity and justice to those he overpowered; others in his gifts and support for his soldiers; all alike in the number of battles he fought and the enemies whom he killed. In ten years in Gaul, according to the record of his own commentaries, he took eight hundred towns by storm, subdued three hundred tribes, and of the three million warriors against whom he fought, he killed one million and captured a second million. Caesar gained the respect of the Gauls, the Germans, the Britons, and the world.

Master of the goodwill and hearty service of his soldiers, he encouraged a love of honor and a passion for glory. He distributed money and honors freely. He eagerly shared the dangers and labors of his soldiers, and frequently fought fiercely beside his men in the midst of the battle. Ordinary men became invincible under Caesar's command. Such a man was Acilius, who in the sea fight at Marseilles, had his right hand cut off by a sword. He continued to fight with his left, striking enemies in the face with his buckler until he gained control of the vessel.

In another battle, Cassius Scaeva had one eye shot out by an arrow, his shoulder pierced by a javelin, and his thigh by another spear. He called to the enemy, as though he wanted to surrender himself. When two of them approached him, he killed one and struck the other in the face.

In Britain some of Caesar's top officers were trapped by Britons in a swamp. A private threw himself into the midst of the barbarians, and by his courage and fierce fighting he beat off the Britons and rescued the officers. After the officers were safe, he jumped into the water and with much difficulty, partly swimming and partly wading, got back safely, but he

CAESAR

lost his shield. When Caesar commended him, he fell on his knees, tearfully begging pardon for losing the shield.

Granius Petro, a quaestor under Caesar, was captured by Scipio, who enslaved some captives, executed others, but offered the quaestor his freedom. Granius then fell on his sword and killed himself, saying it was usual for Caesar's soldiers not to take but to give mercy.

Such displays of courage and loyalty built a tough reputation for Caesar's soldiers. Boldness, and love of honor and distinction were encouraged by Caesar's loyalty to them. All the riches he received became a public fund for the reward and encouragement of valor.

In spite of his brave fighting and displays of energy, Caesar was physically weak. He was subject to epilepsy, and his slender physique and soft white skin made his courage and perseverance unusually remarkable. Difficult battles, long and swift marches, coarse diet, hard work, and sleeping in the open field conditioned him against his diseases.

His men, knowing both his weakness and his courage, his disabilities and his ability, loved him with an intense loyalty. Thus he properly and proudly addressed his troops as "fellow-soldiers" and stirred their enthusiasm and courage.

His tact and efficiency and the humane side of his character are illustrated in anecdotes. Once he and his staff were driven by a storm into a poor man's cottage, where they found room for only one man. Caesar said that though places of honor should be given up to the greater men, necessary accommodations must go to the weaker. He ordered that Oppius, who was in ill health, sleep in the cabin, while he himself slept with the rest of the men under a shed outside the door.

At a supper in Milan a dish of asparagus was served, on which the host had put a strange sweet ointment instead of salad oil. Caesar ate it without any sign of disgust and reprimanded his friends for finding fault with it. "It was enough not to eat what you did not like," he said, "but he who reflects on another man's want of breeding shows he lacks it as much himself."

Caesar was ingenious in communications. It is thought that he was the first to contrive a means for communicating with friends by a code, which he used when business, battle, or great distances left him no opportunity for private conversation about urgent matters.

He disciplined himself to dictate letters while riding horseback or marching and to give directions to two secretaries who took notes simultaneously on different subjects. As he moved forward while conducting various business, a tough and alert Roman soldier followed closely with drawn sword. In this way he produced his book *Commentaries on the Gallic Wars* during his military campaigns.

His first great fight in Gaul was against the Helvetians (Swiss), who had burned their towns and planned to settle in Roman Gaul. They surprised Caesar on the march, but he retreated to a strong position he had remembered from once passing by it. When he had mustered his men and his horse was brought to him, he said, "When I have won the battle, I will use my horse for the chase, but at this moment let us charge the enemy."

He attacked them on foot and cut their main army to pieces in a long and severe fight. The toughest fighting, though, was at their carriages and ramparts, where the women and children fought desperately beside their men until all were crushed. The battle lasted until midnight and the Romans killed nearly half the 190,000 fighting men. He forced those remaining, nearly 100,000 warriors, to reoccupy their burned cities so that the Germans could not occupy the land and thus get closer to Rome. Caesar was extraordinarily thorough about details and he always looked to the future.

CAESAR

The Tenth Legion, led by Labienus, became Caesar's favorite because of the men's intense courage and loyalty to him. When Caesar proposed an early invasion of Germany to fight Ariovistus, the giant king who had been interfering with the Gauls and who threatened to invade Roman Gaul, some of the noble officers in legions other than the Tenth were afraid and cautious. Caesar called them together and advised them to march back to Rome, since they were so weak and unmanly. He said he did not expect the Germans to be tougher enemies than the Cimbri, nor should they find him a general inferior to Marius, who had crushed the Cimbri. He said that he would take only the Tenth Legion and fight the Germans. Of course the Tenth Legion cheered; the other legions blamed their officers and were eager to show Caesar how they could fight. All of them followed Caesar toward the Germans. Ariovistus had expected any Roman army to be on the defensive, and so he was surprised by Caesar's bold, rapid march and sudden attack. His warriors were thrown into confusion, and 80,000 Germans were killed in one day. The rest were driven across the Rhine River.

Caesar then left his army in winter quarters and went to Cisalpine Gaul (northern Italy, on the Roman side of the Alps), where he received delegations from Rome. Caesar was very generous and each delegation left with gifts in hand and promises for the future.

Learning that the Belgae were revolting and attacking the other Gauls, he hastened to rejoin his men. He surprised the Belgae as they were looting a Gallic town and he destroyed their army. Ruthless in his fighting, he records that the swamps were made passable by the many dead bodies.

The Nervii, who were fierce, warlike people who lived in thick forests, surprised Caesar with a force of sixty thousand soon after he had crushed the Belgae. The Roman army was building a camp when the Nervii struck. They routed the

Roman cavalry, surrounded the Twelfth and Seventh legions, and killed all the officers in those legions. Caesar snatched up a shield and fought his way to the center of the battle, thus rallying his men. The Tenth Legion, seeing Caesar in personal danger, broke through the enemy's ranks to rescue him. Under the influence of Caesar's bold example, the Roman soldiers fought with more than human courage. The Nervii would not retreat, so they were cut down on the battlefield. Of the sixty thousand warriors only five hundred survived the battle.

When the Roman Senate had received news of these victories, they voted sacrifices and festivals to the gods, to be strictly observed for fifteen days. The great danger to which they had been exposed by the successive outbreaks of the nations made the people even more grateful to Caesar and gave his successes an additional luster.

Caesar returned to northern Italy and to political war. He gave money and advice to candidates, and made and enforced decisions about what was to be done at Rome. The money he supplied to officeholders was used to corrupt the people and to buy their votes, and thus to advance Caesar's power.

Pompey failed to notice how Caesar used Roman arms to gain favor at home, employing the wealth his conquests brought. At one time two hundred Senators were at his camp seeking favor. It was at that camp that the decision was made that Pompey and Crassus should be Consuls again, that Caesar should be governor of Gaul for five more years, and that Caesar should be voted more money.

It seemed extravagant to thinking men that those who had received so much money from Caesar should persuade the Senate to vote him more as if he needed it. Cato had been sent to Cyprus as governor, but Favonius appealed to the people against the extravagance. The people ignored his pleas because they loved Caesar.

CAESAR

Other German tribes had invaded Gaul and sent ambassadors to Caesar to negotiate peace. While Caesar negotiated with them, the Germans surprised the Roman cavalry and defeated them. Afterwards they sent other ambassadors, whom Caesar imprisoned. He then attacked and routed the Germans, judging that it would be foolish to keep faith with those who had broken their word.

A few Germans, however, escaped across the Rhine, and Caesar seized this as an excuse to invade Germany itself. Although the Rhine was very wide and the current strong, he succeeded in building a marvelous bridge in ten days. His men drove great piles of wood into the bottom of the river upstream from the bridge to stop tree trunks and other floating debris which otherwise would have rapidly destroyed the bridge. In eighteen days Caesar defeated the German tribes, burning the towns of those who opposed him and encouraging those who sided with the Romans, thus teaching the barbarians forceful lessons.

He built a fleet, crossed the English Channel, and successfully invaded Britain twice. Since many had questioned the very existence of the British Isles, he might be said to have carried the Roman empire beyond the limits of the known world. Caesar's pride and ambition led him to do more harm to the Britons than service to Rome, for the Britons were miserably poor and provided little plunder.

Caesar's Gallic army grew so large that he divided it among various camps for winter quarters. One winter, while he was in northern Italy, there was a general outbreak throughout Transalpine Gaul. There were barbarian attacks on many camps, but chiefly on one commanded by Quintus Cicero, the brother of the great orator. Caesar hurried towards the camp, gathering seven thousand men on his way. When the Gauls moved to attack him, confident they could defeat such a small force, Caesar pretended fear, retreated and built walls around his camp. When the overconfident and disorganized Gauls assaulted the walls, Caesar's disciplined army marched forth and cut them to bits.

Vercingetorix, the ablest of the Gallic leaders, began a revolt in the central part of Gaul. He cut off Caesar, who was in northern Italy, from his main army, which was in northern Gaul. In order to join the army Caesar rode in disguise through the country controlled by the rebels. It was bitter cold: some rivers were frozen, others flooded, and the forests and fields were filled with snow. Caesar, who always used everything to his advantage in war, marched his army quickly through the snow and over the ice to attack the rebels. His speed and power made the Gauls think he was invincible; and thus he defeated armies, captured towns, and protected those who declared for Rome.

On the way to the country of the Sequani Caesar was surrounded by swarms of rebels and there ensued a bitter but indecisive battle during which the Aruveni tribe claimed to have captured Caesar's sword. Later the sword was shown to Caesar; the great general smiled, but refused to take it back.

Many of the rebels assembled in the town of Alesia, which Caesar besieged, although the height of its walls and the number of those who defended them made it appear impregnable. There were one hundred and seventy thousand rebels in the town, led by Vercingetorix. During the siege, three hundred thousand warriors picked from all parts of Gaul arrived well-armed to attack the Romans from the outside. Caesar, caught between two dangers, built two walls to keep the two Gallic armies apart. He attacked and crushed the invading army before the Gauls in the town even knew such a battle was being fought. After a long siege, Vercingetorix dramatically surrendered.

Until this point, Pompey had discounted Caesar, thinking it

CAESAR

would not be difficult to put down the young man whom he had himself advanced. On the other hand, Caesar had recognized his need to gain strength for the great combat. Making the Gallic Wars his exercise-ground, he had improved the effectiveness of his soldiers through discipline and tough combat experience. He had heightened his glory by his victories, so that his reputation could now challenge that of the great Pompey. As Caesar had long ago resolved to overthrow Pompey, so had Pompey resolved to crush Caesar.

The Triumvirate of the three ambitious men began to fall apart. Crassus was killed by the Parthians. Caesar's daughter Julia, who had sealed the alliance by her marriage to Pompey, died. In the meantime, the Roman government had become so corrupt, with politicians buying offices and wasting public money, that many called for dictatorship. Cato prevailed upon the Senate to make Pompey sole Consul, rather than dictator. Pompey allied himself with the Senate and the nobility against Caesar and the masses. Caesar asked the Senate for the consulship, for the continuance of his province in Gaul, and for more money.

The Senatorial party opposed Caesar's requests and added insult to injury. Caesar had won for the Gallic city of New Comum the precious right of Roman citizenship, and now the Senate voted to take away this status of citizenship. It was illegal to whip a Roman citizen; therefore the Senator from New Comum, now stripped of Roman citizenship, was whipped and told to show the marks to Caesar. Pompey tried to arrange for someone to succeed Caesar in Gaul. He demanded that Caesar return the legions he had loaned to him, which Caesar did, after giving each soldier a generous cash gift as he left Gaul.

In the meantime the young general had built his strength and popularity by bribes and political favors in Rome and by more victories in Gaul with his own troops. Some officers from Caesar's legions had flattered Pompey by telling him that the soldiers in Gaul were tired of their general and his constant drive, that they would desert to Pompey, as they themselves had done. So Pompey made no preparations against Caesar's possible return other than with speeches and votes, for which Caesar cared nothing.

Caesar proposed to the Senate and to the people that both he and Pompey should lay down their arms and become private citizens. He said that those who wanted to make Pompey dictator were simply establishing the one in the tyranny to which the other was accused of aspiring.

When these proposals were made in Caesar's name, the people applauded, but the Senators resisted. Scipio proposed in the Senate that if Caesar did not lay down his arms within a certain time, he should be voted an enemy of Rome. When one of Caesar's captains was told that the Senate would not give Caesar a longer time as governor, he clapped his hand on the hilt of his sword and said, "But this shall!" The Consuls then called for a vote as to whether Pompey should dismiss his troops; very few Senators assented. They asked whether Caesar should dismiss his soldiers; almost all Senators assented. Antony then proposed that both should lay down their arms, and nearly all the Senate voted "aye." Scipio then became violent and Lentulus cried that the Senate needed arms, not votes, against a robber.

Caesar offered a further compromise. He proposed to keep only part of Gaul and two legions until the people could decide between Pompey and himself in the regular election for Consul. Cicero became the peacemaker and convinced Pompey to accept the compromise, except for allowing Caesar the two legions. Then, for the sake of peace and harmony, Cicero got Caesar's friends to cut him down to only six thousand soldiers.

CAESAR

Pompey wanted to accept this compromise, but Lentulus the Consul drove Caesar's friends Curio and Antony from the Senate floor and out of Rome.

At this time Caesar had only five thousand soldiers with him, but he decided to move suddenly with these few, knowing the rest of his army would follow later. He preferred to surprise and to frighten his enemies immediately, rather than to give them warning and time to organize their forces.

While some of his officers and men went ahead to attack the key town of Ariminum, causing as little disturbance and bloodshed as possible, Caesar spent the day in full view of the unsuspecting people, feasting and watching the gladiators. During the evening banquet, he and his key officers, one by one, slipped away to join the army at Ariminum. At the Rubicon River, the boundary of his province, he stopped to consider the civil war and whether to go ahead toward absolute rule. He wavered during the day, trying to compute how many calamities his passing that river might bring upon mankind. He worried about the many Roman deaths that would follow and wondered what history would say about his decision. Then he considered the greatness of the enterprise and cast aside calculation. Abandoning himself to what might come, he cried, "The die is cast," and plunged into the river.

In passing the limits of his province, Caesar shattered Roman law beyond repair. Once across the river, he sped to Ariminum, arriving there before daylight. The capture of Ariminum opened up northern Italy to Caesar's war. The march of Caesar's growing army towards Rome brought fear to Pompey's party, confusion to the Senate, hope and aggressiveness to the common people, an excuse for looting and violence, and disorder for Rome. The City was overrun as if by a deluge, with both exultant and frightened people entering and leaving Rome.

As he advanced, Caesar announced that he considered all

neutrals his friends. He respected property rights and forgave those who turned to his side. He gladly accepted into his army those formerly enlisted in Pompey's forces.

Favonius now asked Pompey to stamp upon the ground, for earlier Pompey had boasted that with one stamp of his foot he could fill all Italy with soldiers against Caesar. Pompey still had a larger army than his opponent, but he was filled with panic. He was not able to pursue his own thoughts, but was constantly disturbed by false reports, confusion, and alarms. He declared the City in anarchy and left Rome, urging the Senate and all who preferred Rome and liberty over tyranny to follow him out of the City. Many of the Senators and patricians, all who had opposed Caesar, and even many of his former friends deserted Rome in fear of Caesar. Even Labienus, former commander of the Tenth Legion, deserted to Pompey.

Pompey mustered a great fleet and took his supporters to Greece. Caesar wanted to pursue him, but because he had no navy, he went back to Rome. He had in sixty days made himself master of all Italy without bloodshed.

In Rome Caesar found many Senators and others who had returned to take their chances with a victorious Caesar instead of with a retreating Pompey. He also found enthusiastic and happy supporters among the common people, who loved him for his generosity, his boldness, and his achievements. He was respectful towards the Senators and urged them to make peace with Pompey, but they did nothing in this direction. Caesar was a gracious winner when he chose to be, but he wanted complete power.

He demanded control of the public money. When a Tribune opposed him, he said that war and law each had its own time. "If what I do displeases you, leave the place; war allows no free talking. When I have laid down my arms and made peace, come back and make what speeches you please." The Tribune continued to oppose Caesar as Caesar ordered the doors of

CAESAR

the treasury forced open. He threatened to kill the Tribune, saying, "This is more disagreeable for me to say than to do."

Then, with a small army, Caesar invaded Spain to crush Pompey's forces there. He wanted to be able to advance securely against Pompey's main army, with no enemy left behind him. In Spain he was in constant danger from ambush and treachery and from a lack of provisions, but he persisted until he defeated the forces in Spain, with only the generals escaping to Pompey.

Returning to Rome, he was voted dictator. He called home the exiles, gave citizenship rights to the children of those who had suffered under Sulla, and relieved the debtors in Rome. After eleven days, he resigned the dictatorship, declared himself Consul, and hastened after Pompey.

He moved so fast to the port that he left most of his army behind. In January, with only five legions and six hundred cavalrymen, Caesar crossed the Ionian Sea. He then sent his ships back for the rest of his men, under the command of Gabinius and Antony.

One part of the army, slowed down by exhaustion after many fights, complained on their way to the port. "When at last will this Caesar let us rest? He rushes us from place to place and uses us as if it were impossible for us to be exhausted. Even our armor is worn out from many blows. Our wounds should show him that we are mortal men, subject to the same pains and sufferings as other human beings." But when they arrived at the seaport and found that Caesar had gone on without them, they changed. Their loyalty to him was such that they blamed themselves as traitors to their beloved general; they worried about his safety; they blamed their officers for letting them march slowly; and they watched eagerly for ships so that they could join the pursuit of Pompey.

On the other side of the sea Caesar did not have enough

soldiers to attack the giant army of Pompey, who had plenty of provisions because of his vast navy. Caesar, wondering what had happened to his ships and men, daringly disguised himself as a slave and boarded a small boat returning to Italy. He flung himself down like a person of no consequence and lay in the bottom of the vessel. When at the mouth of the river the ship met a fierce gale the master of the ship ordered his men to turn about. At this point Caesar announced his presence, saying, "Go on, my friend, and fear nothing; you carry Caesar and his fortune in your boat." The seamen, when they heard him, pulled on their oars with all their strength but could not overcome the storm; they had to row Caesar back to land. His soldiers ran to him and begged him not to risk his life. They promised to fight to their death for him.

In Italy, Gabinius was afraid to attempt the sea crossing in winter and urged that they march by land to Greece. Antony was more concerned that Caesar was outnumbered; so he gathered all the ships he could, beat back Pompey's fleet, and started for Macedonia. Fighting storms and enemies, he succeeded in bringing the needed reinforcements to Caesar. This enabled the great general to seriously attack Pompey's camp. Yet it was difficult to tell which was besieged and which the besieger, for Pompey was well supplied by his ships and his control of the sea, whereas Caesar's men had little food. His men had to dig for roots, from which they made a coarse bread. In defiance they threw some of the loaves into Pompey's camp, saying that as long as they could make such bread, they would continue to fight Pompey.

Caesar won all the skirmishes and little battles except one, when Pompey's men drove Caesar back, killed many, endangered Caesar's own life, and caused many of his men to panic. And in this skirmish Caesar was unable to rally his men. When Pompey did not follow up his success with a vigorous assault,

CAESAR

Caesar said, "The victory would have gone to our enemies, if they had a general who knew how to take it."

That night he could not sleep. He worried over mistakes he had made in this war: he had allowed Pompey to gain advantage by his superior naval strength. Pompey was controlling the fight. During that night he awakened his camp and marched towards Scipio in Macedonia. He hoped either to get Pompey to follow him into territory where he no longer had the advantage or, if Pompey did not follow, to defeat Scipio. Because the conditions were not favorable, Caesar set out to change them.

Many of Pompey's officers were anxious to pursue Caesar. They thought he could easily be defeated while retreating, but Pompey had no desire to follow. He did not want to risk all his forces on one battle; he thought that Caesar, without supplies, would wear out his army. Cato alone supported Pompey's view, but only because he hated to see Romans kill Romans. Finally Pompey gave in to his officers and followed Caesar to Pharsalia. Pompey's lieutenants were so overconfident that they began to argue about who should be Consul, praetor, quaestor, or Pontifex Maximus when they turned in triumph to Rome.

Pompey had five thousand cavalry to Caesar's one thousand, and forty-five thousand infantry against Caesar's twenty-two thousand veteran "fellow-soldiers." Caesar, understanding the psychology of his men, asked them if they should wait for reinforcements or fight immediately. They cried out to fight at once.

When he sacrificed to the gods and prayed for victory, before the battle of Pharsalia, the Augurs predicted that within three days he should come to a decisive action. Caesar asked the priest if he foresaw a happy event. "That," said the priest, "you can best answer for yourself; for the gods indicate a

LIVES FROM PLUTARCH

great alteration from the present state of affairs. If, therefore, you think yourself well off now, expect worse fortune; if unhappy, hope for better."

As Caesar was just putting his troops into motion for the advance, he passed one of his veteran captains encouraging his men to fight hard. Caesar asked him, "What hopes, good friend, and what grounds for encouragement?"

The captain replied, "We shall conquer nobly, Caesar; and I this day will deserve your praises, either alive or dead." This captain was the first to charge the enemy. Breaking through the ranks with his one hundred and twenty soldiers, he pressed forward, killing many until he himself was struck down by a sword thrust that went in at his mouth and came out at the back of his neck.

Pompey had commanded his foot soldiers to stand their ground and to receive quietly the enemy's first attack until they came within javelin range. Caesar, on the contrary, believed that if the first encounter is made with impetus, this gives force to the charge and inspires the soldiers to bravery.

Caesar commanded the right wing with the Tenth Legion, opposed by Pompey's cavalry and elite soldiers. Caesar's men rushed aggressively towards the cavalry and hurled their javelins, not at the horses or the riders' legs, as usual, but at the faces of the young patricians. Caesar figured the young gentlemen, in the flower of their youth and handsome appearance, would fear such blows and scars for the future even more than present danger. He was right. As the spears began to cut their faces, they tried to cover their heads with their shields and cloaks. They were thus thrown into confusion. Caesar's veterans closed in with fierce fighting. The cream of Rome's nobility thus shamefully forfeited Pompey's hopes when faced by the tough "fellow-soldiers" of Caesar. Pompey himself retreated from the field of battle, disguised himself, and fled to Africa, where he was murdered by an Egyptian.

CAESAR

When Caesar beheld the ruins of Pompey's army and camp, he groaned. "This they would have; they brought me to this necessity. I, Caius Caesar, after succeeding in so many wars, would have been condemned had I dismissed my army." Then he went to Pompey's tent and ate the victory feast that had been prepared in advance for Pompey.

Caesar accepted from Pompey's army the foot soldiers who chose to join his victorious forces. He gave free pardon to many distinguished officers, including Brutus and Cassius, who later murdered him.

Caesar then pursued Pompey to Egypt, and released those of Pompey's men who had been arrested by the Egyptians. When Pompey's head was presented to him, he would not look upon the head or the murderer. He cried, but accepted Pompey's signet ring. In a letter to Rome, he said that his greatest joy was to be able to save the lives of his fellow-citizens who had fought against him—Caesar wanted all Rome on his side.

In Egypt Caesar found palace intrigue among Ptolemy XII, Pothinus the prime minister, and Cleopatra, who had been banished by her brother. Caesar had great trouble from the unfriendly and haughty Pothinus, and succeeded in defeating Pothinus' attempts to murder him only by sitting up all night. Caesar then sent for Cleopatra, who was smuggled into his quarters wrapped in a rich carpet. Captivated by her charm and bold wit, he fell in love with Cleopatra and fought to gain full power in Egypt for her.

In this fight his small army suffered many disadvantages by being in a strange country. The Egyptians diverted the canals and thus cut off his water supply. When they tried to cut off his communications by sea, he set fire to some of his ships and thus accidentally to the docks and to the great Alexandrian library. In a desperate battle he leaped from a sea wall into a small boat to save his soldiers, who were in danger.

When the Egyptians continued to fight hard he had to jump into the sea. He was carrying some valuable documents, which he held out of the water in one hand while swimming with the other. This he accomplished, although he often had to duck his head under water to prevent detection. At last Caesar prevailed and crushed the opposition to Cleopatra.

He left Cleopatra queen of Egypt, with a baby son named Caesarion. He then went to Pontus to suppress a revolt. He so quickly and thoroughly defeated the rebels that he could honestly report *"Veni, Vidi, Vici"*—"I came, I saw, I conquered."

Caesar returned to Rome and there his followers were both envied and opposed because of their extravagance, wildness, and conceit. One supporter was assigned to Pompey's house, but he had it pulled down, claiming it was not magnificent enough for him. Caesar knew the shortcomings of these men and disapproved of their attitudes, but for his own scheme of government he needed them because they were loyal to him.

Cato and Scipio fled to Africa, assembled a strong army, and made an alliance with King Juba of Numidia, who had a superior cavalry. Caesar quickly followed them, but again he lacked provisions. Without forage for his horses, he used seaweed, which he washed to remove its saltiness and mixed with a little grass to make it more palatable.

The Numidians surprise-attacked a large force of Caesar's men and were systematically destroying them as they retreated when Caesar came up and turned his troops back to fight. In another battle, when Scipio's men were winning, Caesar seized a retreating standard-bearer by the neck. He turned him about, saying, "Look, that is the way to the enemy!"

An oracle had said the Scipios would always be victorious in Africa. In Caesar's army was a plain private soldier named Scipio Sallutius—a distant relative of the great Scipio Africanus —whom Caesar put at the head of his troops, as if he were general. It is difficult to say whether this was done to ridicule his enemy Scipio, to bring good luck to Caesar's side, or just to amuse the troops.

Scipio became increasingly confident and finally divided his forces into three armies, intending to surround Caesar and thus win a decisive victory. While Scipio was building a central fortified camp above a lake, Caesar marched rapidly through some thick woods which Juba had thought impassable. He surprised and destroyed each of the three armies, one after another, killing fifty thousand men in one day.

Cato, who had decided to defend the city of Utica, was not in any of the three battles, so Caesar quickly went to Utica to capture him. On learning of the general's approach towards Utica, Cato retired to his room to read Plato. During the evening he killed himself with his own sword. Caesar, upset by news of Cato's suicide, said, "Cato, I must begrudge you your death, as you begrudged me the honor of saving your life." On the other hand, he later answered Cicero's praise of Cato by publishing a response called "Anti-Cato," criticizing the dead Senator. It seems improbable that Caesar would have spared Cato's life, when he was so bitter against his memory. Caesar was merciful to Cicero, Brutus, and others, though, and his "Anti-Cato" may have been written more to justify his own actions than to criticize those of Cato.

Caesar then returned to Rome for three magnificent triumphs—for Egypt, Pontus, and Africa. He distributed cash and grain to his soldiers and treated the people to feasts and shows. For one feast there were twenty-two thousand dining couches. Caesar claimed to have subdued territory which would provide Rome each year with 200,000 bushels of corn and 3,000,000 pounds of oil. He neglected to mention a census showing that Rome's population had been reduced from 320,-000 to 150,000 during the far-flung conflict.

Caesar's next battle was again in Spain, where he subdued Pompey's sons. In this last battle he ran through his ranks, crying out to his soldiers not to let him fall into the hands of boys. After crushing the enemy at Munda, Caesar said he had often fought for victory, but this was the first time he had fought for his life. He killed thirty thousand of Pompey's followers and lost one thousand of his own best men. This was exactly four years after the beginning of Caesar's civil war against Pompey.

Unwisely Caesar celebrated a triumph for this victory in Spain over Pompey's sons and followers. Many Romans resented his celebrating a victory over his fellow-citizens and thought he ought rather to have tendered an explanation for fighting against Romans. Nevertheless, in recognition of his fortune and his achievements, the Romans accepted the bit and voted Caesar dictator for life. They feared his power, yet hoped that a strong government by a single man might bring relief from civil war and confusion. Thus Caesar established a complete tyranny, for his power was absolute and perpetual. Cicero proposed that the Senate confer great honors on him, and others followed with such an exaggeration of honors and titles and privileges that many citizens resented his power. It may be that his enemies joined with his flatterers in bestowing such pretentious honors in order to make him hateful to the public. They thus built up a justification for revolt against Caesar.

Once more Caesar forgave his enemies and appointed many of Pompey's followers to high offices. He set up Pompey's statues which had been thrown down, thus increasing his own honor by respecting Pompey's memory. He refused an armed guard in Rome, saying it was better to suffer death once than to live in fear of it. He thought his popularity with the people was his best safeguard and so he gave them all the benefits he could from the public resources.

CAESAR

In seeking to share honors with as many as possible, he devoted great thought to appointments. When Maximus died one day before the end of his term as Consul, Caesar appointed a new Consul for that one day only. As many went to pay respects to the new Consul, Cicero remarked, "Let's be quick, lest the man be out of his office before we see him."

Caesar was born to do great things and had a passion for honor. His many noble deeds did not allow him to sit still and reap the fruit of his past labors, but made him want to do even greater things. Among his many ambitions was to make war on the Parthians. He also wanted to encircle the boundaries of Rome's possessions, subduing Scythians, Germans, and all who lived between Rome and the oceans. He at one time appointed an engineer to dig a canal across the Corinthian isthmus; and he also proposed to divert the waters of the Tiber in order to provide a good passage from Rome directly to the sea. He planned new harbors and wanted to drain the Italian marshes to provide new farmland.

Although he did not achieve these dreams, he did cause the reformation of the calendar to correct the irregularity of the year. Throughout history there had been a discrepancy between the lunar months and the seasons of the year. Little by little, festivals changed through the year, until a festival originally intended for spring would be celebrated in the dead of winter. The priests who managed the calendar sometimes would slip in a thirteenth month to "adjust" the calendar.

Caesar called in the best philosophers and mathematicians of his time to settle these questions. Out of the systems they developed, he selected a new calendar which seemed to avoid the errors occasioned by the inequality of the cycles. One month in the new calendar, July, was named in his honor.

Still Caesar longed to be king. This desire was the cause of his first quarrel with the people and was the best weapon for his secret enemies to use against him. A rumor was started that there was an old prediction that Rome would defeat the Parthians only when they fought under the leadership of a Roman king, and not before. Caesar shrewdly rejected the title of king until he could gain popular support for it from the masses of the people. Once, on the way from Alba to Rome, a few greeted him as king, but he found that most of the people did not like it; so he told them his name was Caesar, not King.

At the festival of the Lupercalia, young noblemen and magistrates ran through the Forum stripped to the waist. Each carried a leather whip and playfully struck all they met. Many women held out their hands to be struck, in the superstitious hope that childbirth would be thereby made easier. Caesar was seated in a golden chair in the Forum to view these festivities, in which Antony as Consul was participating enthusiastically. Suddenly Antony darted from the arena and offered to Caesar a crown wreathed with laurel. A few, planted in the crowd by Antony, shouted approval, but the great mass of people remained silent. Reluctantly Caesar refused the crown, and there was universal applause for his modesty. Antony tried three times, but Caesar, seeing it would not be popular, ordered the crown to be carried to the Capitol. Afterward crowns were found on the heads of Caesar's statues.

The Tribunes pulled these crowns off the statues and arrested some men who had first called Caesar king. The people cheered them and referred to them as "Brutus," because Brutus was the early Roman who had terminated the rule of kings and transferred the royal power to the hands of the Senate and the people. It is interesting to note that Marcus Brutus, whom Caesar favored as a beloved friend, was to lead the conspiracy to murder Caesar, and that Decimus Brutus Albinus assisted significantly in the plot.

Marcus Brutus was descended from that first Brutus who stood for democracy, but the honors and favors he had received from the dictator reduced his inclination to overthrow

CAESAR

the ruler. Caesar had pardoned him after Pompey's defeat, had made him praetor and nominated him for Consul. When some advisers warned him against Brutus as a conspirator, Caesar said, "Brutus will wait for this skin of mine," meaning that Brutus was worthy to succeed him but would wait for his natural death. On the other hand, when someone warned him against Antony and Dolabella, he said he did not fear such fat, luxurious men but rather the pale, lean, and hungry ones, meaning Cassius and Brutus.

To encourage Marcus Brutus towards the conspiracy, notes were placed on his praetor's chair, saying, "You are asleep, Brutus!" or "You are no longer Brutus." It was Cassius and Brutus who fanned the flames of jealousy and envy and exploited the resentment towards Caesar's conceit and power.

Fate is, to all appearances, more unavoidable than unexpected. At a supper with Lepidus, someone had asked what sort of death was best, and immediately, before anyone else could speak, Caesar said, "A sudden one." Later, his wife Calpurnia dreamed she was holding the dead Caesar butchered in her arms and the next morning she warned Caesar to stay home and not to go to the Senate. The priests had also reported that it was an inauspicious day for him, so Caesar asked Antony to go to the Senate and to dismiss the Senators.

At this point, Decimus Brutus Albinus, who was engaged in the conspiracy with Marcus Brutus and Cassius, mocked the superstition and urged Caesar to go to the Senate: "What will your enemies say if you dismiss the Senate until Calpurnia may have better dreams? If you are so superstitious, at least go yourself to dismiss them!" On the false basis of his one-sided friendship, he persuaded Caesar to go to the Senate. Later that morning, this same Decimus Brutus was to keep the powerful Antony occupied in conversation outside the Senate Hall so that he could not prevent the assassination.

Caesar had been warned to prepare for great danger on this

day, the Ides of March. "Beware the Ides of March," a soothsayer had told him. On the way to the Senate, he met the
same soothsayer who had made that prediction. "The Ides of
March are come," bragged Caesar. He received the answer,
"Yes, they are come, but they are not past."

A Greek logician who had learned of the plot tried to warn
the dictator. He handed him a manuscript, saying, "Read this,
Caesar, alone and quickly, for it contains matter of great sig-
nificance for you." Caesar took it and tried to read it, but he
was interrupted. At the end he still held this paper in his hand.

The conspirators gathered closely around Caesar as he entered the hall, praising him and asking favors. Tillius Cimber
was begging for his exiled brother to be returned to Rome,
and when Caesar refused, he pulled the dictator's robe down
from his neck, a signal to the conspirators. Casca cut his neck
with a dagger, and as Caesar grasped the dagger, he shouted,
"Vile Casca, what does this mean?" Casca cried, "Brother,
help!" and dagger blows struck Caesar from all sides. The rest
of the Senators were so horrified and amazed that they could do
nothing to prevent the murder. The conspirators were resolute
and had agreed that each would share in the assassination and
shed Caesar's blood. He was surrounded like a wild beast in
toil. Whichever way he turned, he was struck by dagger
blows. It is said that he suffered twenty-three wounds. Others
crowded in hastily to kill him and many were wounded by
each other as they struck at Caesar from all sides.

He fought and resisted them, shifting to avoid the blows
and calling for help, until he saw Marcus Brutus stabbing him
in the groin. "You, too, Brutus?" he cried. Covering his head,
he submitted and fell dead at the base of Pompey's statue.

Brutus stood forth to give reasons for what had been done,
but the Senators would not listen. Instead they rushed out of
the hall to lock themselves in their homes. Antony and Lepidus, Caesar's most faithful companions, hid themselves se-

CAESAR

cretly in friends' houses. Brutus and his followers, hot from the murder, marched together from the senate house to the Capitol, not ashamed of the deed, but proud to have ended a tyranny. The next day Brutus made a speech to the people, who showed by their silence that they pitied and missed Caesar, but respected Brutus.

The Senate passed "acts of oblivion" forgiving all for what was past and seeking to reconcile all parties. They ordered that Caesar should be worshiped as a god and that none of his laws should be revoked. Antony helped to develop a compromise by which Brutus and his chief partners were voted positions of trust as governors of provinces.

At Caesar's funeral, Antony made a dramatic oration in an attempt to arouse loyalty to the fallen dictator and vengeance against the assassins. He revealed that Caesar's will left a gift of money to every Roman citizen and he displayed Caesar's bloodstained clothes, showing where the daggers had pierced his garments.

Unable to restrain their emotions, the people built a funeral pyre in the marketplace. Lighting torches from the fire, they hurried to burn the homes of Brutus, Cassius, and the other conspirators.

Antony and Caesar's nephew and heir, Octavian, who later became Augustus Caesar, took an army of Julius Caesar's veterans to defeat and punish the assassins. In the first day of battle at Philippi, Brutus triumphed, but on the second day, the conspirators were crushed. Brutus and Cassius both committed suicide.

· · ·

Julius Caesar was a man of great force, cunning, ambition, and ability. Brave and bold and having an amazing power of concentration, he never quit or relaxed his efforts. Careful observation and thorough planning made him nearly invincible. He was born to do great things.

A master politician, he was generous and at times merciful and kind, though at other times ruthless. He was a vital and thrilling leader, inspiring the thorough loyalty of his "fellow-soldiers," as he called his men. His conceit and selfishness, his desire for absolute power, and his willingness to be dishonest and disloyal if such suited his purpose combined with the envy of little men to cause his downfall.

He contributed much to Rome's greatness through brave conquests, through extending the provinces, through achieving the Gracchi's proposed reforms for the people, through breaking the power of selfish interests in the Senate, through his new calendar, and through winning new respect for Rome. On the other hand, he ended the Republic and substituted government by men for government by law.

ANTONY

83–30 B.C.

*A*ntony's father, although not distinguished in public life, was a worthy and very generous man. His wife objected to his liberality, however, because he could not afford it. Once when he had no cash on hand, a friend in need asked for help; Antony's father called for water in his silver basin and pretended he was going to shave. Dismissing the servant, he handed the basin to his friend to sell. Later, when his wife began looking for the basin, the father humbly acknowledged his deed and begged her pardon.

After his father's death, Antony's mother, Julia, a relative of Julius Caesar, married Lentulus, who was later put to death by Cicero in Catiline's rebellion. Antony bore a constant grudge against Cicero from that time on.

Antony was a handsome, vigorous man. He was charming, attractive, and popular, a natural leader of men and beloved by many women. He often indulged himself in pleasures—drinking and partying and wasting money and time and neglecting his business and career. When he was young he was often in debt. He became involved with Curio, an extravagant playboy, and with Clodius, the demagogue, who was an opponent of Cicero.

Antony finally became tired of these foolish ways. Afraid also of the opposition developing against Clodius, he left Rome and traveled through Greece. There he spent time in military training and studied oratory, developing an ostentatious style of speaking which reflected his personality.

He had earlier rejected the invitation of Gabinius to serve as a private soldier, but now he promptly accepted a commission from him as cavalry commander against the Syrians and the Jews. Antony was the most daring officer and always the first man to scale the walls. Anxious to fight even more heroically, he persuaded Gabinius to march into Egypt to restore Ptolemy to the throne. Antony led the way with the cavalry, securing the passes and capturing the key cities on the way. When Ptolemy entered a captured city, he wanted to kill many Egyptians in revenge, but Antony prevented the executions.

In many of the skirmishes and battles, Antony proved his personal valor and military strength. Once in particular, by wheeling his cavalry about and suddenly attacking the enemy's rear, he clearly won the victory for Rome. Through brave and aggressive leadership he defeated Archelaus who had formerly been his guest. But after the death of Archelaus Antony found his body and gave him a royal funeral, which much impressed the Alexandrians.

Antony gained a great reputation for his courage, energy, graciousness in victory, and generosity of spirit. In his handsome and virile appearance, he was said to resemble statues of Hercules. His athletic physique, full beard, sharp Roman nose, and prominent forehead gave him an appearance of boldness to match his deeds. He was criticized by some citizens for his drinking in public, his wild parties, boasting, and pranks. But his fellowship with his soldiers and their mutual trust, his readiness to eat and fight beside them made him the delight and pleasure of the army. He was free and easy about love affairs and gained many friends by encouraging their romances; he accepted good naturedly other people's jests and banter about his own varied loves.

ANTONY

Like his father, Antony delighted in giving money, presents, and loans to his friends and supporters. On one occasion he decided to give 25 myriads to a friend; his steward, thinking Antony did not understand how great a gift this would be, stacked the coins on the floor where Antony could see them. Antony asked why the money was there. "This is the money you ordered given to your friend," the steward explained. Antony, rejecting the implied criticism, said, "It is too little. Double it!" His generosity supported his first rise to power. Many followed him because of his kindness, his favors, and his lavish gifts to friends and fellow-soldiers. After he became great, his power was sustained by those who had enjoyed his liberality or yet hoped to share it, even while a thousand follies were hastening his downfall.

When Pompey and Caesar moved toward civil war, Caesar's friend Curio won Antony's allegiance to his leader. With Caesar's support and money sent from Gaul, as well as by his own energy and eloquence, Antony was elected Tribune and Augur. Antony became Julius Caesar's chief supporter within the City, reading publicly Caesar's messages which the Senate refused to read or acknowledge. He resisted the Consuls, who wanted to give Pompey arbitrary power and the command of all troops in Rome. As Tribune he diverted troops designated for Pompey and sent them instead into Syria to reinforce Bibulus against the Parthians.

When a Senator proposed that Pompey dismiss his army, many Senators were in favor. Another proposed that Caesar dismiss his army, and more were in favor of this. Thereupon Antony proposed that both Pompey and Caesar dismiss their armies; the Senate gave this their greatest approval and praised Antony. The Senate then called for a vote, but the Consuls blocked it.

Caesar's friends made other generous proposals for compromise, but Cato and others strongly opposed them. The Consuls ordered Antony out of the Senate. He left Rome in disguise to join Caesar in Gaul. Antony reported that order and justice were ignored in Rome, that the Tribunes were denied the privilege of speaking in the Senate, and that the man who spoke for honesty was driven out.

After hearing Antony's report, Caesar started with his army toward Italy and Rome. It has been said that Antony was the immediate cause of Rome's Civil War, as Helen was the cause of the Trojan War. But it would be foolish to underestimate the purposeful Caesar, or to suppose that he would have plunged into civil war merely out of indignation at the treatment Antony had received. Actually Caesar had decided on war long before, and he was just waiting for an excuse to fight Pompey; he seized this situation as a plausible occasion. Caesar's true motive was the same as has driven other ambitious men against all mankind—an unquenchable thirst for empire and the mad ambition to be the greatest man in the world.

Caesar occupied Rome, left the government of the City to Lepidus, the command of his troops in Italy to Antony, and himself pursued Pompey's legions into Spain.

Antony, as Tribune of the people, quickly won over Caesar's soldiers and became second only to Caesar. He lived among the soldiers and joined in their work, exercises, and drills, but at the same time he was too lazy to pay attention to complaints. He was too impatient with the details of government. He was also wild and immoral, and had a bad name for being familiar with other men's wives. He bought Pompey's fine home, loudly complaining about the price. As he traveled through Italy, he scandalized the people by drinking from golden cups which were more suitable in a temple or palace than in the camp of an army officer on the march. He rode sometimes in a chariot drawn by lions when he went to elaborate morning feasts in pavilions set up by riversides or in

ANTONY

groves; he quartered dancing girls and camp followers in the homes of serious parents; the conqueror of Gaul gained a bad reputation through this wildness and the roughness of Caesar's other friends and lieutenants at home. Antony, who had been given the greatest trust by Caesar, committed the worst offenses and hurt Caesar's good name the most. When Caesar returned from Spain, he overlooked the complaints against Antony, whose courage, energy, and military skill seemed more important to Caesar than his faults.

In pursuit of Pompey, Caesar crossed the Ionian Sea with a few troops and then sent his ships back to Brundisium with orders for Antony and Gabinius to bring the rest of the troops to reinforce him in Greece. Gabinius was afraid of the rough, stormy sea and wanted to march around by land, but Antony declared this would be too slow and that they must hurry to support Caesar. Antony beat back Pompey's fleet long enough for the troop transports to start across the Ionian Sea. The enemy followed him, but he turned in close to the rocky shore to evade them. There he avoided the gales which wrecked most of Pompey's western fleet, as they remained in the open water. Antony captured many men and much military equipment from this battle. He was able to transport 20,000 infantrymen and 800 cavalry across the sea to Caesar. His seasonable arrival with so large a reinforcement gave Caesar the strength and encouragement to attack Pompey.

In the battles against Pompey, Antony distinguished himself for bravery—twice he stopped the army from full retreat and led them back to charge. His reputation for courage was second only to Caesar's. In the great battle of Pharsalia, Caesar showed his confidence in Antony by giving him command of the entire left wing while he himself led the right.

After the battle, Caesar became dictator of Rome, but he followed Pompey to Egypt. He sent Antony back to Rome as his representative, with the title of Master of the Horse, a position of power second only to that of the dictator. Except for the Tribunes, all other magistrates ceased to exercise authority in Rome. Antony soon began to disagree with the Tribune Dolabella; he attacked with Caesar's troops and captured Dolabella and his supporters. The imprisonment of the Tribune antagonized the common people. The responsible citizens were already disgusted by Antony's wild living, heavy spending, and arbitrary measures, for it seemed unreasonable to them that he should live in such luxury in Rome while Caesar fought the end of a dangerous war under circumstances of fatigue and hardship.

When Caesar returned he restored Dolabella and took Lepidus, rather than Antony, as his fellow Consul. In resentment, Antony remained in Rome instead of following Caesar with the army to Libya. But Caesar dealt gently with Antony's errors and tried to cure him of his folly and extravagance.

Apparently settling down, Antony married Fulvia, the widow of Clodius the demagogue. She was an ambitious woman who was not content with housework or a private husband; instead she wanted to dominate her husband in a vital public career. Although she tried to tame Antony, he loved her and enjoyed her, playing boyish and sportive tricks to keep her amused. Once, when she was afraid he was in danger, he disguised himself as a messenger bringing her a letter. When she asked about Antony's safety, he grabbed her and kissed her.

When Caesar returned from Spain again, all Romans of rank went several days journey outside of Rome to meet the all-victorious dictator. Antony was the best received of all and was invited to ride back to the City with Caesar while Octavian and Brutus Albinus rode behind in the next chariot.

When Caesar was made Consul for the fifth time, he chose

Antony as his colleague. Soon, however, Caesar informed the Senate that he would give up the office himself and make Dolabella Antony's colleague. Antony opposed this move with violent criticism of Dolabella, and when Caesar went before the people to proclaim Dolabella, Antony shouted that the auspices were unfavorable. At last Caesar gave up in disgust, as much with Antony as with Dolabella, because of their childish and petty contentions.

The dissension between Antony and Dolabella caused a great deal of trouble for Caesar. When someone warned him about their ambitions, Caesar said, "It is not these well-fed, long-haired men that I fear, but the pale and hungry-looking ones," meaning Brutus and Cassius, who later conspired for his murder. During a festival, Caesar was seated in triumphal regalia above the rostra in the Forum, watching the sports, when the young patricians and officeholders ran into the Forum, stripped to the waist, lashing with leather whips in sport at any they could reach. Antony, participating enthusiastically in this custom as the young Consul, suddenly ran up to Caesar and tried to place a crown of laurel on the dictator's head, as if he were declaring him king. Caesar pushed the crown aside and was applauded with great shouts by the people. Each time Antony tried to crown him, Caesar received only a weak cheer from those planted by Antony to support the move. Each time he refused the crown Caesar received a mighty ovation. The people accepted the fact of Caesar's absolute power but they still dreaded the title of king as a symbol of the destruction of their liberty.

This offering of the crown was used by Brutus and the other conspirators as evidence that Caesar wanted to be king. Some of the conspirators reported that Antony knew of the assassination plot, but that he neither encouraged it nor reported it to Caesar. Some of the conspirators wanted to kill

Antony also, but Brutus blocked this, saying that an action undertaken in defense of right and law must be kept pure and free of injustice.

On the Ides of March, Brutus Albinus kept Antony occupied outside the Senate so that he could not prevent Caesar's murder. The conspirators were concerned lest his bodily strength, his courage, and his prestige might interfere with their plans. Immediately after the assassination, Antony hid. When he learned later that day that the conspirators had assembled in the Capitol and that they planned no further purge, Antony persuaded them to come forth, sending them his own son as hostage for their safety. That night Cassius dined with Antony and Brutus with Lepidus.

The next day Antony convened the Senate and urged that Brutus and Cassius be given command of provinces, that all of Caesar's laws and appointments remain in force, and that no action of punishment be taken concerning the assassination.

Antony was praised as a peacemaker and credited with having prevented civil war because he had settled a difficult and embarrassing situation with wisdom and statesmanship. The praise went to Antony's head; he saw a chance to inherit Julius Caesar's power and authority.

As Caesar's body was carried to his tomb, Antony made the customary funeral oration in the marketplace. He announced that Caesar's will had left a gift of money to every Roman citizen. Sensing the emotional response of the crowd, Antony began to mingle with his praises of Caesar expressions of sympathy for him and indignation at his murder. Holding up Caesar's bloodstained clothes, Antony called those who committed the deed villains and bloody murderers. This emotional oration led the people to make an immediate funeral pyre for Caesar and to vengefully burn the homes of Brutus, Cassius, and the other assassins, who fled from Rome.

The dictator's widow had entrusted to Antony Caesar's money, his plans, and all his papers. Antony was then able to announce that Caesar had wanted certain men rewarded and others punished; in that way Antony accomplished in Caesar's name all he himself wanted done. It was as if Charon, the boatman of the river Styx, had brought commissions from the dead, and so the Romans called those who were thus appointed to office "Charonites" because they owed their office to the dead dictator.

Octavian, son of Caesar's niece, came back to Rome to claim his designated place as Caesar's heir, since Caesar had adopted him. He went to Antony as his father's friend and spoke to him of the money in Antony's trust and the need to make the cash payments to all the citizens, according to Caesar's will. Antony refused, ridiculing Octavian as a silly youth and opposing his efforts to honor Caesar and his wishes.

Cicero was at this time the most influential man in the Senate. He spoke eloquently to turn people against Antony, making a series of orations against Antony which they called "Philippics" because they reminded scholars of the bitter tirades by which Demosthenes aroused the Athenians against Philip of Macedon. Cicero persuaded the Senate to declare Antony a public enemy and to send Caesar Octavian and the Consuls to wage war against him to subdue him.

Young Octavian allied himself with Cicero, and both of them were elected Consuls. Cicero's eloquence and political influence strengthened Octavian's bid for power. Octavian borrowed money and distributed it among Caesar's veterans, quickly recruiting soldiers in Italy before they joined Antony. As he gained support among the veterans and among those who hated Antony, he pushed his campaign to Modena, where he defeated Antony's army.

In adversity Antony was most nearly a virtuous man. Although he had been used to luxury he provided an excellent example for his soldiers, eating roots and tree bark and living in misery during his retreat. He marched toward the army of Lepidus, hoping for a strong ally, but Lepidus was slow to join him. When Antony went into the large army camp, unshaven and unkempt from his long retreat, he addressed Lepidus' soldiers directly. Lepidus ordered the trumpets to sound, so that the men would be unable to hear Antony, but this only aroused sympathy and pity for him. Many of the soldiers assured Antony that they wanted to join him, so the next day he marched into the camp and took command, enlisting the reluctant Lepidus as his general and treating him with respect and friendship. They gathered other troops and then sought an alliance with Octavian. The young Caesar, realizing that Cicero was sincerely for the Republic, deserted him to make an alliance of power. Thus do ambitious men change sides when it suits their purpose, their greed, and their fancy.

Octavian, Antony, and Lepidus met on an island for three days. They divided Julius Caesar's empire, formed the Second Triumvirate, and condemned 300 Roman leaders to death. Each agreed to give up his former favorites to the vengeance of the other two Triumvirs. Antony insisted on the death of Cicero, although he had helped Octavian significantly. He gave orders that Cicero's head and the hand that had written the "Philippics" should be cut off and nailed above the rostra. Antony agreed to the execution of his uncle, Lucius Caesar. Antony's mother prevented this murder by shielding her brother and saying, "You shall not kill Lucius Caesar until you first kill me, who gave birth to your general."

The Romans hated this Triumvirate. Antony bore most of the blame, because he was older than Octavian and had more authority than Lepidus. The people resented the vengeance, and they criticized Antony for shutting his doors—which had once been those of Pompey—to officers, envoys, and sober citizens, while behind those doors he entertained actors and actresses, play girls and drunken flatterers. Antony spent the public money carelessly; when it was clear that there was no limit to his extravagance, Octavian called for a division of the property and the armies.

When the Triumvirate defeated Brutus and Cassius at Philippi, Antony took all the credit, since Octavian was ill before the battle. Octavian was taken back to Rome, and Antony went on to Asia to raise money for the army's expenses. He was popular with the Greeks, who compared him to Bacchus, god of wine and revelry. When he demanded a second tribute of all the Asian cities under his control, a spokesman for the cities answered, "If you can take two tributes in a year, no doubt you can give us a couple of summers and double harvest time." He reported to Antony that Asia had raised 200,000 talents for him. "If this has not been paid to you, ask your collectors for it; if it has, and is all gone, then we are ruined." Antony was very touched by these words, for he was basically a simple man and was unaware of the wrongs that were done in his name. He lived so wildly that he could not detect flattery and dishonesty. He found it difficult to understand how men who seemed good fellows in drinking and relaxing could flatter or deceive him in serious matters. He was rarely aware of his own faults, but when he did see them, he was extremely repentant and ready to ask pardon and to make reparations. Although he was severe in his punishments, he was extravagantly generous.

Antony's love for Cleopatra, added to his other weaknesses, completed his ruin. Cleopatra awakened and kindled the latent passions in his nature and stifled and corrupted his goodness and sound judgment. As he prepared for the Parthian war, he commanded her to appear before him to answer charges that she had helped Cassius against the Triumvirate. She ignored his orders, but came on her own terms and in her own time, confident of her charms and cleverness. She made elaborate preparations and dramatized her arrival by floating down the river to Tarsus in a magnificent gilded barge with purple sails, and with silver oars beating time to the music of flutes and fifes. She lay under a canopy of gold, dressed as Venus and surrounded by beautiful young boys who were supposed to be Cupids. Her maids were dressed like Sea Nymphs and Graces, some steering at the rudder and some working at the ropes. Perfume from the barge enveloped the crowds who deserted Antony and ran to see the spectacular sight. It was said that Venus had come to Bacchus for the joy of Asia. Antony invited her to supper, but she thought it better for him to come to her barge. Willing to show his good humor and courtesy, he accepted her invitation. That evening he was astounded by the magnificence of her preparations and the spectacular illumination she had contrived for his entertainment, with many chandeliers lighted at once in patterns of squares and circles.

Cleopatra was bright and entrancing, less remarkable for her actual beauty than for her personality. Her conversation had irresistible charm; the natural grace and beauty of her speech and movements were bewitching. She used the intriguing sound of her voice in many languages and rarely needed an interpreter. Antony was so captivated that he forgot his wife and family, his competition with Octavian, and his wars against Rome's enemies.

He went to Alexandria and wasted his most valuable asset, time. Cleopatra used flattery, charm, cleverness, and fantastic entertainments to tie Antony passionately to her. She played dice with him, drank with him, hunted with him, and played violent pranks with him on the people of Alexandria. They accepted the foolishness well, saying they were glad he acted his tragic parts in Rome and saved the comedy for them.

ANTONY

One day when he had bad luck in fishing, he ordered divers to attach fish to his hooks so that he could seem to Cleopatra to be a great fisherman. She realized what he was doing, but praised him highly; and the next day she invited others to watch Antony fish. An Egyptian diver then submerged and put a salted fish on his hook, to the merriment of all. "Leave the fishing to us," she said, "your game is cities, provinces, and kingdoms."

While he was playing in Egypt, two messages arrived: his wife Fulvia had started a revolution in Italy against Octavian, had lost, had fled from Rome, and now begged him to join her in fighting back; the other message was that young Labienus and the Parthians were overrunning the province of Asia. With a terrible hangover, Antony impulsively started toward Parthia to fight. When he got to Phoenicia, he changed his mind and headed for Italy in response to Fulvia's plea. By the time he arrived there, his wife had become ill and died.

Octavian received Antony in friendship, and both of them blamed Antony's late wife for their differences. They agreed on the Ionian Sea as a boundary between their areas of control, Octavian taking the western provinces, Antony the eastern, and leaving Africa for Lepidus. They also decided that each of the three in turn should make their friends Consuls when they did not choose to take the office for themselves. Because it seemed wise to establish a closer tie between the Triumvirs, Antony married Octavian's sister, Octavia, a wonderful woman of great beauty, honor, and prudence. The Romans all hoped that this marriage would seal the Triumvirate and influence Antony to lead a more respectable life.

Although Octavian and Antony conferred together and celebrated happily, Antony developed an intense jealousy of Octavian. Antony and Octavia, therefore, left for Greece. During Antony's absence, his lieutenant Ventidius won great victories over the Parthians. Then Ventidius, not wishing to arouse Antony's jealousy, decided to punish those allies who had forsaken Rome's interests. He surrounded and besieged Antiochus, who offered to submit to Antony's orders and to pay a thousand talents for his pardon. Ventidius told him he had to wait for Antony, who had ordered him to make no terms until his arrival. When Antony arrived, Antiochus stiffened his defense and frustrated the Roman's attempts to capture the fort. Antony shamefully had to settle for 300 talents instead of a thousand. This kind of incident gave both Antony and Octavian the reputation for achieving more through their lieutenants than they could accomplish themselves.

Listening to Italian rumors heightened Antony's resentment against Octavian; he decided to return to deal with him. He was refused admittance to the port of Brundisium, so he headed for Tarentum. There Octavia received permission to visit her brother. She pleaded separately with both Octavian and Antony, saying that from being the most fortunate woman on earth she was in danger of becoming the most unhappy. "I shall be miserable," she cried, "for no matter on whichever side victory falls, I shall lose." Octavian marched his army to Tarentum and then, in deference to his sister, presented an unusual and dignified spectacle: the vast army met as great a fleet, not with hostility, but with only friendship, joy, and kindness between the two. After they exchanged gifts, legions, and promises, Antony left Octavia and his children with Octavian and sailed for Asia.

Then more trouble started. Antony sent for Cleopatra and made her queen of vast provinces that had been conquered by the Roman army. He acknowledged her two children as his own, which infuriated and shamed the Romans. Antony tried to excuse his misconduct by saying that the greatness of the Roman empire consisted more in giving than in taking kingdoms and in begetting in every place a new line of kings.

ANTONY

He then sent Cleopatra back to Egypt and he assembled an army of 100,000 soldiers in Armenia to attack the dreaded Parthians. The war was hastened without proper thought and preparation, in the hope that Antony could quickly defeat the Parthians and return to Cleopatra for the winter. In his haste he negligently left behind some equipment, including an eighty-foot battering ram. When he tried to capture the city of Phraata, he failed because he did not have the necessary siege equipment. His Armenian allies withdrew, although their king had been the chief promoter of the war, and Antony was deprived of valuable cavalry and archers. The Parthians, encouraged by their successes and Antony's errors, began a series of small attacks on the Romans.

Antony tried to draw the Parthians into a major engagement. He marched out ten legions, three cohorts of heavy infantry, and all his cavalry, and then encamped. The Parthians were hovering about, so he marched all his army past them, as though he intended to return home. As the Romans marched in front of them in perfect order and silence, the Parthians stood still and admired their precision drill, military bearing, and discipline. When the Roman forces were in the most advantageous position, Antony gave the signal for a fierce attack by the cavalry and infantry. Antony fought hard, hoping that this victory might settle the war; he scattered the Parthians, but killed only eighty men and took only thirty prisoners. The Romans were extremely discouraged that their victory had gained such a small advantage, whereas when they were beaten, they had lost such a great number of men.

The next day, with great difficulty because of cavalry charges and ambush on the way, they returned to their camp site near Phraata. There Antony found that the men he had left to guard the camp had deserted in panic during an attack by the Medes. To punish them he decimated the guards. In this infrequent Roman punishment, the commander divided his men into groups of ten and put one of each ten to death, choosing by lot as a horrible example to those remaining.

The Parthians used every propaganda device and deceit to demoralize the Romans. They criticized Antony to his men for his obstinacy and told them they would soon face their two worst enemies, winter and famine. They claimed that the Parthian king wanted only peace and an opportunity to save the lives of brave soldiers like themselves. Antony therefore decided to demand the Roman standards and prisoners captured from Crassus' army as a basis for withdrawing from the Parthian territory. The King replied that he need not trouble himself about the standards and prisoners but that if he wished to retreat, he could do so in peace and safety. Although ordinarily he was eloquent and effective in addressing his troops, this time Antony was so shamed and saddened that he asked another officer to order the retreat. He could not find the heart to face his loyal soldiers.

A friendly scout advised Antony to keep his retreat close to the mountains, for even though the march would be rougher, he would be safer than if he exposed his army in open country to the Parthian cavalry and archers. This native volunteered to be bound as a hostage and in this way guide Antony through the mountains.

The retreat was painful; the Parthians attacked them every day with arrows and darts; they lacked food and water, and had to eat vegetables and roots they could not identify. Many of them ate unknowingly a poisonous herb that made them lose their minds. They forgot everything and were content to occupy themselves endlessly by moving stones from one place to another until they died. Some of the men drank brackish water that incapacitated them with intensely painful stomach cramps.

Antony learned not to allow his patrols to go far from his

ANTONY

main army. Though the Roman patrols might seem to be initially successful, the Parthians would soon lure them beyond Antony's help. Then the Parthians would systematically destroy them.

Antony's leadership and resourcefulness saved his men repeatedly in this miserable twenty-seven-day retreat. His soldiers remained intensely loyal during this trial, calling him emperor and saying that as long as he was well they were safe. They loved him for his courage, eloquence, nobility of spirit, frank manners, and his liberal and magnificent habits. He visited his wounded men, crying in grief over their condition. They appreciated his friendliness, kindness and consideration for the sick and wounded, who seemed even more eager to serve than those who were whole and strong.

After about twenty days of retreat, the Parthians came closer with more troops, expecting the Romans to give up. Antony assembled his men and addressed them, praising those who had fought well, reproaching those who had fled, and praying to the gods to punish him alone but to grant victory and safety to his soldiers. The next day the Romans amazed the Parthians by their spirit, discipline and courage. When they were attacked by archers, the first rank kneeled to hold their shields close to the ground, the second rank held their shields above those of the first rank, and the shields of the third rank were above those of the second, like tiles on a roof. In this way they provided excellent protection against the arrows. The Parthians, seeing Romans on their knees, thought they must be weary. They made a confident, fierce assault, but the Romans arose, killing many Parthians with javelins and causing the rest to retreat.

Finally Antony's army reached the Araxes River and crossed safely into Armenia. The Parthians praised the Romans' courage and went back to their homes. Antony had lost

24,000 Romans in this bitter and humiliating twenty-seven-day retreat. He had won eighteen battles, but he had been unable to follow up any victory. Then he lost 8,000 more men by hurrying through a snow storm to meet Cleopatra, who was bringing clothes and money for the army.

When the Medes, who had a strong force of cavalry and archers, invited Antony to ally himself with them against the Parthians, he accepted. Octavia in the meantime had left Rome to join him, but he ordered her to wait for him in Athens. She asked where she should send the provisions she was bringing for his army.

At this point Cleopatra thwarted all hopes. Pretending heartsickness, she said she could not bear to be out of his sight and made him believe that she would die if he left for Media, for Greece, for Octavia, for anywhere or anyone. He therefore postponed the war and returned with Cleopatra to Egypt, even though the Parthians had been weakened by internal disputes and therefore were vulnerable.

Octavia returned to Rome, and her brother vowed revenge against Antony for the insulting neglect of his true wife. Octavia pleaded in vain that it would be intolerable for the world's two greatest commanders to involve Rome in civil war, one out of passion for a woman and the other out of resentment about a woman. She remained in Antony's house, reared his children, managed his business, and helped his interests in Rome. She received his friends and supporters and aided them as Antony's representative, which only made the Romans more disgusted with Antony's neglect of this fine woman.

Reports of Antony's wild, extravagant life with Cleopatra and of his gifts to her further inflamed the Roman people against him. In a theatrical piece of insolence against Rome, he dramatically bestowed hollow honors and unconquered king-

ANTONY

doms upon Cleopatra and her children. In Alexandria they posed on golden thrones on a platform of silver; each of Cleopatra's children appeared in the costume of the kingdom Antony arbitrarily decreed he was to inherit. At Rome Octavian exploited this scene to undermine what little support Antony still had there.

Octavian had put Lepidus out of the government because of misconduct and had assumed control of his provinces without consulting or sharing with Antony. When Antony began to quickly mobilize his armies and fleets to attack, Octavian became alarmed, as he was afraid he might be forced to fight that summer, before he was prepared. The Roman citizens resented having to pay for an army and navy which was going to fight against other Romans.

Antony had the advantage of time but his great mistake was that he ignored it. With Cleopatra at his side, he converted his war preparations into one continuous drunken celebration, mobilizing the chefs and bakers, actors, musicians, and dancing girls to provide entertainment. The men speculated as to what could be expected for a victory celebration if they went to such elaborate expense and festivity before starting a war. When Antony peevishly sent word to Rome for Octavia to leave their home, his noble wife meekly complied, grieving that she must be one of the causes of the war.

While Antony feasted and played with Cleopatra, Octavian used the time for military preparations and for overcoming the people's resentment at the high taxes. While the taxes were being collected, the people were mutinous and violent; but, having paid their money, they held their peace and cooperated loyally with Octavian.

Antony had the advantage that his forces were better prepared and more experienced in war. If he had struck quickly and decisively, he might have won. But he wasted his opportunities by delaying for more parties and play. In the meantime, Octavian seized Antony's will and read it publicly to the shocked Senators. Antony had willed great riches to Cleopatra and had arranged to be buried in Alexandria rather than Rome.

Time, wise planning, and clever propaganda had prepared Octavian's forces for the conflict. As soon as Octavian was ready, he declared war on Cleopatra and announced that Antony had forfeited his power and authority by letting a foreign woman control his decisions. Octavian ridiculed Antony's allies and generals as eunuchs and maid-servants of Cleopatra.

At first Antony ordered Cleopatra to wait in Alexandria until after the war, but she insisted that she was as wise and brave as any of his allies and deserved to be with him in the battle. She referred to her experience as ruler of Egypt and reminded him of the sixty ships she had added to his navy. She also flattered him by saying she had learned a great deal from him.

Antony had 500 ships, 112,000 fighting men, and numerous Eastern allies, while Octavian had only 250 ships and 92,000 soldiers. Antony's veterans had a good chance to win a land battle, but he chose to fight at sea to please Cleopatra. His captains had to impress Greek farmers, who knew nothing of the sea, into service as sailors to man the 500 heavy ships. Octavian, on the other hand, had Roman ships which were built for battle and were light and swift and well-manned by loyal Romans.

Antony's generals urged him to leave the sea to Octavian, who had long experience in sea-fighting during the Sicilian war. It seemed foolish for Antony, the most experienced army commander living, to waste his disciplined infantry, parcelling them out onto ships. His generals even made new allies who

ANTONY

agreed to meet him in Thrace or Macedon to fight by land, whereas some of his other allies deserted with their ships just before the battle and joined Octavian. Throughout all these arguments Cleopatra's wish for a naval battle prevailed.

Octavian sent word to Antony to stop delaying and made a peace offer, promising him land for his army in Italy as far inland as a horse could run in a single course. Antony refused, but offered to meet Octavian in single combat. Then Octavian crossed to Actium, where Antony's ships were assembled. Antony was afraid his fleet would be defeated before he could get his soldiers on board, so he faked readiness by crowding armed men, including rowers, onto the decks of his leading ships, where Octavian could see them. Octavian was deceived and retired temporarily.

Antony had so much trouble organizing his recruits on the ships that he was tempted to go back to the land to fight. An infantry captain cried to Antony, "Oh, my general, what have our battle scars and swords done to displease you, that you have given your confidence to rotten timbers?" But Cleopatra again insisted on a sea battle. Selfishly she relied upon her flagship and her navy to provide for her a secure retreat to Egypt in case of a defeat. Antony posted his ships at the harbor entrance and went from ship to ship in a small boat, encouraging his men to stand fast and to fight on deck as they had on land. He ordered his sea captains to hold still and defend the harbor entrance.

They waited through three days of rough weather, and then at noon of the fourth day a strong breeze tempted Antony's men to advance the left squadron. Octavian, to encourage them out, ordered a retreat. He wanted to fight in the open sea, where his small, fast ships could circle and maneuver around the tall Oriental galleys. When the battle began, the ships did not charge into one another. Antony's men were not

able to charge because they were not skilled enough to maneuver their ships, and Octavian knew his small ships would be
shattered if they rammed the huge galleys, which were heav-
ily armed with brass spikes. The battle resembled many attacks on forts: three or four of Octavian's ships would surround one of Antony's big galleys, attacking with spears,
arrows, poles, and catapults of fire. When the battle was still
equal and undecided, Cleopatra's sixty Egyptian ships suddenly hoisted full sail, went right through Antony's other
ships, and headed for the open sea in retreat. The rest of Antony's ships were thrown into disorder, and Octavian's men
were encouraged.

Antony proved that he had lost his spirit as a commander
and a man, for he hoisted sail, abandoned his men, and followed Cleopatra in a single ship. What had earlier been said as
a jest, "that the soul of a lover lives in someone else's body,"
he proved to be a serious truth. Cleopatra took him on board
her ship, but while they returned to Egypt he sulked on deck
for three days before he would visit her.

At Actium, Caesar captured 300 of Antony's ships. Many
of Antony's men could not believe that their leader had deserted them, and his army stayed together for seven days, hoping he would return. Finally, deserted by most of their officers
as well as by Antony, they surrendered to Octavian; thus Antony forfeited his strong army and his chance for empire.

Cleopatra then started a project to drag her fleet across the
Isthmus of Suez and set it afloat in the Red Sea. There she
hoped to make a home where she might live in peace, away
from war and turmoil. When the Arabians burned the first
ships she brought across, she abandoned the project. She then
started fortifying the approaches to Egypt. Antony took no
part in all this, but withdrew in solitude to a small island in the
mouth of the Nile, brooding over his defeat and failure. Here

he learned that his armies had surrendered themselves and his provinces to Octavian, now called Caesar. Completely despondent, Antony decided to commit suicide but was prevented by his friends.

He soon returned to the palace and to Cleopatra, and spent his time drinking, feasting, loving Cleopatra, and celebrating any little excuse for festivities. He started an organization of "Diers Together," who were men dedicated to dying with him when Caesar's legions would arrive. In the meantime they devoted themselves to enjoying the transitory luxury of Egypt. Cleopatra was busy researching drugs and poisons, in the hope of finding the least painful way to die. She tried them all on prisoners but found that the quick poisons caused the sharpest pains and that the less painful ones worked slowly. Next she tried poisonous animals and insects and watched the death of many prisoners in her experiments, until she finally decided the asp was the best, because its poison produced a heavy drowsiness and a gentle sweat while it dulled the senses by degrees.

Antony and Cleopatra then sent messages to Caesar, begging for mercy. He would not answer Antony, but replied to Cleopatra that there was no reasonable favor she might not expect if first she would kill Antony or expel him from Egypt. He sent this message to her by his own personal servant, who because of his long audiences with Cleopatra and her courtesies to him made Antony extremely jealous. He had the messenger seized, whipped and returned, telling Caesar that the man's impertinent ways had provoked him. "But if it offend you, you have my servant Hipparchus with you; hang him up and scourge him to make us even."

Cleopatra moved many of her treasures into a monument that had been prepared for her tomb. She planned to die there, but Octavian wanted to capture her alive so that he could secure all of her riches. He therefore sent her assurances of his good intentions, while at the same time Antony won several small skirmishes against Caesar's approaching army. After one such encounter he returned optimistically to the palace. Meeting Cleopatra, he kissed her happily and commended one of his men for bravery. She gave the soldier a gold helmet and breastplate. That night the man deserted to Caesar.

In this desperate plight, Antony again challenged Caesar to fight him hand to hand. Caesar replied that Antony could most likely find several other ways to die. Antony decided to die fighting in battle. That night he drank much. The next morning he ordered his fleet and his army both to attack. As soon as the ships came near each other, Antony's men saluted Caesar with their oars, fell in line behind Octavian's fleet and followed it into the harbor. Next Antony's cavalry deserted to the enemy, and he was defeated in a minor infantry skirmish. Antony retreated to the palace, crying that Cleopatra had betrayed him. She, afraid of his vengeance, fled to her monument, let down the heavy-falling doors and secured them with bars and bolts. She sent messengers to tell Antony that she was dead. Believing this, he cried, "Now, Antony, why delay any longer? Fate has snatched away the only pretext for living." He continued, "I am not troubled, Cleopatra, to be bereaved of you at present, for I shall soon be with you; but it distresses me that a great general should be slower in finding his courage than a woman." He ordered a faithful servant to kill him, but the servant took the sword and killed himself instead. "It is well done," said Antony. "You show your master how to do what you had not the heart to do yourself." Then he plunged his sword into his own belly.

As he lay dying, Cleopatra's servants came to take him to her in the monument. She would not open the door, but she and the two women pulled him up by ropes to a window in the top of the monument. Antony, covered with blood and on

ANTONY

the verge of death, extended his hands towards Cleopatra and lifted up his body towards her with the little force he had left. It was difficult for the three women to pull him up, but Cleopatra clung to the rope with all her might, straining with her head towards the ground, while those below encouraged her with their cries.

When she got him up into the monument, she laid him on a bed and cried, beating her breasts and tearing her clothes. She called him her lord, her husband, her emperor. She embraced him and smeared herself with his blood. Indeed, she was so distraught over Antony that she seemed to have forgotten her own troubles. When he had drunk some wine she gave him, he advised her to trust certain of Caesar's advisers, whom he named. He told her not to pity him but rather to be happy because of his own past happiness. He said that he was consoled because he had fallen "not ignobly, a Roman by a Roman overcome." And then he died.

While Caesar's ambassadors were talking to Cleopatra through the door of the monument, others scaled the wall to the window through which Antony had been lifted. The clever Queen attempted suicide, but the Romans seized her dagger, captured her, and took every precaution to keep her alive.

Caesar addressed the people of Alexandria and forgave them "for the sake of Alexander, for the beauty of their city, and to gratify his friend Areius, the Alexandrian philosopher." When Cleopatra buried Antony's body in royal splendor, her extreme grief and sorrow led to a high fever. She tried to abstain from food so as to die quietly, but by threats concerning the safety of her children, Caesar persuaded her to take food and medicine. He conferred with her personally to comfort her, but he was neither influenced by her charms nor deceived by her cleverness when she tried to justify her actions by blaming

LIVES FROM PLUTARCH

Antony and her fear of him. Caesar got an inventory of her riches, and when one of her stewards revealed certain omissions, Cleopatra protested that she had saved these articles to present them to Caesar's wife.

She visited Antony's tomb, where she flung herself to the ground, embraced the tomb, and cried and lamented the fact that she was no longer free, that she was guarded by Romans even as she grieved over his death. She cried, "Nothing could part us while both lived, but death threatens to divide us. You, a Roman born, have found a grave in Egypt; I, an Egyptian, am to seek that favor only in your country." She deplored Caesar's efforts to keep her alive for his triumph in Rome. Calling to the dead Antony, she pleaded, "Let me not be led in triumph to shame you, but hide me and bury me here with you, since of all my misfortunes, nothing has been worse than this brief time that I have lived away from you."

Completing her lamentations, she ordered a bath to be prepared, after which she ate a delicious dinner, and received a basket of figs an Egyptian brought to her. An asp was hidden among those figs, and she allowed it to poison her, thus avoiding the humiliation of Caesar's Roman triumph.

Antony left seven children by his three wives. The oldest of these was put to death, and Octavia reared the others. Descended from Antony and Octavia were the emperors Claudius, Caligula, and Nero, three of the most infamous rulers in history.

About the Editors

JOHN W. McFARLAND was born in Galveston, Texas, where he was graduated from Ball High School. After receiving his degree from The University of Texas, Dr. McFarland taught in elementary and high school in Galveston and then served in the artillery in World War II. He returned to teaching after the war, and in 1951 he was awarded the degree of Doctor of Education. Later, when he was Superintendent of Schools, the meetings of the Houston School Board were televised in full; thus his philosophy of education became well-known in Texas. In July, 1966, Dr. McFarland became Dean of Education for Texas Western College, El Paso, where he is particularly interested in the development of methods of teaching deprived and impoverished pupils.

PLEASANT GRAVES was born in Houston, Texas, educated there, and graduated from The University of Texas and Columbia University School of Law. In World War II he served as a lieutenant in the Navy, and has practiced law in Houston since 1946. In addition to his work in civil law he has worked with a community group presenting classics of children's literature as plays which were performed before a thousand young people a year. He is married to Audrey Graves and they live in Houston with their son.

AUDREY GRAVES was born in Pipestone, Minnesota, was graduated cum laude from Augustana College, Sioux Falls, South Dakota, and received her master's degree in education from the University of Houston. As an elementary schoolteacher in Houston, Mrs. Graves helped start television teaching with her programs "The Art Cart" and "Phenomena," both national award-winning series. After serving as a principal and supervisor in Houston's elementary schools she resigned in 1962, and now lectures at the University of Houston. As well as working with her husband and Dr. John McFarland on the Modern American Edition of LIVES FROM PLUTARCH, Mrs. Graves has continued her work in teaching and educational television.